This is W.S. Ishida's debut novel. You [illegible] media at the following places:

Facebook ~ **WSIshida**
Instagram ~ **ishidawrites**
Twitter ~ **@IshidaAuthor**

~

If you would like to stay up to date with the author's latest projects, blogs posts or find out more about this particular novel, please visit the website.

Author website ~ **wsishida.com**

You can also sign-up for the author's exclusive newsletter and take advantage of free books and other special offers, when available.

IMPORTANT NOTE FROM THE AUTHOR

Thank you for giving my book a try, I hope you enjoy it as much as I enjoyed (for the most part!) writing it. This historical, family drama is set in the Norfolk countryside and is narrated in the first person perspective by the protagonist, Rosemary Page. **Please note**: the narration sometimes includes specific Norfolk vocabulary. It is not essential to know the meaning of these words to follow and enjoy this novel. However, if you are interested, please go to my website to discover more about the wonderful world of the Norfolk dialect.

The narration also includes elements of the Norfolk vernacular, as well as deliberate use of the passive tense and erroneous grammar to further reflect this. Whereas all other errors and typos I gratefully attribute to my editors and proofreaders (of course not, I love you really).

W.S. Ishida

GOODBYE TO RIBBONS

W.S. ISHIDA

Faux Crow Publishing

ISBN 978-1-8381953-0-4

'Her temper is our terrier, in a barrel of panicking rats
Her tongue, the cowhide that whips me inta shape
Her mercy, the pike that ate the day-old goslings
Whose wit is the playful kittens, torturing a bishy barnaby'

— From the poem - *My Old Gel: A Norfolk Union*

PROLOGUE

AGED 65 (2010)

I wouldn't ever say it's easy watching a person die, no matter what the circumstances. But it's also hard for me to say that there wasn't a part of me that was glad when he did. Well, maybe glad ent quite right, but I never have been that good with getting my thoughts down. Me, I prefer to talk.

Actually, I've been talking to one of them psychiatrist people, would you believe. She's actually quite nice. I like her. She listens to me. In fact, she was the one who said I should do this—you know, write it all down, like a proper story.

Mostly, she listens with her legs crossed, leaning forwards, head cocked to one side and her thin eyebrows raised. Sometimes she nods along, and sometimes she asks me questions too.

"And how does that make you feel now?" she might say.

Or, "If that were to happen today, what would you think, or how would you react? In fact, tell me, what would the Rosemary sitting here *now,* say to the Rosemary *back then*?"

But my answer is always the same. Okay, I'm slowly losing the use of my hands, what with the rheumatoid arthritis, and walking isn't getting any easier, but I got my own house, my own husband, two little dogs and a fair few friends. In fact, every summer we have a big party here in the garden—which if you'll forgive me for being a braggart—is slowly becoming quite the event on some people's calendars.

So I gotta say, I'm happy. And if I changed any one little thing from my past, then who's to say I would've even got to where I am now.

Yeah, things did go—if you'll 'scuse my French—horribly tits up for a long, long while, but here I am. And, there was even one or two laughs that were had along the way, so you know what—I'll take that.

Anyway, listen to me waffling on already and I haven't even got started. Now, I do want to say one final thing—please be warned, I'm gonna tell it how it was, warts and all. And I ent gonna pull any punches, so to speak, that just isn't me. So, if you care to listen, here it is. This is my story from the very beginning.

PART I

MY MARVELLOUS MOTHER

1

THE GOOD LITTLE GIRL

AGED 3 (1948)

If I only had one thing going for me throughout my life, it was being as tough as a pair of old leather boots that'd been left out in the rain too long. You see, I'd quietly put up with things that most others wouldn't. And so even though they thought I might never walk again, I listened and I did as I was told—just like a good little girl should.

"Keep your head up and always look forward," they kept telling me, when at 3 years old I had to learn to walk for the second time in my life.

And it wasn't long before I was able to straighten my knees. And a short while after that, hobble about with the help of a frame. Then, after five long bedridden-months spent alone in a dark room, the day eventually came when it was all over and I could once again stand on my own two feet.

The old clothes peg was finally removed from the curtains and the lights turned on. I was jiggling with excitement knowing that I was going to be with my family again, that I was going home. They dressed me up in the clothes I came in with, the only ones that weren't hospital issue. Then I waited.

I remember it so clearly, sitting on that bed. The sunshine warming my back. My pale skinny legs swinging free as the excitement tickled away at the inside of my belly.

I heard her first—a distant voice booming through the corridors. Then there was the odd moment of silence, which was when the staff got their turn to speak before she started up again.

My legs stopped swinging.

"Uh yes, she's just in here, we urm—"

But before they could finish, in she stomped. A big-bosomed, bolshie woman with waves of thick, light-brown hair and the most striking red lipstick you ever did see. She stood towering over me, swamped in a lavish fox-fur coat, hands on hips.

My tiny fingers gripped at the bedsheet.

"Right. Come on then. We ent got all day," she said with a weariness, as if we'd already outstayed our welcome.

I didn't reply.

I didn't even move.

"Come on. Let's not hang about. Don't want to keep these busy people waiting, do yuh."

I looked to the doctor, who gave me a nod and an over-practiced smile. But all I could do was pull the sheet up from the bed and hold it in front of my face, my eyes barely peeping over the top. The doctor looked to the woman and then back to me. He wanted to say something but clearly wasn't sure of himself. She often had that effect on people.

"It's... it's just your mother, she's come to take you home Rosemary. You... you do want to go home, don't you?"

Of course I wanted to go home, more than anything in the world. However, something just didn't feel right.

All I can think of now, is perhaps the picture I'd built up in my mind over those last five months wasn't marrying-up to the one who stood towering over me there and then.

2

EARLIEST MEMORIES

People often like to ask what your earliest memory is, but how can we ever really be sure. It's always so hazy when you're young, and then of course you have other people's memories and their stories thrown into the mix. Then soon enough things get all clouded up and before you know it you're not really sure you can believe your own mind anymore.

I was only 3 years old when I went to stay at that small hospital in Cromer. I don't remember all that much before it. It was the rheumatic fever that landed me there, so I was told. They reckon I got it by absorbing dampness up through my knees while playing in the sand heap. And so at the age most kids were getting to master their legs, I went back to being pushed around in a pram.

I remember my hospital room always being so gloomy.

"We told you already, the light's no good for it," they'd say as they re-fastened the curtains. But the curtains didn't just keep the light out, but also any chance of having company in the empty bed next to mine. After all, who in their right mind would be able to handle being shut away like that in the darkness every hour of the waking day.

Occasionally they'd wheel me down Cromer Pier for some fresh air, and that would be as much as I saw of the outside world for a good while. They'd push me along, the wheels *buddum, buddumming* across the wooden slats all the way to the very end. I mostly liked to watch the gulls wheeling through the sky. Their cries blocking out the heavy sighs of the sea coming up through the slats, as it swayed non-stop back and forth between the pier's dark stained legs.

Looking out at the sea caused me to have funny feelings at times. I didn't like the way it went on forever and ever, how there was no end in sight. A nurse once told me not to worry, that even though I couldn't see it yet, if I kept going I'd eventually get to Holland.

"And you know something else, if you just keep on going without ever changing your course, you'll go all the way around and eventually end up exactly where you started from," she said smiling down at my unblinking face. "Now isn't that something to think about."

3

THE PUB SINGER

I never had no fancy dreams like the other kids of being a movie star, a singer, an astronaut or even a famous figure skater. All I ever wanted was to be like my mother. And for her to like me.

"Salt of the earth she is," they'd say.

"Do anything for anyone," others would tell me.

"A real good'un, and that's not for arguing with."

Everybody loved her, and even in the small town of East Rudham where I spent most of my childhood, *everybody* was a whole lot of people, so I had no choice but to believe it. But if that was the truth, it left me with only one answer—that it was me, that I was the problem.

I was born on Monday the 1st of May 1945, the day after Hitler killed himself and the day before the German forces in Italy surrendered. With the war all but done, there was a positivity in the air and a feeling of a new beginning for most folks.

When I arrived into the world I already had two older brothers, Karl and Billy, and another three brothers and a sister still to come. We grew up in a tiny village deep in the Norfolk countryside—all of us crammed into a busy council house that seemed to shrink every year.

We were lucky to have a bit of a garden. With seven kids under one roof, it acted like the release spout on our disgruntled pressure cooker that would rattle away on top of the paint-chipped stove. The garden was split into two by a row of conifers, and although both bits were at the rear of the house we still called them the front garden and the back garden. The "front garden" being the grassy lawn right outside the back door. Most of this was taken up by the junk-filled shed and the two old caravans—where we stored all the junk that we couldn't fit in the shed. Behind the conifers was the "back garden" where we had the old veg patch, the compost heap, the bonfire pit and then at the very end our rather unique double outhouse that my dad built with his own two hands.

The back garden was mostly where you'd find my dad, Trevor. It was a place he could get away from it all and go for a quiet smoke. He was a tall, rangy man, not much one for words, preferring a grunt if he could get away with it. His face thin and weathered, as were his hands that never seemed to scrub up much better than grimy. He worked his whole life as a farm labourer but wore a shirt and waistcoat to work every single day, as well as his beige flat cap that hid his thinning light-brown hair. Despite being as quiet as a dormouse hiding from a cat, I always knew when he was at home by the familiar smell of stale tobacco smoke and faint whiff of oil. Everything was kept well oiled at our house, there was never a squeak or groan to be heard from hinge nor spindle. In fact, there were only four things I ever remember seeing in his hands. If he was outdoors, it was a rolled-up cigarette and the narrow-spouted oilcan. If he was indoors, it was the newspaper. And if one of us kids had got wrong, it was the old leather belt that despite my best efforts I was no stranger to.

By no stretch of the imagination was I a naughty kid—none of us were, really. We never set out to do anything bad, never had no ill-intentions, yet the belt still managed to find the back of our legs on a regular basis. I feared my dad but never blamed him for the punishments. I was always able to see our blame in the matters. I soon understood that if something got broke, even accidentally, then someone got the belt. Sometimes, it would be everyone who happened to be in the room of the wrongdoing, that way he knew the real culprit wouldn't get away with it. But a day or two after the pain had faded, it was forgotten and things carried on as normal like they always did.

Later in my childhood, when I was able to process things better, there was one thing I couldn't forget, one thing that I struggled to get past, and that was the way I'd treated my mum the day she came to pick me up from the hospital. I cursed myself for it because I could only think this was the reason, this was the cause, this was the seed from where it all started. How must it have felt, to be shunned in front of all those people by her own flesh and blood, by a being that she made, that came from her, that was part of her? But little did I know, or could I've known, the poisoned seed had already been sown before my existence had even come to be.

I tried my damnedest to make things right and win back her love—that famous love that all others got so easily and for free. I accepted it was my fault and forgave her time and time again for the way she was and the things she said, the things she did. I lied for her, betraying myself and my own family. I even covered for her when she didn't have the will or the want to do it for herself. I gave her everything and got nothing back, and all cos I accepted the blame. But for some reason, what I never thought about was that in those five months that her infant daughter had been sick in the hospital, my marvellous mother hadn't visited her once.

Of course, I knew she was busy. It'd be impossible not to be with a house full of kids and the regular visitors and whatnot.

We were never short of having random folks stay at ours, so much so for a time I actually thought we ran some kind of guesthouse. I believe it all started when the war was on. With London taking the brunt of the German bombing raids, the call soon went out for people living deeper in the countryside to take in the evacuees. And my mother, with a love for anything to do with London and never being one to say no, stepped forward.

Many of the evacuees who stayed with us, still came by for visits long after the war was wrapped up, such as Linga-Linga-Low-Low as us young'uns called her—her real name being Belinda Lowell. My mum knew the Lowell's from way back when she used to work as a pub singer down in London. It was Belinda's aunt who ran one of the pubs that my mum had a regular spot at. I don't know all that much about my mum's life down there. From what little she told me I think she had a right good time of it though and always longed to go back one day to recapture it all. She had quite the pipes on her and the reputation to match. It seems she was doing rather well for a young lady in those times, on good money and getting well known on the circuit. But then the war broke out and it all came to an abrupt end. She tried to stick at it for a while but was eventually left with no choice but to trundle her way back to sleepy old Norfolk.

It was a year or so after that when young Belinda had to follow the same path. When Bell arrived to find nothing but fields, farms and simple country folk, she wasn't best pleased to be there either. She told me one time that she found it all too slow and quiet away from London, so spent most of the early days crying her eyes out. However, my mum looked after her well enough by all accounts, really took her under her wing. Then years later when the war was done, Bell chose to come back of her own willing to look after us kids in the summers, and that's how I come to know her.

She was like our nanny, taking us kids out and about all the while. Us older ones walking or toddling and little Perry (or Little Pea, as we called him) being pushed in the pram. I once asked why she did it, why she wanted to come up to Norfolk and look after a whole bunch of snotty kids for her summer. She said it was because she got lonely down in London—can you imagine? Lonely in London? Working in a busy pub in the biggest city in the country?

"I like it in Norfolk," she said, "I got a family 'ere. It makes me feel part of something, dunnit."

She said sometimes you get a liking for things that are different or opposite to what you're used to. She liked the way everyone knew you and took the time to say hello. Also, how there was always someone looking out for you and someone for you to look after whether young or old—a real sense of togetherness. But I guess she didn't really get to see the warts-an-all version, mind. I certainly wouldn't have bet against her singing quite a different tune if she had.

4

THE GOOD SAMARITAN

AGED 7 (1952)

It wasn't just evacuees the war sent to Norfolk, there were also a lot of POWs. You'd have thought they would've sent them back home to their families afterwards, but instead many were kept on. They had them working on the farms in the summer and then shovelling snow off the roads and hedges in the winter, booking them in and out just like you would a library book.

They were mostly solemn souls but hard workers to boot. Seeing them quietly drift about their toils like tame ghosts, I realised it doesn't matter what side you were on, good or bad, war would always have its way with you whether you liked it or not. And they certainly didn't seem like the evil killers the radio and papers would have you believe. I remember them being in people's houses at times, fixing things up. My mum would even make them a cup of tea or sometimes send me out to give them some home-baked goods. They were always very grateful and gentle and looked so sad when they had to go back to wherever it was they kept them.

My mum loved to bake and often gave away more than half of what she made. During the winters, when the snow came down especially hard, my older brothers, Karl and Billy, would be sent out on the bike to get some yeast. On their return, she'd then spend the rest of the day baking bread for all the neighbours.

"Oh, bless her!" people would say when us kids arrived with the freshly baked warm parcels. "She ent just a pretty face and a bright smile, is she, eh."

"She's the Good Samaritan all right, your mother is. You're very lucky children, y'know."

I remember one elderly lady who lived by herself was brought to tears because she was so happy. In fact, she was so overcome, she could barely finish her sentences. "Your mother... your mother... oh look at me now..." was as much as she managed each time, before having to dab at her eyes.

Even though the words weren't for me, they'd leave me feeling ever so proud and all warm and fuzzy inside. She was just one of those people who lit up any room she bustled into. Yes, she could be brisk and bossy but she was always pleasant with it, and most people seemed to like it, liked being told what to do, liked her no-nonsense approach. And more often than not, they'd be left with a daft smile still plastered across their face long after she'd blown her way through.

I knew at the time, I was just a kid and I weren't so important, but it didn't stop me imagining that one day I could be just like her and that all the neighbours would be talking about me in the same way. But you know what they say, *hindsight's a wonderful thing* and *be careful what you wish for* and all that. Because, as it would turn out, that's exactly what happened. Don't worry though, we'll get to all that later, I'm sure.

In the meantime, how's this for a start—I remember one February when the snow was humming down thick and fast, Mum had finished baking the bread and had a bit of dough leftover. I asked her if I could eat it raw, but she refused me in no uncertain terms. Instead, she made it into a couple of platted rolls and brushed them with a beaten egg before putting them in the oven. Once they were done, she sent me off to give them to the snow-powdered POWs who were clearing the hedges outside.

There were two of them, Germans I think, been working without stop all morning. I was too shy to say anything, so I just held out the steaming wrapped rolls that had been warming my hands. The one who took them nodded a thanks, and even today I remember his eyes. They were a brilliant blue, so pure against the white all around us, and although he managed a smile, there was no hiding the deep-set loneliness in them. Just like the look in the eyes of the scraggly old donkey that was forever tied to the walnut tree on Weasel's farm.

As I went to leave, I felt a hand rest on my shoulder causing me to let out a startled cloud of breath. When I turned to meet those sorrowful eyes, the prisoner slipped his hand inside his pocket and pulled out a small wooden chicken he'd carved. Without saying anything, he showed me how it worked. How you had to pull a small knotted-string at the bottom to make the chicken bob his head down as if pecking for grain. He made me hold my palm out flat and then made the chicken's little wooden beak tap, tap, tap at my hand. It tickled some, and the way it moved was just like that of a real chicken. It caused me to giggle and made the top of his red cheeks press against his eyes as he smiled, and I swear there was a brief sparkle in them that seemed to fade as quickly as it appeared. I honestly didn't know what to say when he passed it to me and folded my hand around it; my chest was tingling with absolute joy.

When I got back in, Mum was waiting.

"What's that he give you?" she said, hand outstretched.

I hesitated. Then cursed myself for not being more secretive, knowing full well she'd have been peering out the window.

"Come on, give it here. Whatever it is, you ent deserving of it."

Wordlessly, I handed it over and never did see it again.

My mum gave a weary sigh and a shake of the head. I could feel my bottom lip go and the lump rise in my throat. I didn't want her to see me cry, so I went to my room. And I wouldn't say I was wrong in thinking at that time, in that place, there were two lonely, solemn souls secretly shedding tears that longed for lost love.

At that age, why I wasn't deserving of having the toy I could only guess. I was a quiet kid who did what she was told without fuss. I wasn't the brightest of buttons, but I was definitely a hard worker. And I was at least bright enough to realise my four brothers didn't get treated with such short shrift.

I was surrounded by two brothers either side of my age until I was

12, so it also occurred to me that perhaps I was deserving of the special treatment cos I was a girl. Maybe she'd never wanted me. I mean, I was dressed as a boy for most of my childhood. There was no gymslip for me—it was shorts, shirt and necktie, and off to school I went, when in truth I'd always preferred ribbons.

But this theory fell by the wayside when the sixth of my siblings came along. It took us all by surprise when out popped little Valerie. We'd all just been assuming it would be another boy going by my parent's track record.

It left me quite confused for a while. Half of me was excited—another girl—I wasn't alone anymore. But the other half was fearful, knowing what was in store for her. I also thought that maybe we could help each other, be partners and get through things together, a burden shared and all that.

However, my fears were for nothing, as my mum was absolutely smitten with her. I never did harbour a bad thought about Valerie, but that doesn't mean I didn't feel jealous or that it wasn't jarring to see them together, my mother cooing and snuggling her face into her belly. She was ever so proud of her and never shy in letting all and sundry know it. She even had a man come round with a camera every so often to have Valerie's picture done, which weren't so cheap in those days. She'd dress her up all nice, polish her tiny shoes, brush the few teeth she had and do her hair with one of my ribbons. The man would also make a fuss over her—and rightly so, as there was no denying she was a proper little cutie. On the first few occasions he came over, he spied me hovering behind the door and asked if I was to have my photo done too.

"What? Nah, not her," my mum would say. "Be a waste on an ugly ol' stick like that."

That's honestly what she used to say—I mean, can you even believe it. Imagine, saying something like that, not just to a kid, but to your own daughter. I don't know who was more embarrassed, the man or me. But even being in the presence of a flustered and blushing near-stranger didn't stop her.

"I don't know what happened to that one," she'd carry on as if I weren't there, "must've also been behind the door when they were giving out the looks," she said, before roaring away at her own joke.

As a kid, adults are like gods, they are never wrong and never lie—only kids do those things, so I accepted everything that came from them like it was the gospel itself. I could plainly see it myself that Valerie was all pretty and cute, and worthy of being fussed over, and so I also accepted the truth that—I wasn't.

Now, just because I accepted it, it didn't mean it was any less crushing and the heartache any less painful. I'd tell myself that being one face in a family of many was always going to mean there were times when someone would feel left out. However, being in a big family was probably also my saving grace. Partly cos it meant there was always some kind of distraction going on to help steer your thoughts away from the troubled waters, and also because of our family rule—that each kid was responsible for the next one down in age. And so what this meant was, was that I had my very own hero looking out for me when no one else would.

5

RIBBONS IN MY HAIR

AGED 9 (1954)

Billy, being only a year and a half older, was my partner in crime for most of my earliest memories. He looked out for me, fussed over me, protected me. Admittedly, this was partly due to him being duty-bound to the role, but I always felt it was more than that, that he had a naturally caring heart, even when it came to looking after his annoying kid sister.

My mum loved to cook all year round, so even in the summer, she'd be pleasing everyone with her platted rolls and scones delivered by us kids. She even baked for the local pub down the road. They gave her old milk tins for collecting blackberries, and in return, she'd bake them apple and blackberry pies. Of course, the donkey work of picking the berries was done by us kids. Not that we minded, it was always such a grand adventure when we were allowed to roam the Norfolk countryside. As a child, it was like we had a whole world to explore, and seemingly all to ourselves. On the occasions when we did meet someone, it was always a great thrill. Although, being a shy child, at first I was usually a bit skittish. However, I always felt safe when I had my hero with me.

One such time, Billy and me had been sent out picking and managed to find ourselves all the way down by the airfield. We'd been at it for a good hour, our fingers and mouths stained purple, our milk tins half empty but our bellies half full. It was a bright summer's day with insects buzzing lazily on a breeze so thick you thought you could taste it. The sun was warm on your skin, but not so hot that you felt all icky under your clothes. Birds hopped in and out of the hedgerow, busily chattering away with their nonsensical chirps.

I'd reached a gap in the hedge when I first saw them across the way. The hole, large enough for a pony to pass through, was a tangle of twigs and leaves leading onto a grassy field. The field stretched all the way to a steel fence with great menacing rolls of barbed wire sat on top of it. This marked the boundary of the American airbase, RAF Marham.

We hadn't spoken for some minutes, both lost in our daydreams, enjoying the heavy summer warmth. I was deep into my usual fantasy of pretending I was out on a hack on my very own horse—Bessie the bay roan with a white blaze and four white socks. But I was snapped out of it in an instant when I saw the first one. One second it was there, the next it was gone. I craned my head forward, squinting.

"Oy," was all Billy said when he realised I was dawdling. He beckoned me on with a nod of his head, but I paid him no mind, determined not to miss it should it happen again.

I heard him let out a weary sigh. "What you gawping at anyhow?"

"I... don't know."

"Well, come on then."

I risked a quick glance at him. He glared back, brow furrowed, trying to be all serious, but his purple-stained mouth made him look like more like a toddler who'd found his mother's make-up bag, than the stern big brother he was imagining.

I promised myself I'd give it up after the count of five, but by three it happened again.

"There. There. I saw it again." I pointed, not daring to take my eyes from the spot. There was no mistaking it this time. I'd seen... something. No more than head height to a child. There, and then just as quickly not.

Billy ambled over, all huffing and gruffing. "What? What was there?"

“Something in the air, something sparkly. I saw it.”

“You ent seeing fairies again are yuh?”

“No. I really saw it. I really did this time.”

He stood, shoulders slumped, in no mood to humour his annoying younger sister.

“There. Again.” My arm was shaking, I was pointing so hard. “Look! And another one. And there.” I was so happy I clapped.

“What? What is it?” he said, shielding his eyes with a purple hand. “I don't see nothin.”

I could tell from the edge in his voice that I had him now. He’d bought his ticket, he was on board, his interest had been got and he was in for the adventure—whatever it would turn out to be.

“There! And they're coming this way,” and I started forward.

Billy reached out for my shoulder, “Careful yet.”

“It's all right, come on.” I shrugged free, causing berries to tumble from his tin. But I didn’t care because I was off. I ducked through the hole in the hedge, leapt the overgrown ditch, and went galloping across that field.

“Oy. Rosemary. Come back, comeback this minute.”

But I paid him no mind, and the next thing I knew he was giving chase.

Soon the both of us were racing across the grassy scrub. I could see hundreds of them now, flittering and glittering in the breeze. The first one I managed to touch appeared in front of me in a blink. I reached up too late and felt it flick against my hand with a fishtail slap.

“Grab it, Billy. Grab it.”

“What? Where?” he said, turning on the spot. “Wait... I see it! I see it!” he shouted. And just like that, he remembered he too was still but a child.

I watched him tear about in zigzags, chasing the tumbling silver eel that danced in the wind, teasing and turning just out of his reach. I certainly laughed some—laughed until I couldn’t see through my tears. With his frustrations gone, Billy was laughing too, and he wouldn't give it up. He must have run a marathon and a half, but still couldn't get hold of the blighter. Eventually, he stopped, bent over double, trying to get his breath.

"Don't worry, look, there's more, there's hundreds more! Come on." I waved him on as I skipped towards the swirling swarm of silver.

Once we were amongst them proper, it was impossible *not* to catch them as the wind pressed them against our clothes and wrapped them around our legs. Even so, we mostly jumped for the ones teasing us in the air, then stuffed the crinkled strips of foil in our pockets until they were bulging.

We went back the next day armed with potato sacks, still not knowing what we were collecting or even why. We managed to fill both our sacks and drag them home. In those days nothing was wasted; folks always found a good use for anything and everything. And so we went back a third time, but this was the day the man with the Alsatian came and we finally discovered the truth about our spoils.

The dog was huge. It had a long dark muzzle, thick shaggy coat, and pointed ears. It pulled against the leash, its front legs rising into the air, causing it to let out a series of rasping chokes like some sort of possessed demon. But worst of all was its eyes and the way they locked onto us, tracking our every movement.

"So you're the culprits," came the airmen's American accent. "Stealing from the US Air Force, tut, tut."

We didn't know what to say.

We just stood there, either side of the potato sack, caught silver-handed.

The man didn't sound as angry as I thought he might, but it didn't matter because I knew we'd be in for it when we got home. Half of me was praying for him to loose the dog and put us out of our misery.

The first time we lugged home sacks of the wind's silver treasure, Dad had been sat on the front wall rolling a cigarette.

"What you got?" he said without looking up.

"Dunno," replied Billy.

"Where d'you get it?" came the next weary question.

"Found it."

"Where?"

"In a field." We waited for the next one, but it didn't come, so we continued dragging the sacks round to the coal shed.

However, being brought home in shame by a man in uniform

meant a damn good hiding and no mistake. Dad was a man of few words, who I feared more than anything when I was a child. Although quiet, he always carried great anger like the threat of darkening thunderclouds on the horizon.

"So what we gonna do wit the pair of you then?" said the airman.

Still, neither of us could find anything to say. I was trying my hardest to hold it together, but I could already see the disappointed scowl on my dad's tired face and... that was enough. My bottom lip started trembling, my eyes welled and my chest juddered, and I knew there was no stopping it.

"Hey honey, it's all right, don't be upset. I'm just kidding wit you." His face broke into a soft smile.

A couple of sobs escaped before I could catch my breath again.

"In fact, you're doing us a favour. It saves us having to collect it all. I'll tell you what, I'll even give you a hand." He gave the dog a command, but it didn't move. He then took a step towards us as he unwrapped the leash from his hand, dropping it to the floor.

Billy and me took a backward step. The airman looked from us to the dog. He told us not to worry and gave the dog another command and it lowered itself to the ground.

The airman was one of the tallest people I'd ever met, and even when he was bent over to pick up the silver foil, he towered above me.

"Well, come on," he said, "I'm not gonna do it all myself."

Soon, we'd stuffed the sack so full it was nearly too heavy to carry. The airman liked to talk, but all we had for him were one-word answers. The dog was resting its head on his huge paws, its eyes blinking sleepily shut.

As the airman pushed down the final handful of foil, Billy eventually found the courage to pipe up.

"Your dog, Sir, it's called a... German shepherd dog ent it?"

"That's correct. You're a smart kid. But actually, we don't call them that anymore. We call them Alsatian wolfhounds. Because of the war," he explained.

We both nodded slowly as if we understood. Seeing my brother's success, I asked a question of my own. "Sir? What are these things anyhow?"

"Well, well, Missy. That is top secret military information." Then he smiled, clearly enjoying himself. "But... you look like a couple of stand-up kids," he said, and then in a hushed voice, "so if you can keep a secret I'll tell yah."

Using his hands and putting in a few aeroplane noises and other sound effects, he told us how they dropped the silver in big long streams from the back of the "airplanes" to create a huge metal storm that confused the enemy's radar.

As we readied to leave, he suddenly told us to wait. We watched as he and the dog strolled away. I turned and looked up at Billy. He sucked at his bottom lip for a moment.

"...I think it's okay, maybe we should wait," came the verdict.

And we were glad we did. He came back with another uniformed airman but without the dog. He had a grain sack swinging from his hand and his friend had an armful of white cloth.

"Thought you might like this old gear too."

The sack was full of different coloured silk ribbons, and the white cloth was from old silk parachutes. We were too stunned to say thank you, but our gormless fishlike gapes spoke for us. He told us he did regular patrols around the airfield and we should come say hi if we were out that way again, but we never went back. As nice as he was, we couldn't help but feel that somehow we'd got away with one. We'd got caught, yet still come away with a bumper load of swag.

Back at home, we found no shortage of uses for our booty. In the summer, Dad had us thread the silver strips and ribbons with garden string, then tie them around the fruit trees and veg garden to scare off the birds. Come the winter, we'd wipe them clean, pull them tight on the string and hang them up as Christmas trimmings. Mum made good use of the parachute material, sewing dresses and what have you from it. And, after that day at the airfield, it was a rare occasion if you didn't see me with a coloured ribbon in my hair.

Though I got to keep some of the ribbons, the parachute silk dresses never found their way to me. I weren't deserving of them, she'd say as usual.

"I mean she can't even keep her hands clean, let alone her clothes," she once told our neighbour. "In fact, there's barely much point in me washing hers at all."

Not being deserving of nice things was something I quickly accepted. Anytime anything good happened to me it was just a matter of waiting before something larger came along and plonked itself on the other end of the seesaw, causing it to go—scuse my French again—tits up. Therefore, I shouldn't really have been surprised when the day came that my very own knight in shining armour betrayed me and left me abandoned in a castle tower.

6

NEW ALLIES

AGED 10 (1955)

It seemed to happen so suddenly and easily. If I hadn't known better, I might've thought it had all been planned.

Sir Billy of Rudham, who was now 12, had been at grammar school a year, settled in and started to make friends. His best friend being Wiggy, a tall thick-limbed boy with dusty hair and a front lip that turned up—making him look like he was always a little bit angry and confused. It weren't long before Wiggy started to come over and muck about with us, and so the terrible twosome became the trio of trouble.

At first, not much was different. Of course, Billy was keener on Wiggy as he was a fella and they were at school together. But then soon, whether Wiggy was there or not, Billy started to turn his nose up at our usual fantasies and made-up games—unless they involved throwing stones at something. I tried to follow suit as best I could, but the one thing I could never change was the lack of a dangly thing between my legs. It was no good having me about if they wanted to look at the saucy pictures Wiggy stole from his uncle, or if they wanted to talk about which "birds" they thought were prettiest. I tried my best to fit in with the rest of the stuff, and pretty soon I could throw a stone without them laughing at the way I did it.

I didn't know it at the time, but my mum rang the death knell one morning as we were putting on our shoes ready to go roaming. She shouted through from the kitchen that from now on we had to take little Perry with us every time we went out. Of course, with me being the next one up in age from him, it meant he was my responsibility. At first, I didn't think anything of it—Perry was a good wee fella. He liked to muck about and could always make you laugh by making farting noises with his hand in his armpit.

Had it just been Billy, Perry, and me, I think it would've been okay. But with Wiggy thrown into the mix, Billy stopped being Billy, or at least the Billy we'd always known. And it didn't take long to see that the pair of them were getting fed up of having so much extra lumber to lug around. And because I was the one who had to help Perry climb the gates and jump the ditches, I also became marked as extra lumber.

They'd stand shaking their heads, rolling their eyes, sighing, or kicking at stones while they waited. I kept thinking about having a moan at Perry so they knew I was in the same boat, but I didn't have the heart. You could see the little fella was trying his hardest to keep up and be part of the gang. I wasn't stupid enough that I didn't see myself mirrored in his struggle—quietly tagging along, trying not to be a nuisance.

Eventually, we had to stop to let Perry have a breather and take a widdle. The older boys found a lean oak tree they thought would be a good climber. It was trickier than they'd first thought, having no low branches to hoike themselves up on. They struggled some, but got there in the end, whereas Perry and me knew we were too short to even bother trying.

They sat hidden amongst the branches, talking quietly, only their legs to be seen dangling above our heads. I thought it would be okay, that we just had to wait until they got bored and came down again, then we'd all continue on our way.

"Hey, why dunt you two be useful and just scarper off home, eh," Wiggy called down.

I heard Billy sigh, "I'd get wrong if they came home without me."

This was when I realised my station had changed. *"They"* Billy had said.

The two tree-dwellers went back to their whispering. I wanted to do something to Perry; I wanted to annoy him or make him cry. I thought I could get a stinger and brush his ankles with it, make it look like an accident.

"All right then, Billy, you win," Wiggy said loudly. And then to us, "Oy, you two. C'mon then."

I looked up to see the olive branch being held out in the form of a thick oil-stained hand reaching down from the leaves.

"Billy says we shouldn't be leaving you out none, so reach up will yuh."

Good ol' Billy! I thought to myself as I lifted Perry up. I knew his good side would win out in the end.

Once in the tree, we were safely hidden away from the outside world. The sun reflected off the flittering leaves and gave everything a green glow that made me think we were in a magical woodland ball, with the speckles of sunlight being fairies dancing all around us. Of course, I kept this to myself.

The boys didn't seem that upset about sharing their new den, in fact, Wiggy was smiling away like the Cheshire Cat with a new bowtie. We sat quietly, not much being said until Wiggy stretched his back.

"Cor, I dunno about you, but I'm kinda bored up here all of a sudden." He stretched again. Then lifting his bum he slipped down, grabbed the branch in front of him, swung on it for a second before dropping nimbly onto the grass. Billy didn't say anything, but he followed straight after.

Wiggy peered up at us, "You two coming as well?"

I got ready to hang from the branch, but looking down it was further than I'd thought. "You gonna have to catch us."

"What? Nah, you're big enough to do it yourselves, ent yuh?"

"It's too high," I said. "You'll have to reach for us."

"What say you, Billy?"

Billy shrugged. "They look safe enough, I s'pose."

"That's what I was thinking," Wiggy said with a grin.

"Help us down again. We'll turn an ankle if we jump."

"Should keep them out of trouble for a bit, you reckon?" Wiggy continued, talking as if we weren't even there.

"Yeah, I reckon."

"Come on then."

And with that, they sauntered off.

"Where they going?" Perry said turning to me.

"Don't you worry, they're just playing. They'll be back in a bit, just you watch."

We did...

...they didn't.

We sat up there a good few minutes before thinking about getting ourselves down. But there weren't no doing, it was just too high.

Perry had begun to chew on his bottom lip. "What we gonna do?"

"It's all right. They're probably hiding on the other side of the hedge, spying on us."

Perry looked around, then back to me, his nose twitching.

"All right. We can see you," I called out. "Ent no use hiding." But my calls went unanswered.

"They really have gone, hent they?"

"They'll be back. Billy knows he'll get the belt if he don't."

Come the afternoon, Billy returned home to ask Mum if he could go eat at Wiggy's, then off they went. I guess once she saw Billy, her mind automatically clocked us all back in. Then an hour later she called us in for dinner. Half an hour after that, the whole village was out searching for her two missing children.

It wasn't until she sent someone to fetch Billy to help search that he remembered about leaving us in that tree. For quite some time, Billy held a grudge against me for the hiding he got that night. Things weren't right between us for a long time. I didn't quite have the gumption to work it out, to realise that, of course, a young boy of Billy's age was gonna be going through changes, was gonna need to break free from his childhood shackles and all the reminders of them too. Instead, I was left thinking it was something I'd done, or was, or wasn't. I couldn't quite figure it out, but could only think it had been my fault again.

He didn't even try and hide his annoyance with me. It was as if my very existence was a constant reminder of what he was trying to leave behind. Very soon I started to clam up and not say a word when we happened to be in a room together. I even stopped talking to the others during dinner, and still it didn't seem to be enough. For me, nothing had changed, he was still my hero, I still looked up to him. But to him, I was nothing more than a pain in the backside. After some time, I got used to the fact that this was the way things would be. And so eventually, he went from being my hero to just being my grumpy older brother. Therefore, I can't say I wasn't a bit glad the day Little Pea and me were able to get a small measure of payback on him and Wiggy.

7

THE DIRT TUMBLER

AGED 11 (1956)

It was just me and Perry from there on out. Nothing said, no ceremony, no explanation, it just happened. I guess that's the way it is with kids. Even though you imagine everything will carry on forever and ever, things are changing all the time. And as a kid, you mostly got no choice but to accept it without complaint.

It was strange not having Billy no more; not having someone who told us where to go and what we were doing. I could handle the looking after Perry part no problem, but what I did struggle with was having to magic up some great adventure each time. I could always feel him looking to me, expecting from me, always waiting for... something. But to be honest, I didn't have all that much tucked up my sleeve.

However, it wasn't long before we found a new ally, this time from outside the family in the shape of young Weasel. He was a year younger than me and a good few inches shorter. Scrawny as a stick in winter, but as strong as a branch in summer, with dirty blonde straw-like hair which I doubt had ever seen a comb, and he always seemed to have a grease smudge on his face somewhere too.

As with most kids back in those days, we had a good lot of daily chores to get through. But once they were done we had a fair bit of freedom, especially during the endless summer holidays.

Now, Weasel, well... he was a completely different animal. You see, his father had done a runner when he was but a baby, and his mother spent most of her life in bed feeling poorly. This meant it was left to Wease and his older brother, Donny, to run the family farm. His brother was the one who really did all the work, and because of this, he was too busy to worry about what little ol' Wease was up to. Therefore Weasel was free to roam the countryside causing mischief with almost no comeback. And we didn't half love and envy that boy for those special powers he had.

We'd go along with almost anything he did, even though he rarely asked us to. To be honest, he just did things and we followed. He was always on the go; if he weren't busy with one thing it was the next.

Having an entire farm as our kingdom, we didn't always need to roam too far for our adventures. On hot summer days, you'd most likely find us taking shade in the tall barn where they kept the ol' dirt tumbler. The dirt tumbler was a big wooden cart that could either be hooked up to a horse or tractor so the manure could be lugged around the farm.

One afternoon, we were up in the hayloft trying to throw pebbles down into it. It wasn't much of a game; the only aim was to hit a spot where the dry crust gave way to the fresh stuff beneath, making a satisfying squelch. You got a bonus if it made a farting noise that caused Perry to giggle like a little girl. Once our pocketful of stones ran out the game ended, and no one was of the mind to climb down the wooden ladder to restock our munitions. But, like I said, Weasel was never still for long and he soon darted off, scurrying down the ladder and out of the big barn. Next second, he was back dragging in a gret ol' length of rope. Me and Perry didn't bother to ask what, we just watched and wondered. He dumped it on the floor, tied one end around his waist, and then like a monkey on a mission, he scrambled up the inside of the barn with the rope trailing behind him like the longest tail you ever did see.

"He's a rum'un all right," I said, turning to Perry. "He's got that all wrong, y'know. That rope ent gonna save him none if comes a cropper." But we both knew he weren't about to fall, and if he did, he'd land on his feet like a cat. I was wrong anyhow. The rope wasn't tied to him for safety, but as a way of hauling it up there.

Soon, he was no more than a dusty brown movement high amongst the shadows inching across the main beam. All we could see was the occasional shower of dust as the dangling rope shifted and danced across the barn like an Indian rope trick. It stopped in the middle and then he finally spoke.

"Well?" he called down.

"Well, what?"

"Give it a good ol' tug is what."

"What, you trying to pull the barn down, are yuh?"

"No! It's a swing, ent it. A rope swing."

And there we had it, in a matter of minutes, Weasel had made the shade—and for that matter the rest of the summer—a whole lot less boring.

Well, almost the rest of the summer. As I said before, no good thing ever lasted that long when I was involved. We did manage to get a fair bit of mileage out of it, though. First, we tied a big knot so you could put your feet either side of it and swing out from the top of the hayloft, soaring right out over the barn, just like we were really flying.

"I'm Peterrrrrrrr Paaaaaan!"

We played a game where you had to shout out who you were as you swung.

"I'm Superrrrrrr-maaaaaan!"

"I'm Wonderrrrr Womaaaaan!" We'd call out, before swinging back and landing on a pile of hay in fits of giggles.

"Wonder Woman? That's not a real one," Weasel complained.

"Is too, I got one of her comics, hent I Little Pea?"

Perry nodded uncertainly.

One of the benefits of having the airbase nearby was that, amongst other things, we got all the very latest American comics passed around our sleepy Norfolk village.

We made up loads of different games using that swing, like Roger the Dodger—as the swinger swung back over the loft you had to run between them and edge without get bowled over it and falling fifteen feet onto the concrete. I didn't have much of an appetite for this game, but it was definitely Weasel's favourite.

But anyhow, like I said, the fun had to come to an end at some point. How they found us I don't know, it seemed like they had a sixth-sense, that every time we were having fun it would ping up on their radars and they'd sniff us out. And so, one afternoon they came strutting into that barn, Wiggy and Billy, like it was their farm, like they had a right to be there. They then climbed the ladder and shoved us off. I didn't see why they couldn't just join us and share, why they always had to be mean, and why we always had to scarper. They didn't even like us hanging around watching them, and half the time they didn't even use the swing, they would just laze in the hay quietly mumbling to each other.

It annoyed me because I knew only a few months earlier Billy would've been helping me onto the rope and fussing that I might fall.

Weasel was annoyed because he'd only given the swing its latest upgrade the day before. We'd found the knot had started to rub smooth by the wear of our shoes, and a couple of times we had heart-stopping near slips. Weasel's answer had been to tie on a large branch so you could either stand or sit on it. And for a day the swing had become like a whole new toy.

We discovered that while you were swinging, you could grip the rope tight, and by pulling it towards your chest and pushing out with your feet you could lean your head right back. For a few wonderful moments, it was like you were flying upside down—the world no longer as you knew it.

"I should've left the knot so one of those lummoxes would slip right off," Weasel said, swinging a stick half-heartedly at the long grass. "Or better still—" Then he stopped.

Me and Perry looked at him and we knew, we knew that imaginative and sometimes downright devious mind of his was well at work.

He never got on so well at school, mostly because he didn't go. The teachers had no time for him, saw him as a no-hoper, a waste of space. He couldn't read so good and had no mind for sums and all the rest, but I've never known anyone since who was sharper of mind or could solve a logic problem like that boy could.

We caught up with him in the tractor shed where he was stood atop the workbench stumbling over discarded tools as he rummaged amongst the rusty tins of the upper shelves.

"What you got there Wease?"

"Good old tratt'ur grease," he beamed, proudly holding out the dirty tin. "We'll cover it good and see how well they can hang on arter that!"

"But...?"

"But what?"

I almost didn't say anything as he usually had everything thought out before I'd even realised what the start of the plan was.

"But won't they realise? I mean... the first thing you do is hold the rope ready. They'll know before they take off. Won't they?"

His smile dropped. I felt bad, as if it were my fault.

He slung the grease pot, sending it clattering onto the workbench, then hopped down and traipsed off. We stood watching a large glob of grease slowly ooze from the upturned pot and slide off the edge of the bench. It landed on the dusty floor with a dull *glump*.

"Come on Pea." He followed me out and we started to head home. "Don't worry," I said, "Weasel will come up with something."

Come the next morning, Weasel had found his rascal grin once more. He briefed us on the plan and we got everything ready before the boys finished work. Once we were all set, we hid the watering can and waited. Then, sure as sunrise, they turned up and pushed us out the way. This time we didn't sidle off, instead, we climbed down and sat on the (now empty) upturned water pails. Perry sat with his mouth tightly shut and his lips folded inside. He occasionally looked from Wease to me. All day I'd been telling Perry he had to keep *completely* schtum, as he wasn't quite at the age to know all about the subtleties of lying. I sat on my hands to stop myself fidgeting, while Weasel sat there with the faintest of smiles as he whittled a stick with his hunting knife.

We didn't have to wait long before they decided to have a swing. I closed my eyes and made a quick wish. *Please, please, please let it be Billy who goes first.* And lo and behold, my prayer was answered.

Billy grabbed the rope.

He walked backwards.

He placed his left foot on the branch.

He pulled himself up.

Placed his other foot on the branch.

And took off.

He swooooooshed through the air. Away from the hayloft. Away from safety. Soaring over the freshly watered, steaming muck pile that wallowed in the dirt tumbler beneath.

I allowed my smile to break free. It didn't matter now—it was too late.

We watched as he soared further... and further... and further away from the ledge. We watched as he reached the end of his swing. Then, we watched as he began to... come back? All the way back, back over the hayloft and back to safety.

Perry looked to me. I looked to Weasel. His half-smile now upside down.

"Come on, my go now, Billy," said Wiggy, as Billy continued to swing back and forth.

He landed neatly and passed the rope to Wiggy. Wiggy took his turn. Also swinging safely back and forth.

Weasel got up and kicked his pail across the barn.

"Oooooh," laughed Wiggy, as he swung above him. "Someone's throwing their toys out the pram today, ent they."

I stood up to follow, then stopped. An idea of my own was forming.

"So what," I shouted up to them, "you'll never be as good as Wease."

Hearing his name, Weasel turned around. I gave him a quick wink and saw his brow crease in confusion.

"You'll never even be as good as me and Little Pea neither," I continued.

Wiggy just laughed, paying me no mind.

"We can even swing with two people on it," I said, putting my hands on my hips.

"Keep a lid on it, Wonder Woman," said Billy.

Wiggy landed. "Yeah, you think we can't do that? We already do that, don't we Bill?"

"Yeah. We done it loads afore."

"Bet you hent never," said Weasel, coming back into the barn. "I think you two hent never done it and would never dare."

"We don't need to prove nothing to a scrawny rat like you."

"See, told you they hent," I said and turned to leave. "Come on, Pea, let's leave these girls to play by themselves."

"All right then," Billy said, grabbing the rope off Wiggy, "let's show 'em how it's done."

Billy pulled it back on to the ledge. They began to hop around and struggle as they tried to work out how to get both of them on it. They were trying to get on each side of the branch, but all they managed was to turn it into a seesaw. I started to think maybe it wasn't possible after all.

"You doing it wrong," Weasel sighed.

Even if we didn't have a hastily made-up plan unfolding, he wouldn't have been able to stop himself helping them out. He'd seen a way it was possible and he'd never have been able to keep it to himself. "One of yous needs to sit on the branch backwards, the other has to pull it, then jump up on the knot and a way y'go."

"Yeah," said Billy, "that's how we usually do it. We're just getting it the right way is all."

Eventually, they got themselves sorted—Wiggy on the branch and Billy as the take-off man.

"Ready? One... Two... Three." And they pushed off.

As they swung out, the extra weight was already showing. The rope stretched like it had never done before, causing Wiggy's bum to brush the ledge clean of the loose hay, sending it fluttering delicately towards the steaming dirt tumbler.

As they continued to swing out, the rope began to creak and groan as it rubbed on the beam above. Then, from high up in the darkness of the barn eaves—where earlier that morning, Weasel had clambered up with his hunting knife and cut through half of the thick platted rope strands—there came a *snap*.

A cloud of dust exploded as the rope pinged away like a rubber band and went slack.

The boys continued past the usual point of return for half a second, and then all was quiet.

There was a surprised half-grunt from one of the astronauts, followed by a pause... before they simply fell out of the sky. Down they went. Plummeting like stones into wet cement, splotting straight into the stinking mess of cow crud.

"Wooooohooooo!" Weasel screamed, jumping with his arms in the air like he'd won the football final cup. Perry was chuckling away like when I tickled his feet in the mornings, and I found myself just clapping my hands wildly and bouncing on my toes.

Slowly, a two-headed bog monster began to struggle up out of the muck. It was hard to tell who was who until they spoke.

"What the hell." Billy tried to wipe his face clean, but his hand was dirtier still.

"It bloody snapped," snarled Wiggy.

For a moment I thought we'd done it, the perfect crime, that we wouldn't even need phase two.

...that was until Wease piped up, "Or maybe... someone cut it. Ha-ha-ha."

"You what...?" And then it dawned. "It was... you lot!"

"You come here." They started to scramble out of the cart.

"Ha-ha. Let's go. Let's go. Phase two. Phase two," said Weasel, pretending to shout into a walkie-talkie while beckoning us on. "Move it, men. Move it."

We turned and ran the short distance to the tractor and trailer that he'd readied outside. He hopped into the driving seat and started her up. It belched out a dirty clot of smoke and rattled into life.

"All aboard! *Waaaht-waaaht*," Weasel shouted, as he pulled the rope of an imaginary air horn.

The Bog Boys had got themselves free of the tumbler. All covered in wet manure, with bits dripping and falling off them, they set after us. As I was trying to help Perry on to the trailer, I turned to see them coming, but I didn't wait. I grabbed his legs and slung the rest of him on, then hopped up myself just as Weasel hit the throttle.

Now, let me tell you, there's good reason why you never hear about bank robbers making their getaways in a tractor and trailer.

Chugga, chugga, chugga, it went as we began to crawl away at a tortoise pace. The Bog Boys were upon us, but not soon enough as the old girl finally gathered her wits, picked up her skirt hem and we were off.

They chased us as we rattled and bumped along the farm track, but several times it looked like they'd given up. So Weasel, the little devil, eased off the throttle, just enough to keep them interested, then as they got within spitting distance he'd gas it again and off we'd rattle once more. They only fell for this a few times before they gave up and we left them bent over double gasping for air. Billy scraped a thick lump of muck off his arm and threw it at us, but it landed short and only caused us to belly laugh even more. I'm not sure what was funnier —them covered in muck, Weasel teasing them by slowing down and speeding up, or even just the very sight of tiny little Weasel (who could hardly see over the steering wheel) bouncing around in the huge old tractor seat.

I knew Perry and me would be safe at home. Billy wouldn't dare say nothing to Dad, fearing he'd get in just as much trouble as us. And even if he had've done, it would've been worth it.

One thing we couldn't avoid, though, was the end of the rope swing. Before we'd done it, I'd said to Weasel that we could just untie the rope from the beam and leave it loose so it was easier to fix afterwards, but Weasel wouldn't listen, insisting it be cut. It seemed his love for making stuff always needed to be balanced by an equal want for destroying things.

As is often the way in a child's life, friends seem to fade in and out as we grow, and at times we hardly notice they're gone until we chance to look back. Whilst the episode with the dirt tumbler wasn't the last time I mucked about with Weasel, it was the last time I remember clearly. It was some years later, and a fair few after I'd last seen him, when his older brother came into the tractor shed one afternoon to find young Weasel on the floor in front of the workbench. It seems he'd accidentally electrocuted himself trying to fix an old arc-welder he'd bought secondhand. He was a week shy of his fifteenth birthday, and that day the world lost a true little genius.

It caused quite a stir in the surrounding neighbourhoods. By then, we had moved a couple of villages away, but still everyone was talking about it and had an opinion—which I always thought was a bit off since no one had the slightest interest in the boy before his passing. You'd hear people in the shops telling one another how they once bought a car from his great uncle, and then felt this allowed them to pass some sort of judgment on him and his family.

"I blame the absent father, myself."

"Well, if his mother wasn't playing hooky in bed all day, maybe she'd have been there to keep him safe."

"It's the older brother I feel sorry for, y'know."

"He was a good boy really, just misguided."

"I don't care what people say; he was off the rails from the start. Was always gonna end in just one way."

However, this only really lasted for a week until he was forgotten about once again. Though, it nearly got my brother Billy the sack from his job, mind you. I don't know exactly what was said, and I never cared to find out, but some fella made a smart-arse remark about Weasel's passing. This caused Billy to flip his lid and fly at him. I don't think any real punches were thrown before they were pulled apart, and luckily he was shown leniency by his bosses and our parents alike because of the circumstances. Good ol' Billy.

The happenings with the dirt tumbler turned out to be one of my last big adventures as a carefree kid. The arrival of the sixth, and last but one, edition to our family in the shape of young Valerie changed everything for me at the tender age of 12. The day she was born, was the day I took my first step onto the express-train headed straight to adulthood with no stops scheduled along the way.

8

A NEW MOTHER

AGED 12 (1957)

Whilst she may have been sparing with her time and love for me, I have to say she never let me go hungry. Whenever Aunt Sylvie and her went out to the pictures, they'd always come back with plenty of goodies to share out amongst us all.

Aunt Sylvie, not my real Aunt, *was* truly marvellous. She was a short lady, but she always made quite the impression with her rich auburn hair, big hazel eyes, and the most beautiful angelic smile you ever did see. She was brought up in Blackpool and therefore was always calling everyone *duck*.

She was the closest thing to a real-life fairy godmother in my eyes. She'd wink at me when no one was looking—sometimes for no reason at all, no joke or secret being shared, she'd just wink at me and smile. It made me feel giddy inside whenever she did.

Sylvie and my mum were thick as thieves, so she was often over at our house. When they came back from the pictures, Aunt Sylvie always made a big deal about sharing the treats out fairly amongst us kids, then later she'd slip me an extra one, saying, "Oh, look what I just found in me pocket, duck. Don't be telling the others now." Of course, this time she had good reason to wink.

At school, you always knew the teachers had favourites, even though they weren't meant to. And they always thought the other kids didn't notice, but we did—or at least the quiet kids who hid behind doors did. I spent most of my childhood being invisible to adults, through a mix of shyness and trying to avoid trouble. However, Aunt Sylvie could see me, and that was enough for me to be sure that I wasn't just a figment of my own imagination, that I did at least exist. She'd actually take time to talk to me, have actual conversations, ask me questions and tell me things. In fact, if it wasn't for Aunt Sylvie, I might never have known about baby Valerie existing until the day she popped out.

"What you reckon, duck? Do you want a boy or little girl?" she said to me as she sat brushing my hair at the end of the bed.

"I ent really thought about it yet. I'm only twelve," I told her, quite surprised by the question.

"Not you, you silly. Your mam."

"Mum?"

"You know, her being in the puddin club again."

But I was still none the wiser.

"You know, being pregnant again." She could see from my confuddled look I wasn't up to speed. "Oh... she hasn't told you yet then? She's a card ent she, duck."

"So...?"

"Yes! You're gonna have another little brother or sister in six months or so. How about that? Exciting isn't it?" she said, placing a hand over her belly.

"Yeah." I was excited, but also just surprised, and wondering how I hadn't realised. Maths wasn't one of my strong points, but I knew enough of the world to realise this news was nearly three months old. At first, I felt hurt, but wasn't even sure why. Then me being me, this soon turned to guilt. Guilt because I hadn't noticed, because I hadn't been treating my mum according to her condition. She was a big lady, but you'd still thought I would have noticed the change in my own mother.

"She don't half pop 'em out hey, your mother," Sylvie carried on. "Your dad must be eating something right, I tell you, duck. Imagine though, I haven't even had one yet and your mother's on her sixth, isn't she?" she said, almost idly as she re-brushed the same length of hair for the tenth time. "Hm, I wouldn't be surprised if this one just falls out when it's ready, hey? She'll be in and out of that hospital the same way as what your dad must be like in the sack," she finished with a slightly different type of wink.

I didn't always understand everything Sylvie said, but she never checked herself and always talked to me honestly, just like I was a real adult. Which turned out to be good practice, seeing as six months later when Valerie arrived, I pretty much *had to* become a real adult overnight.

Almost from the outset I was playing second mother to baby Val. My mum doted on her for sure, but she also liked her free time and managed to keep herself busy. She was always popping round to check on an elderly neighbour, or popping off to the shops, or popping out to catch up with an old friend. Whereas I was no longer even allowed out at all, not like the other kids. Unless it was to take the young'uns for a walk—Valerie in the pram, and Perry and Puddin dawdling along in tow. Most weekends I had to take them by bus to the beach at Sheringham. Out by 9 am and not allowed back until 4:30 pm whether it rained, hailed, blowed or snowed. And if it wasn't the beach, then I'd have to pack us all a lunch and struggle with the pram across the rough ground at the heath.

Having to play mother aged 12, meant growing up fast. I did my best, and I like to think I did Valerie fine most of the time. But of course, there were mistakes and worries along the way, and she wasn't my only responsibility. In the mornings when Karl and Billy couldn't get themselves out of bed for work—which was nearly every morning —I'd go in with cold wet flannels and fling them on their faces before scarpering quick sharp. And when I wasn't looking after the family, well, then I'd be cleaning around the house, which was no mean feat for a family of our size. The place seemed to get dirty as quickly as you could clean it, like a never-ending cycle it was.

"Poor little bugger," Aunt Sylvie once said to my mum, upon seeing me on my hands and knees scrubbing the outside toilet. "What you make a pretty little girl like her, do that for, duck?"

"She uses it, she can clean it," was all Mum would say.

I wanted to live with Aunt Sylvie so much that I secretly wished that she could be my mother. But this thought then left me awash with guilt, so I tried not to entertain it all too often.

Our outhouse was different to most, my dad had built it himself and made it a double one, so if you wanted to, you could sit side by side while you did your business. Heavens knows why you might want that option, but it did make for an often-retold family story involving my two real aunts, Polly and Evie. We didn't always see them that often as they married two Americans, Burt and Ned, and ended up moving over to California in the States. I missed them; they liked to have fun and were always, always laughing. I don't think they spoke a single sentence without it ending in laughter.

Anyway, one day they were all over visiting when I sensed some excitement going on around the kitchen table. I was washing-up after lunch, and Burt and Ned were trying to talk all quiet but couldn't keep themselves from chuckling. Being a curious kid I tried to listen in. Peering over my shoulder I saw Burt had something in his hands. My mum gave me a scowl and a nod of the head sending me back to the dishes. Next, they were all getting their shoes on and going out the door trying not to giggle. I couldn't help myself and followed close behind—having the power of invisibility isn't always so bad. We all sneaked down to the bottom of the garden, and then I stood back watching while they gathered themselves around the toilet shed.

Meanwhile, Ned had got himself set by the door, while Burt had the camera at the ready. On a whispered count of three, Ned yanked the door open to reveal Aunt Polly and Evie sat side by side with their knickers around their ankles, and Burt took the photo. Well, there was laughter, and mind you, some screaming from my aunts too, but they were loving it really.

Even though I wasn't properly involved, it was a beautiful moment. A family getting along and having fun, making stories that'd be retold whenever they got together, and be laughed at all over again as if it happened that very day.

At times like that, you never imagine you'll get older and that things will change. As a kid, time doesn't seem to move so fast and you think everything will always remain the same, so it came as quite the shock when our parents told us we were moving to a new house in High Kelling some twenty-odd miles away. I'd never even entertained the idea of living anywhere different, everything was so familiar and comfortable, so why on earth would we. But our ever-growing family had finally pushed that old council house's seams to bursting point, and so with a bit of help from the grandparents, they bought a house we could finally call our own.

However, given the choice, I would've taken the one owned by the council any day. Even though it wasn't actually ours, it felt like a member of the family. And it wasn't until after we moved that I realised it wasn't just the house you left behind but your whole life. The friends you'd made, the camps you'd built, the streams you went paddling in, everything that you were familiar with. But my dad had got himself a new job as a cowman with slightly better pay, and the new house, although colder, older, and a little bit more ramshackle, was slightly larger. Inevitably, a larger house meant more work in order to keep it spick and span and everything running as smoothly as possible. Of course, with me being the only female big enough to wield a mop and a plunger, all the extra work fell to me. This suddenly left me with very little free time, and when I did I was expected to use it for the babysitting duties. Even if it was a school day, I had to stay off and look after Valerie. My dad only got one regular day off a week, Tuesdays, and so my parents would use it to visit my mother's mum and dad. They lived a lot further afield after we moved, so generally, just the two of them would go on the motorbike.

I can't say I really minded missing school. Coming in as the new kid halfway through a term meant I had no friends, and I was too shy to try and make new ones. Sometimes I could go almost an entire day without speaking to anyone. It wasn't long though before the school realised it was always Tuesdays that I was absent. And very soon the school inspector, Mr Dimsdale, came out to see what was going on.

He was a tall man, always well-dressed and always very serious. And sure enough, he found me at home alone with the baby and said he'd have to come back at the weekend to speak to my parents.

I didn't tell them he'd come because I wasn't sure whether I'd be in trouble for it or not. In the end, I decided to forget about it, hoping he'd do likewise. But the very next Sunday I was putting the clean sheets on the bed when I saw him from the top window coming up the path. I raced down to try and give my mum some warning, telling her I recognised him from school.

"Well, what's he gonna want? What have you been up to?" she said with her eyes narrowing in on me.

Then came the knock on the door, giving me the opportunity to scarper back up the stairs out of harm's way. Stopping at the top, I peeped down from between the banisters, my hands already clamming up. I really feared for Mr Dimsdale. I remember thinking, he doesn't know what he's got himself into, or *who* he is about to take on.

9

THE MAD MOTHER OF HIGH KELLING

I couldn't catch the exact goings-on of their conversation, other than Mum being all jolly and trying to tell Mr Dimsdale not to be so daft and that I was just a bit of sickly child was all.

"What, and it just so happens to be every Tuesday?" he said, in his clipped proper voice. "No, it won't do. I'm simply not having it."

"Well, Mr... Sir. It's not as though it is *every*—"

"No. It stops here. And that is going to be the end of this conversation."

Honestly, I hadn't seen it coming, but my mother was in a total fluster and all apologetic. As big and bolshie as she was, it seemed there were times when she feared authority, and so Mr Dimsdale put pay to their Tuesday outings.

It was almost an eye-opener for me, sitting atop the stairs, watching in disbelief. I thought maybe it would change things, that the telling-off would change her, that there was hope she could be the mother I wanted.

These thoughts didn't live long though, once the belt came out. Again, somehow, it was all my fault. Not only did I get the belt, but it also meant an extra day at school for me every week.

It was never her who dished out the punishments; it was always

Dad who was cast as the executioner. Mum was just the judge and jury. It almost seemed as if it was beneath her to do it herself.

Despite being treated like a maid by my own mother, I did at least get a sense of pride and satisfaction from the housework and looking after everybody. I got good at it too. I knew what I was doing and I had my little systems. I did the work without complaint, mostly because it needed to be done, but also because I thought it was the only way to make her like me. If I just concentrated on not upsetting her, keeping my head down and doing whatever she needed and whatever she told me, she'd soon see I was a good little girl after all. The other plus point was that it kept my mind busy, and that way I didn't have much chance to rue the end of my childhood.

School, on the other hand, wasn't something I did so well at. Even before the move, my only friends had been my brothers or their friends. It took me almost a year to shake that feeling of being the new kid. I wasn't particularly academic either; I always tried my utmost and did the best I could. The only thing I wasn't so bad at was staying out of trouble, but this was rather easy when you didn't have any friends to play with. I realised this tactic worked well at home too, so if I ever had time to myself I'd spend it playing quietly in my room, and if my parents were out, I'd sneak into their room and pretend their old clothes horse was a real one. A couple of times I even managed to go a whole month without a belting, can you believe.

School mornings were always a hectic occasion in our house with so many kids. Of course, I had to be up earliest so I could get the little'uns awake and ready. And because Mum had recently started working voluntarily at the local children's hospital a couple of days a week, it meant that first I had to run Valerie round to our kindly neighbours, Keith and Elaine, then take Perry and Puddin to primary school before finally getting myself off to secondary school, hoping after all that I wouldn't be too late.

We only had the one pushbike for me to use for the school run, but somehow we managed. I'd put Perry on the crossbar, Puddin on the back seat, and then stuffed all our school satchels in between us wherever we could. It was tough to get started, but once we got a head of steam up we were all right. We must've looked a sight though, piled high like one of those trains you see in India. So of course the other kids from school never missed a chance to call out names at me.

"Here she comes! The Little Mother of High Kelling!"

I got the same when I had to take Valerie out in the pram, too. I tried to ignore them and pretend I didn't care, but my blushing face always told the truer story.

After a few months of riding the bike in this way, I got pretty good at it. Even fully laden I could fair whiz about. One morning we were on our way when I saw a gang of school kids opposite the corner near the pub. I could already see one of them pointing me out as we came down the hill.

Don't blush now, Rosie, don't blush, I was telling myself, but could already feel the burn creeping up my neck and down from my ears. Then the calls started.

"Look out, here comes Little Mother!"

"Where's your pram Little Mother?"

"Mind you don't fall off."

I didn't look at them. Instead, I started to pedal faster and build up speed. Perry grabbed for the handlebars to steady himself, but I told him to grip the frame instead. With the tyres whirring we came whizzing down the hill, and just before we passed the gang of kids I let go of the handlebars, folded my arms across my chest, and raised my head up all casual-like.

The gang went silent as the pub on the corner came at us fast.

"Rosieeee!" came Perry's urgent whisper.

"Just you keep still, Little Pea," I told him.

Puddin on the back couldn't see so was none the wiser.

The gang stood as one to get a better look at the forthcoming crash.

As we hit the corner I shifted my weight to the left and began to lean ever so slightly. At the right speed, I knew it didn't take a lot to steer that old bike. Three-up, arms folded, we glided round that there corner.

"Woh."

"Blimey."

They couldn't help but be impressed.

"Did you see that?" I heard the last voice trail off.

But as I told you before, it was just a matter of waiting. Nothing ever came good for me. With the wind in my hair and a hard to hide smile, I continued, arms folded. After the pub was the post office. As we came to it, the door opened and, looking down into her bag, Mrs Webster came trundling out.

"Watch it," I screamed.

I lent right and made a grab for the handlebars, managing to skim past her. However, Puddin's knee must have caught her bag. Of course, it went flying. The contents spilling all over the road as we wobbled away, much to the laughter of the gang.

I had to put up with taunts all day at school. Kids would brush by me, then suddenly pretend to drop all their belongings before running away shouting, "Look out, no one's safe from the Mad Mother of High Kelling."

I was so relieved to finish school that day—until on the way home we saw Mrs Webster outside the post office waiting for us. And she wasn't alone.

"You're nothing but an embarrassment," my mother said. "What... first of all it's the school inspector and now a bloody policeman come round. And to think you'd been doing better of late as well. Well, you ruined it all now, that's for sure. Just you wait 'til your father gets home."

10

ALL CHANGE

AGED 13 (1958)

I was 13 years old when the world, or what little I knew of it, began sliding away from me. It all started with two pieces of news. One seemingly good, and one the worst I could have imagined at that time. The first was that Mum was pregnant for the seventh and final time with little Daniel. You'd think I'd have been sick of babies already, but I couldn't have been happier. However, it was a case of one in, one out. The other news was that Aunt Sylvie was going back to Blackpool. I was devastated.

I didn't know what to do when she came round ours to tell us, except put my hands over my ears, hoping I'd done it quick enough to stop the words happening. If I didn't hear them they couldn't be true, was my thinking, but I knew it was too late, that I couldn't pretend this one away.

"I'm gonna miss you too, duck," she said to me as we sat on the rusty grass-roller in the back garden.

"Don't go then, stay here. Come live with us."

"I have to, I'm afraid. All my family is back in Blackpool, you see."

But I'm your family too! I wanted to say, but I didn't because then I'd have to hear her say the truth.

"Do you want to go back?" I asked instead.

She straightened the ribbon in my hair and sighed. "What I really want is to meet me a nice fella and have a daughter who is even half as lovely and pretty as you, duck."

I felt my chest go and wanted to cry. *You don't need no fella for that. I'll be your daughter.*

~

The next day the taxi came to take her away. I gripped onto her as tight as I could and buried my face into her coat, refusing to let go. I wanted to melt into her so she had no choice but to take me. I felt a gentle hand on my shoulder pull me in closer, then I heard the taxi door being opened. Then a second hand, gripping my arm, firm and determined. The hand kept tightening though, tightening until I hurt. Then it began pulling, but not pulling me tighter into the hug, but pulling me away. I tried to hold against it, but it started yanking at me until finally I was torn away from the warmth and comfort of Sylvie.

"Look what you're doing to her coat. Stop being such a drama queen."

I still had a handful of it, but I didn't want Sylvie to leave being angry at me, so I let go. As I did, I was pulled off my feet and went down grazing my knee on the gravel.

"Now look what you done to yourself," said Mum, shaking her head.

Clutching my knee, I sat up to see the door shut Sylvie away from me. I reached out for her. The taxi started up and began to move away.

She pushed down the window and waved to everyone, gave a brave laugh and wiped a tear from her face. Then as the taxi pulled away, even through the blur of tears, she gave me one of her famous smiles and a wink. "Ta-ra, duck. Don't worry, I'll be back one day." She was good to her promise and did come back for a visit a few years later.

Many, many years later, quite recent in fact, my husband told me he had a surprise for me. Gawd knows how, but he'd found out where she was living, and so off to Blackpool we went.

It had been such a long time and so much had happened that I wasn't sure what I'd say to her, how long we were going to stay or even what we would do together.

We found the address easy enough after asking around a bit. She lived on a small rise of terraced houses. I paused at the gate, but my husband urged me on. Then, just as I was about to knock, the door opened. My heart fluttered; it was as if some special bond had told her I was coming, as if she sensed it. Even at 86, in an old apron and worn-out slippers, clutching a bag of rubbish, you knew she was a real beauty in her day.

"Aunt Sylvie?"

She smiled her beautiful warming smile, but I could see it in her face.

"Sylvie?"

"Sorry, duck, there isn't anything I want today, and I don't even have the money besides," she sighed and began to shuffle back into the house.

"Sylvie, it's... Rose."

She paused a moment. "Oh, wait a minute...." and after another moment of shuffling, the door widened again. "I just remembered. You couldn't be a dear and put this in the wheelie bin for me, could you, duck?"

She handed me the rubbish bag and was already turning to go back in. It was a chilly October day, so I didn't want to keep her at the door while I tried to explain who I was and why I'd come. Maybe I should have used my mum's name—of all the people, surely she couldn't have forgotten her. But for some reason I didn't, I didn't want to. I wanted to ask her if she found her fella and had the daughter she'd longed for, but I didn't.

I don't think my husband could quite understand it, and couldn't hide his own disappointment that after going all that way and after all his effort things hadn't worked out as they were supposed to. But just to see her again, see that smile, being close to her, and that brief moment when I felt the warmth of her hand as it touched mine after more than 50 years, that was enough for me.

Back when I was a child though, parting from her had been a totally different matter. I hardly spoke the week after she left. Just quietly got on with my jobs. Then the week after that I went around calling everyone duck—that was until my mum put a stop to it in no uncertain terms.

A deep loneliness swamped me. It seemed everything I knew and liked was gradually being taken from me and it was my fault and it was what I deserved. If only I was a better person, if only I didn't always mess things up, if only I wasn't so quiet and dull—then maybe Billy would've liked me still, my Mum too, and of course... Sylvie would've liked me enough not to want to move away.

With nothing going on inside, I began to shut down like an empty husk. I went about my chores like the ghostly POWs clearing snow from the hedges. I felt like I wasn't really a person anymore; I didn't have time to think, except for what my next chore was and worrying if I'd made any mistakes on the last. Had I forgot anything? Had I hung up the laundry? Did the little'uns have their school clothes ironed? Had I left the mop in the outhouse? Had I bought everything for dinner? Had I packed everyone's lunches?

At least being busy meant I wasn't able to dwell too much on why I was no good and what it was that I'd done wrong. It meant I could concentrate on getting my jobs done and trying to stay invisible, hoping eventually things might come good on their own accord.

11

BED AND BREAKFAST

It worked—keeping my head down and waiting and hoping—at school at least. Things soon improved. The other kids got bored of teasing me when there was no reaction to it. I'd just kinda shut down, stare at my feet, do my beetroot impression, and take it. And soon enough they'd move onto the next kid who'd give them something better to work with.

Lo and behold, I even started to make a few friends. I never had time to see them outside of school, so I often had to wait every morning just listening to what they'd got up to the night before or at the weekend, and only after that had finally run dry could I join in. To be honest, they weren't always doing interesting things, but that didn't stop them having lots to say about it nonetheless.

Sometimes I practiced in the bathroom mirror, asking Mum if I could go out after school with my friends, *Just one day a week is all? I'll get all my jobs done first, I promise.* But just like the fairies, this fantasy stayed where it belonged too. Besides, with the half-term holiday fast approaching, I didn't want to rock the boat, as I'd soon have the best part of a week free. The kids at school had already made lots of plans for adventures. I also tried throwing my tuppence worth in too, as if I was definitely going—though I wasn't stupid enough to think it was a given.

The first Saturday of the half-term I made sure I was up early and went through my jobs quickly, thinking if I worked hard all weekend, by Monday I would've earned my freedom. But come Sunday evening, my hopes were dashed all across the well-mopped floor.

"Right, Rosemary. Best get them kids and their bags packed. We wanna be off in a couple of hours."

"Off? Where?"

"It's not yours to ask, is it now? C'mon." Then over her shoulder as she walked away, "Lowestoft."

"Lowestoft? How long for?" I asked, praying it was just a day trip.

"What's it matter to you?" she said, turning back.

"So... so I know what I need to pack for them."

"Well, what do you bloomin think? Half-term is a week, the last time I checked."

A week! The whole week. I was all in a fluster and I couldn't think. Had she told me before about a holiday? Usually, they'd tell us so they could use it as a threat to keep us in line in the run-up.

"...Should I pack yours and Dad's things in the same case?"

"Your father? He ent coming. Some of us have to graft in this world, y'know. Just like we'll be doing."

It turned out one of Mum's old friends ran a bed-and-breakfast and they were off on their holidays, so we were to run it in their stead. Deep down I'd known my dreams of freedom were always going to be no more than that. I guess I always tried to give myself something to look toward, some sort of horizon, like owning my own horse one day. And even though I knew the sun would always set before I could reach the horizon, it was important, it at least gave me something to sustain myself on. A bit of hope each time.

Working at the bed and breakfast had its ups and downs. Mum was in her element with all the different people coming and going; she loved being the centre of attention. For me, it only meant ten times more beds to make and wash, ten times the dishes to clean—basically ten times the everything. But I guess it was different from home. And don't they say a change is as good as a rest.

One perk of working in a bigger place meant I wasn't under my mum's feet so much, so there was less chance of getting wrong by her. The guests were always pleasant people. They often tried to chat with me, but I was always aware of my mother's hawkish eye, so I usually nodded back to them politely and carried on with what I was doing.

For the little'uns it was just like having their very own life-sized doll's house. Karl and Billy had stayed at home with Dad, because of their jobs. They'd started to leave me further behind, now they had money of their own. It didn't seem fair that they could buy themselves things and go out, while I worked every spare minute for the house and family but got nothing back. I guessed that I was just unlucky in being the oldest girl.

The week in Lowestoft flew by and soon it was Friday. We'd be back home on Sunday, then Monday I'd be back to school to hear all about the adventures I'd missed out on. The week hadn't been a complete washout though as Mum finally fed me some much-needed crumbs. A guest who'd spoke to me the day before was chatting to her as they were checking out.

"Here comes the little darlin," said the man as I walked through with an armful of bed sheets.

"Cor, hardly," scoffed Mum.

"You're too hard on her. She's been working like a trooper non-stop ever since we been here."

"Well, that much is true," came the golden words from my mother's mouth. "She knows her jobs. I guess she takes after me in that respect."

I couldn't believe what I had just heard. I hurried out of the entrance hall so I could set free my smile. It may not sound much to you as I tell it now, but back then it meant everything to hear these words. When I got into the laundry room I felt like throwing the sheets into the air in celebration and dancing under them as they floated serenely all around me. For the rest of the day I worked with a skip in my step and a smile on my face.

Come Saturday morning, I was right proud of myself. I'd managed a whole week without doing-a-Rosemary and ruining it all. I got up early and was down in the kitchen chucking bread in the toaster, and while that was toasting I set the dining room out, napkins straight, cutlery polished, then poured the milk and juice into the jugs. In fact, I had it all done before Mum had even got out of bed. When she saw what a few good nourishing words could do for me I knew they'd be plenty more to come.

The early risers started coming down and quietly eating their breakfast. Once they all had some food on their tables I went around and checked that no one was in want of anything before going to rouse the little'uns.

Us kids were all staying in the one room—the two boys in one bed, me and Val in the other, and little Danny's cot by the window. I opened up the curtains to the usual moans and groans as the lumps in the beds began to stir.

Once I'd given little Daniel his morning feed, I pulled the covers off the others.

"Come along now, up you all get. I want you all dressed ready for breakfast. Quick, quick now."

Val was still in nappies but was talking and toddling. I had to get her dressed fast so I could get back to the customers, realising that I still hadn't heard Mum get up yet. She normally came down before the customers had finished breakfast so I'd then be free to raise the rabble. As it was the last full day of work and because of her good words the day before, I didn't mind or think nothing of her not being about yet.

Val was being niggly as I tried to get her dressed in quick time.

"Valerie. Come on. I gotta get back downstairs, stop being so silly."

Being the last day, I decided to put her in a pretty little dress with bunny rabbits on it. As I was trying to pull it over her head I caught her arm, and in my rush didn't realise. I kept yanking it down, which of course set her off bawling.

"Mummmmy. Mummmmy," she started wailing.

"Now just you be quiet, Mummy's sleeping."

Even though I did more for her than our mum ever did, whenever she got upset it was always straight into her arms that she ran. Mum would pick her up and Val would bury her head into Mum's giant bosom, big arms coming round and holding her tight. Then the soothing words would come, and more times than not Val would soon fall into a blissful slumber.

"I want Mummy," she continued.

"Look, if you weren't being so troublesome, you wouldn't be bawling in the first place. You gonna do it yourself then?" I said and stepped back, leaving her half tangled in her dress. She sat scowling at me, all in a huff.

I turned my attention to the boys next, "And boys, come on. You gotta..." As I spoke, Valerie, minus her dress, toddled past me out of the door.

"Muuuuumy!" she bawled again as she made her way down the corridor.

I took off after her but couldn't get to her before she reached Mum's room.

"Valerie. No," I barked, but the knob was just within her reach, and she was already turning it.

Blurting out my apology I scooped her up, but the door had made up its mind that it was going to swing fully open.

"I'm sorry, I'm sorry," I said, "I couldn't—"

Then silence.

It's times like that, that you doubt your own eyes. All I could think to do was cup my hand over Valerie's, hoping she hadn't already seen.

I stood, frozen, speechless. Eventually, I felt Valerie's hands fussing at my arm, trying to pull it from her face. I turned us both away and slowly closed the door again. In a daze, the corridor seemed long and cold and unfamiliar. I became all too aware that we were living in somebody else's house, that we were far from home, that things weren't as they should be. Strange things in strange places.

Finally, I let Valerie pull my arm away, but my efforts had been for nothing.

"Rosieee?" she said. "Who was that man in Mummy's bed?"

12

THERE WAS NO MAN

Back then, it wasn't all so different from how it is now. Most people would have you believe that jumping in and out of bed with each other is a modern invention. Well, let me tell you, you'd just be plain wrong to think that folks weren't at it in those days too, or that everybody was waiting until they were wed first. The only real difference was, even though it still got gossiped about, most folks just pretended it wasn't going on. Ignorance is bliss and all that.

Now, if you don't mind bearing with me for a bit, I'd like to tell you a story—however, before I do I must warn you it ent going to be one of these ones that ends all nicely. So, here we go—there was once this couple, Uncle Denny and Aunt June, who lived next door to my mum's parents for a while. They were a lovely pair apparently, and used to look in on my grandparents all the while—whether it was cutting wood for their fire, baking them bread or helping them with the house cleaning. Absolute angels so it's told—you see this all happened before my time—in fact just around the time my mum found out she was pregnant with me. Aunt June was also pregnant, ahead of my mum by almost three months, but that still didn't stop her helping out with the axe and mop. As close to a real-life saint as you can get, people would say about Aunt June. The original good Samaritan. A proper Florence Nightingale, they called her.

They called Uncle Denny, Horse, on account of him being as fit as a butcher's dog. He worked at the wood yard, and would pushbike eleven miles there and back again six days a week, and then played for the local football team on his day off. I once heard the old boys say that on the days it was blizzarding and impossible to cycle, Horse would run to the lumberyard. And they said he always turned up dry as bone cos even the falling snow wasn't quick enough to catch him.

Anyway, as it's told, one night Uncle Denny was coming back from the pub on his pushbike, possibly a little worse for wear, making his way down the country lanes to June and their unborn child. Now, if you've ever been out this way, you'll know most Norfolk country roads are narrow and high-hedged affairs, often with little enough room for a car and pushbike. A small lorry, however—that wouldn't even leave room for a cigarette paper as poor Uncle Denny found out to his cost that evening.

He was knocked clean off his bike; the bike left crushed and mangled and Denny fairing no better—though he was still breathing. He could never be sure of the exact details, but he was certain it was a small lorry cos it stopped. There was a man and a woman, and he felt sure he heard them say his name at some point. Other than that though, there was only a lot of maybes.

Maybe neither of them quite sure what'd happened—what they'd hit. Maybe the driver gets out praying it was a deer, at worst a dog... Then they hear the moans and the driver calls out to his passenger.

"Come, come quick!"

She doesn't want to, it's dark and she can hear that edge in his voice, that edge that tells her all is not right. Maybe she lowers herself out of the cab, clutching her arms across her chest even though it's early autumn.

"What... what happened? What... is it?" she asks.

The driver looks back at her. His pale face, lit up in the lorry's lights, speaks for him.

"*Who*... is it?"

He doesn't want to answer.

They stand looking down at the heap of broken bones and battered flesh that was once the sprightly Uncle Denny, once the Horse. Recognising him, the lady puts her hand to her mouth and turns away. "No. Not Denny."

Maybe Uncle Denny looks up at the dark figures and tries to speak, but there ent no doing—his jaw is smashed. But he tries, and he tries again cos he's a fighter.

"Help me," says the driver, as he bends down and grips under Denny's shoulders.

The lady doesn't want to, doesn't want to touch this pitiful creature, all bloodied and twisted.

"I said help me!" The urgency and anger in the man's voice makes her move. They pick him up. They carry him. As they cross the lights of the lorry, his true state is revealed. The lady wants to cry, wants to drop him, wants to let herself be sick, but the man forces her to keep it together. They keep walking. Down the road. Away.

Away from the lorry? Denny doesn't know what's going on. He feels like he's been struck by lightning. Doesn't understand why he's being carried down the road? Away from the lorry? Away from the light.

Then everything starts to sway, the dark dizzying sky moving above him. Is he floating? Is he dead? He doesn't know...

Then he feels lighter, colder, the sky is coming towards him, or... he is going up to the sky? This must be it for him, he thinks. If it is, then so be it, he's ready. But then the sky stops. It starts to recede, getting further away, and he's not going up no more, he's going down. *It can't be, not me,* he thinks, *what did I ever*—then the impact.

Already-broken bones crack and clatter as he hits the ground. The pain is too much. It's dark and cold and he's all alone. His eyes close.

The couple walk back to the lorry. Nothing said. Unable to meet each other's eyes. The lady sobs into the sleeve of her dress. With a trembling hand, she pulls herself back into the warmth of the cab. The man follows shortly after, but not before picking up the crumpled pushbike, throwing it in the back of the lorry and covering it over with empty grain sacking.

The man drops the lady off round the corner—out of sight from her house, as always. He stops her as she's about to get out; he talks to her, tells her to keep it together.

"There was no man, right?"

Tells her that everything will be okay.

"There was no man," she repeats solemnly.

She goes back home, back to her husband. And the man goes back to his wife. And Denny lays in the field dying.

The following morning a young girl is on her way to work when she hears something. Slowing down... she hears it again... at first, she thinks it's an animal. Injured?

She stops her bike, and when she hears it a third time, she knows it ent no noise that an animal could make.

Whether by miracle or curse, Uncle Denny survived that night. The young girl found him shaking and moaning on the other side of the hedge in the stubble field.

It took all of two months for him to regain full consciousness. His jaw, his arm and hip were all broken, his shoulder dislocated. He eventually lost his right leg, and Aunt June lost the baby. She was never able to have children again and never did get over it. She spent the rest of her days in and out of mental homes. My grandparents did their best trying to care for the pair of them who once looked after them so well.

Who could ever really know, but maybe things could've been so much better for Denny had he not be thrown in a field and left there in the hopes that the lovers' secret would die quietly. They made a decision to ignore it, to go on living their lives as always, pretending it never happened.

At first, I couldn't accept what I'd seen at the guesthouse. I did my best to blank it out, close my eyes to it and pretend it didn't happen. Hoping that it too would quietly die and there would be no side effects rippling far into the future.

Mum never said anything about it, never shouted at me, never tried to explain, didn't even warn or threaten me to keep schtum.

"Who was that man?" little Valerie kept asking, but I kept denying, telling her there was no man. *There was no man, there was no man...* if I said it enough I was sure I could make it true.

We got back on the Sunday evening. I was so scared and confused, not sure what would happen. Would us kids be sent to bed so we didn't witness the row? Would one of them have to leave that night? Would my dad shout at her? Cry? Beat her? I'd never seen him do any of these, so I had no idea. Would I be dragged into it, forced to take a side, to choose?

We humped our bags to the front door in silence. Mum had barely spoken a word to me since the morning. She paused at the door and turned and looked at me. There wasn't much of an expression other than her usual steely scowl. She held my eye for a moment and that was it. We went in.

"Cor!" she announced, bold as brass. "Can't say I'm not glad to be home," she called out all cheery as if she'd simply flicked a switch.

Dad and the two boys were sat about the kitchen table with a pot of tea and an oily motorbike part on a newspaper.

"Not that it weren't a good time, but your home is your home after all," Mum sighed as she put down her bag. She then turned to me, "Better get the dinner started, Rosemary, these boys must be hungry, bet they ent eaten proper all week." She walked over to the table and ruffled Karl's hair. "Have you mice been behaving while the cat's been away, huh?"

There was no man, there was no man, there was no man.

13

THEM POOR KIDS

AGED 14 (1959)

When Perry, Puddin, and Valerie all came down with the whooping cough I had to stay off school to look after them—what with Mum working at the children's hospital part-time. If it weren't so serious, it would've been funny. Once one of them started a bout of coughing, they'd all be set-off. It sounded like they were having a competition at times, or like they were an audience coughing instead of clapping at the end of a performance. Of course, it was only a matter of time before it got me too. For the most part, it was bearable, but then when it hit you, it hit you hard. You'd cough and cough 'til you couldn't breathe. At times Perry would go blue before he'd finished.

Dad was fuming when he arrived home to hear me at it as well. "Where's yuh mother? All these sick kids here."

"She's at the Children's Hospital today."

"At the hospital? What, when we got our own kids 'ere suffering. There's nothing for it, go fetch her home."

And so off I went.

After I arrived, I waited a good few minutes outside until a bout of the coughing came on, got through it, then went in.

They must have thought I was a rum'un all right. On account of me not wanting anyone to catch my cough or even knowing I had it, I spoke with my mouth pointing anywhere but towards the people.

"Dear, I can't hear yuh, you need to speak up, speak towards me," the lady at the desk kept saying.

I thought about it for a second, then pulled up the front of my dress over my mouth and spoke through it like a half-daft twit. This way I could at least face her rather than keep turning my head like an owl having a fit.

"I come to get my mum, we need her at home," I said and then lowered the dress again.

"Okay. What's her name, love?"

"Shirley, Shirley Page,?" I replied. Dress back up.

"Sorry... Shirley? Page you say?"

"Yeah, she's my mum," I said, forgetting to speak into my dress.

"And how long she been working here?" The lady was watching me carefully. I figured she couldn't quite place me as Shirley's daughter—being too small and timid and that.

"Five months and a week,"

"You know this is the *children's* hospital?"

"Oh yes."

"Well... there ent no one called Shirley, or Page for that matter, who works here."

"Yeah, it's my mum. Shirley - Page," I said more clearly, wondering if maybe she was the daft twit.

"No, not here. I think you may have the wrong place, my dear."

Well, I tell you, I was completely flummoxed all right. I mean, adults always know what they're on about, so could this lady really be getting it wrong?

She gave a sigh, her large chest heaving, then she looked down at me with a gentle smile. "Are you okay, my dear? Would yuh like to... speak to someone?" She said it all slow as if I was hard of hearing.

"So... she don't work here!"

"Nope, no Shirley works here. I worked here myself, ooh... best part of ten year."

"And this is the children's hospital?"

"That much is right."

"Ah. I think... oh yeah, I think I got it wrong," I said, starting to back away. "That's what I've done all right."

"Dear, just wait a minute. We got a doctor you can see if you want?"

"No, no. Uh... I just got all confused, was all. Sorry, sorry, bye." And with that, I made my escape.

I hurried out, looking back to double-check it really was the children's hospital. And sure enough, that's what the sign said.

I was so confuddled and tired. Combined with my illness, it felt like I was stuck in some weird dream. Where could she be? I began to worry. Had something happened to her? But they definitely said she'd *never* worked there... so not only did nobody know where she was, they didn't even know *who* she was. I wasn't sure what to do next, who to ask or where to even start looking. In the end, I decided the only thing for it was to go to the police station.

When I got there, I looked up at the word *Police* carved into the stone above the door. What was I to say to them? Would they think I was fruit-loop like the lady at the hospital must have? Was I just gonna get myself in more trouble if I brought the police home again? But I couldn't go home alone, what would I tell my dad.

I slowly wandered in the direction of my house, thinking the longer I leave it the more chance I had of making sense of her disappearance, and maybe coming up with a reason why I was returning without her.

The closer I got to home, the slower I walked and the more the dread built inside me.

I stopped at the end of the lane before it turned down towards our house. I said a quick prayer asking God for some kind of help, but was only answered by another bout of coughing. When I finished, I looked up to see a large figure striding down the road towards me. I couldn't quite believe it. Had he heard me after all?

"What the heck you doing loitering 'bout here?" she said without breaking her stride.

"I—"

She grabbed my arm as she brisked past, dragging me along with her and sweeping me into our lane.

"But, Mum. I've been looking all over for you," I blurted out.

She stopped.

She eyed me warily. “Why d’you be doing that for?”

“Dad sent me,” I said, hardly able to get my words out fast enough.

She checked towards the house, then yanked me back around the corner out of sight.

“Did he say why?”

“We all got the cough now. Me too. He didn't know what to do. So he sent me... y’know, to get yuh.”

“I see...” She let go of my arm and straightened the dress that was showing beneath her coat. “Well, I'm here now ent I.”

“But—”

Her head turned sharply to face me. “But. What. Rosemary?”

I took a breath, feeling the same as I did the day we went ice-skating on Blickling Lake. I could see it must be safe, there were already people skating and sledging on the thick layer of ice, but when it came to my turn to step onto the frozen lake something in my heart was telling me not to do it, not to take that step.

“I... I went to the... children's hospital.”

Her eyes narrowed. “Why the hell would you do that? I told you, ent no one should disturb me at work. That's your problem, you never listen do yuh.” She raised her palm to clip me.

“Dad said so,” I blurted out as I turned my face, bracing for the strike, “said I had to.”

It didn't come.

“And you spoke to them?”

I nodded.

“And what’d they say?”

I opened my eyes and looked up at her. “They said...”

“Go on...”

“They said that...” I swallowed and stepped onto the ice. “...that you don't work there.”

In a strange way, I think I actually wanted her to hit me. She’d never done so before. In fact, it was a rare day if she touched me at all.

Her elbow lowered, but her hand didn’t. I waited.

Her fingers slowly folded into a fist. And still I waited. But instead of striking me, she put it to her mouth and rested her teeth on her knuckles. She stared past me, over the top of my head. I'd never seen her lost for words before.

"Right, you listen," she said, grabbing the collar of my dress and pushing me against the hawthorn hedge. Tiny jagged thorns pierced through my coat and into my back, making me whimper. "You came down to the Children's Hospital and you spoke to Betty at reception right, Beh - tee. She come and fetched me and now we're here, aren't we? You got it?"

I tried my hardest not to scream as she shifted her weight, slowly pushing me harder onto the thorns. Biting my lip, I managed to give a hurried nod.

"What's the matter?" she asked, looking at me carefully. She was watching my face with what looked like curiosity as she very slowly increased the pressure through her arms. It was like she was pressing her foot down on a snail, waiting to feel the point at which its shell would give way and crack.

But then, a sudden change came over her face, it softened and she stopped pushing. "That hedge spiking your back, is it?" She let me come forward and then tidied my collar.

I gathered my breath. Not sure what to say, my lips only trembled.

"Oh come here, you silly sausage," she said as her big arms came round me and pulled me into her bosom.

A huge stopper was released and I started crying. I reached my arms as far around her as they'd go. She was warm and I could smell the familiar scent of her favourite perfume and fried bacon. I closed my eyes, wanting to stay there forever and then some. I felt her hand cup my head, her warm fingers stroking my black hair. "Come on then, can't stay out here forever can we or we might catch a cold, eh."

I ent never taken drugs or the like, but as we walked back to the house together it felt like I had. I was in a giddy daze, no tension in my body, feeling all glowy and light-headed like nothing mattered anymore and nothing ever would.

It was a rare thing, but that night my parents rowed something fierce. My dad was angry cos it was only a voluntary job she was doing, and weren't her own kids more important? My mum was saying she was doing a good thing, and that it was important to help others and an important lesson for us kids to be seeing.

"Right then," she finished up, "if that's what you want, I'll stay at home 'til they get better. Them poor kids at the hospital will have to go without for a week or two is all."

My father gave an angry nod, then took his hat and went outside for a smoke.

14

PARTNERS IN CRIME

The following day, Mum let me stay in bed while she was busy round the house doing my usual jobs. Even with the regular bouts from the coughing chorus, I managed to fall into a deep sleep.

I slept and slept and slept, before waking early evening to the comforting, muffled sound of Mum busily clinking and clunking around in the kitchen below. I lay snoozing in bed until the smell of food found its way upstairs and called me back to the land of the living.

We all sat down for a cottage pie and boiled veg smothered in a thick onion gravy.

"Come on, come on, tuck in before it gets cold. Don't want all my hard work to be for nothing," Mum said as she ferried over the jug of water.

"But Dad ent home yet?" piped up Karl.

"Well, that's his choice if the silly bugger don't get home in time for his dinner."

I looked at the kitchen clock and saw it wasn't even quarter to five yet.

Having missed lunch, I tucked in good and proper—we all did. We chattered away and laughed as Puddin chased his buttered peas around the plate with a fork before Mum eventually got him a spoon.

Dad got home at twenty past five.

"Yours is in the oven," he was told.

He looked to the clock but didn't say anything. He fetched his plate and dropped it on the table. The chatter went silent.

I saw Perry shifting in his seat as though he was about to get up, so I gave him the eyes. He settled back down, dipping his head and crossing his arms.

Mum began to clear away our empty plates. "Go on you lot, you can scarper, *you* weren't late."

Dad looked up at the clock but still didn't say anything.

Wednesday morning, Mum got us up and cooked breakfast, then at eleven she came into the coughing chamber. "Right, Rosemary, I think you're okay to do lunch today, ent yuh?"

This seemed fair enough. Seeing that she'd changed her dress and done her hair, I knew she must be going out for the groceries. "What time shall I get it ready for?"

"Well, whenever you like," she said as if I'd asked a stupid question.

"I mean... how long will you be?"

"Oh, not for me. I gotta go to work hent I," she said, stooping to take a look in the small mirror that Karl had cracked several years before with his marble catapult.

Rosemary... I warned myself *...stay off that frozen lake now.*

"Work...?" I found myself asking.

Creaaaaaaak went the ice.

"Yes. Work," she said, turning back to face me. "My job—at the children's hospital. What? Has that cough struck you dumb or something?"

"But...?"

Crrrrck.

Her eyes began to glower. Even if I didn't crack the ice with my clumsy foot, the heat from her glare was going to melt it. I closed my mouth.

There was no man.

"Good," she finished, turning back to the mirror and making a final adjustment to her hair. "Now, I will be back for dinner, mind. So it needs to be ready by the usual time—twenty past five, no later." And with that she was gone, leaving only the trailing wisps of her perfume behind.

At quarter past four, I started to put the dinner on. Then just as I was finishing up, at ten past five, Mum strolled in.

"Better all be done."

I nodded.

"Good, your father will be home any minute. Now listen, we're not to let him know that I've been working today, unless you want us at it again. So, I've been here the whole time and you just now helped me get the dinner on, ent that right?"

I nodded.

"Good. Lay the table, I'll be getting myself changed then."

The next week the whooping cough had got bored of torturing us, packed its bags and moved on. We all started back at school, and Mum started back at the children's hospital two days a week. This meant I had to rush home quick-sharp each day, pick up the little'uns from Keith and Elaine's, do a quick tidy around, lay the table then get the dinner on. Then when Mum came home she'd put on her apron and serve it up as if it was her doing.

Billy and Karl never noticed cos they were working full time and so didn't get home 'til just gone five. Plus, they didn't even live in the house no more. The pair of them, no longer wanting to share digs with a bunch of kids, had moved into one of the old caravans in the garden. Perry and Puddin never noticed—just because they never noticed anything. They weren't troubled with what other people were up to and accepted whatever they were told. On the rare occasion they said something that might suggest Mum had been out, she'd say it was for shopping.

Being the only one who knew what was going on turned me into a bag of nerves, thinking it was only a matter of time before we got found out. However, it soon became the normal way of things. In fact, we soon had everything running so smoothly that Mum was able to increase her work to four days a week.

There was no man.

It was a confusing time for me, to say the least. Even though we weren't directly telling lies, it didn't sit right. If I allowed myself to think on it too much, I'd get terrible stomach pains, like my guts were tying themselves in knots, so I did my best to steer my mind away from that path as often as I could. But, on the other hand... it was something I shared with my mum, something that made me feel valued, like we were actually a team, working together. I never did get much in the way of thanks though, except for the occasional knowing nod. But that was more than enough payment for my part.

There was no man.

Her birthday was the closest we came to getting rumbled. I'd picked up the boys from primary school, picked up some groceries from the shop, scooted over to Keith and Elaine's to pick up Valerie and Daniel, got home, rushed into the kitchen—and then strike me dead, sitting quietly at the table, there was a man.

I completely froze.

"What, yuh seen a ghost?" he said.

"What are you...? What time—"

"Where's yuh mother?"

"Well... she must've popped to the shop."

"So what you got in the bag then? Kittens?"

"No..."

"Rocks?"

"No. It's dinner. For tonight."

"So, she ent at the shops then. Right?"

"I don't know... maybe she just popped out, I guess."

He looked up at the kitchen clock. "I've been sat here since half two. Where is she, Rose?"

There was just silence. Dad not moving, just staring right at me. I had to say something... but nothing was coming. I couldn't think, this wasn't fair, this wasn't even my game.

"The hospital," I finally blurted out. "I remember, she has to work today at the hospital." I knew this might set him off, but it was all I had and it felt enough like the truth.

"On her birthday?"

"Uh... they called her in cos err... cos Beh— Betty was sick, she had to cover for her."

"That's utter nonsense," he said, standing up, his chair scraping on the stone floor.

I wanted to cry. I wanted to run away, bury my head and cry.

"I'm not having her working on her birthday when she's not even getting paid for it," he said as he paced the kitchen. Then he turned suddenly. "Nothin for it, you go down there now and get her home. I don't care what they say."

"Now?"

"What you got cotton in your lugs? Yes, now."

"But... I gotta get the dinner on."

"I'm taking your mum out for dinner. Enough time's been wasted, now go already."

I walked slowly out of the kitchen and started to put on my coat. What was I to do? I didn't have a clue where she might be. The only thing I did know was that she wasn't at the bloomin hospital.

"Come on. Get your arse into gear," Dad hollered through from the kitchen.

I hurried up the lane crying, holding my coat closed. After I turned the corner I stopped and sat on the verge sniffling as I hugged my knees to my chest. It was no use traipsing around town looking for her, and what if I missed her and she came home before me, telling a different story. By now it was gone four o'clock, so all I could hope for was that she'd be back soon. So I waited.

Occasionally, I peaked down at the house to check Dad weren't coming. Then finally, to my utter relief, I saw Mum ambling down the lane towards me. The painful knots in my belly began to loosen in an instant.

"What the hell you doing?" she said, her stride changing to a march. "The dinner better be done, your dad's gonna be home soon."

"He already got home."

"What? What you prattlin on about?"

"He got off work early. Wanted to know where you was. Sent me to get you again."

"Slow you down a minute. So... so he's at home?"

I nodded quickly.

"Whatever for? When he'd get back?"

"He says he was let off early to take you out for your birthday."

She stepped closer to me. "And what d'you say to him?" Her face inches from mine.

"Nothin."

"Nothin? You must've told him something. Dint you say I'd gone to the shops?"

"No, he says he's been there since two. So I said you was working. I said Betty was ill and they got you to fill in."

"What d'you say a daft thing like that for?" I watched her face ticking through the differing emotions as she tried to work things out. "Well... well, hang on... then, I'm fine then ent I. Cos you come and got me and here I am."

"I'm sorry," I said quietly. I wasn't sure for what.

"Well, you're lucky this time," she paused. "Mind... he dint see yuh hiding here did he?"

"No. No. I been checking," I said. "And I was right careful when I did," I quickly added.

She glared at me good. "You better be right." Then after a long sniff. "Now, stop that blabbing and we'll get ourselves in, shall we."

As soon as we were inside, she played it as being all angry at the hospital for getting her in on her birthday, and then said some more things about Betty being so poorly, saying she couldn't possibly have said no.

Then they went straight out—seeing as Mum was already in a dress and had her best make-up on.

15

I'M NOT AFRAID OF THE DARK

This close call didn't put her off—if anything, it made her more brazen. I guess she started to think she could do anything and get away with it. And the more she did, the deeper she dragged me into it.

It shames me now, thinking back on it, but the longer it went on, the closer I felt to her. Just the two of us, not having to share it with anyone else, just me and her, our very own special little secret, our own special bond. Maybe it was like the thing that Uncle Sidney Barrett always said to us, if life hands you a bucket of—well... as he said it—shit, then best you go out to the garden and use it to grow some roses. And so our new routine became firmly set.

This went on for some time, until one Thursday evening after dinner while I was doing the dishes, something changed. The boys were upstairs making a rumpus, Dad was at the table reading the paper, and Mum was on the sofa, head back, feet up, eyes closed. "You done with them dishes yet?" she called through to the kitchen.

"Well... nearly." Give me a bloomin chance, I thought. If I did them too quickly, she'd only say I hadn't done a good enough job. And why'd she suddenly care when they got finished, anyhow.

"Good, cos once you have, you can get your coat and shoes on."

"But... I... I cleaned the outhouse this morning," I called back.

"No you prinny, it's cos I'm taking you out, ent I." Even from the kitchen, I heard her give a reluctant sigh. "You've been doing all right of late, so thought you deserve a treat. How's the pictures sound, eh?"

"What? The pictures? Me...?"

"Well, if you don't wanna go..."

"What. No. Yes!" I stammered, almost dropping a bowl. "I'd very much like to go, I mean."

"Well, hurry up and get them dishes done then," she said, this time with a bit more bite to her voice.

I rushed the last of the plates. Dried my hands, then called out to Mum that I'd finished and made to go upstairs to get ready.

"What you changed you mind," she said, as she came yawning through from the lounge.

"But my clothes... Can I put a dress on?"

"We're going to the pictures, not bloody ballroom dancing. Now let's get going, unless of course you don't want to get popcorn, eh? No, thought not. Come on then."

After putting on our coats and shoes, she got a torch and a big tartan picnic blanket from the hamper by the backdoor—I didn't ask—and off we set for the bus stop.

It seemed she was determined not to miss out on the popcorn going by the pace she stomped away at. I had to occasionally scamper to keep from being left behind.

"What picture we gonna see?"

"I dunno."

"What they showing?"

"Hent got the foggiest."

Clearly in no mood for idle chitter-chatter, I decided to keep schtum for the rest of the journey, unless spoken to. I nearly broke this promise though when we reached the top of Almer Hill and she turned down the right fork toward the beck, rather than the left down towards the bus stop. She continued marching at a purposeful pace, so I didn't say nothing. We kept troshin until we got all the way to the corner of Almer Woods.

"Right," she said, taking a quick glance about, "you stay here, just inside, behind the trees a bit. Cos we don't want no one seeing you and asking questions, do we now?"

I nodded slowly, having no idea what she was on about. I thought it best to just wait and see. I was thinking, maybe she just needed to go to the loo quickly in the bush.

"Now, take this," she said, handing me a rusted pocket watch. "You know how to tell the time don't yuh?"

I nodded more vigorously this time.

"Good, the last bus comes through at 10:50 pm, so when it gets to 10:45 you come down and meet me at the bus stop. But make sure no one sees you coming right. Maybe just wait behind the bus shelter or something 'til I get off and it goes again."

Now I was completely flummoxed. I couldn't for the life of me work out what she was on about. Why did I need to worry about bus times and people seeing me?

"Right then, best I get going," she said, turning back up the hill.

My mouth opened, wanting to ask, but I was so confused I didn't even know *what* to ask.

She paused and looked at me, "Now, you be a good little girl while I'm gone. Don't be getting up to any mischief, you hear me?"

I nodded. Then watched her march her way back up the hill, blanket under arm, torchlight swaying with her every stride, then she was gone.

She left me there. Stood just inside those blasted woods with the rusted watch slowly *tick-tick-ticking* away in my outstretched palm. It took a while for it all to sink in.

Only a few minutes before, my mind was all off wandering and imagining about the glitz, glam and hubbub of the picture house, but instead, it seemed I was to spend the evening stood alone in a dark forest. Finally, the tears caught up with what was going on. I tried to fight 'em off, tried not to think about it, tried to ignore it.

There was no man, there was no man. I tried to distract myself by singing a nursery rhyme. *Mary had a little lamb, its fleece was white as snow, and everywhere that Mary went the lamb was sure to go.*

And that was the first time.

16

THE DOCTOR

Of course, me being the 'good little girl' that my mum wanted me to be, meant the visits to the pictures and other places became a regular thing. Mum going off and doing... whatever it was she was doing, and me waiting in those woods. At the agreed time, I'd then wander down to meet her at the bus stop. After a while, it became so normal I stopped feeling sorry for myself and just accepted it as another one of my duties. I've never been afraid of the dark, not sure why. Maybe cos I always had so many other things to worry about. In fact, whilst waiting in those woods I was mostly worried for my mum, can you believe. I always felt so relieved to see her getting off the bus, knowing she was safe. I could never shake the dreadful feeling that something bad might happen to her, seeing as none of us knew where or what she was doing. If something did happen, we'd likely just never see her again and be left with not even a hint.

We never talked much as we walked back home. She always seemed a bit disgruntled. It almost felt as if I were the mum who'd come and picked her up from a party she didn't want to leave. However, always the performer, as soon as we reached the front door she was able to turn it on. As we walked in, she'd start some mid-conversation nonsense about what we'd been up to. She made it sound like a right good time, loud and laughing, sounded like me and her were the best of friends, it did.

Now, you're gonna think of me as very strange when I tell you this next bit, but I have to admit it, it always made me feel so good when we walked in—just for that one moment. I always looked forward to it and treasured it, even though I knew it was only pretend. Despite it not being the truth, I still got to experience it as if it was. Just for those few seconds, it felt like everything was right in my world. I also liked that the others in the family must've thought Mum and me were getting so close. Thick as thieves you might even say—just like her and Sylvie used to be.

On those nights, I'd go to bed happy, and always managed to get off to sleep much better than I did on most others.

When they started I can't quite remember, but even on the nights I fell asleep thinking I was happy, a short time later I'd be trying to wake the dead with my night terrors. It always seemed to be within an hour or so after I nodded off. I never could remember much about it when I woke, only that Valerie would be in tears and Perry hiding under his sheets and everyone else annoyed to high hell. I'd be thrashing around and screaming the house down, they said, often with my eyes open—which didn't half put the spookers up the young'uns. It was a job to rouse me out of it at times and when they did, I was all sweaty and panicked but not really sure what was going on or what was even scaring me so bad.

Realising how much it disturbed the rest of the family, I found it difficult to sleep. I'd be waking every few minutes full of worry that I might be about to do it again. At school, I got so tired I couldn't concentrate and kept getting wrong off the teachers. At home, I never had a chance to properly rest. Every minute was used for covering for Mum, doing work she claimed as her own, or waiting and worrying for her in the dark woods.

Eventually, it all got too much. At the age of 14, I was on the verge of a mental breakdown. I had no meat on my bones; I was down to five and a half stone. Always had dull bags under my eyes, and my skin was as pale as a ghost. I'd get all nervous and jittery, acting like a spooked horse that'd seen a plastic bag fluttering in the hedge. I told Mum I needed to see the doctor—but she told me I didn't.

"Well, if you ent really sick, what on earth do you wanna see a doctor for, huh? Wasting his time is what."

The following week I didn't care anymore, I had to get help. I begged her to let me see the doctor, told her I couldn't carry on with our... thing, so she finally let me go. But of course, she came with me.

With her there, I couldn't say all that was going on. I even played down my night terrors, saying they were just the odd bad dream. He told me I had to make sure I ate and slept properly, said many girls my age go through troubles at this time of their lives. Mum tutted and agreed in all the right places.

"I've been tellin her the very same thing. But she dun't always want to listen to her mum though, does she? Teenagers, huh."

"You'll do well to listen to your mother. After all, she was a teenager too, once upon a time."

"Well, there's no need for that. I ent that old you cheeky bugger!" And we all laughed, and that was that.

Even if she hadn't been there, I don't know if I'd have said much more. I was ashamed about the whole thing, ashamed of myself. I felt like I was some sort of wanted criminal and that I mustn't let on, that I had to keep schtum. So like a good little girl, I did. And so things continued in the way that had become the new 'normal'.

17

THE LAST TIME

The cauliflower was boiled, the potatoes were peeled, cut, salted and simmering. I still had to do the carrots, lay the table, boil the tea, and all the while remember to stir the cheese sauce. I heard the door, but I daren't look at the clock. I just hoped she was home early rather than me being late, and so started rushing around even faster. I heard the stamping of boots, then a muffled voice complaining about the wind. I heard the door close again, then the bustle of a coat being put on the peg. I paused mid stir of the cheese sauce. I knew for sure it wasn't Mum, but... who else would just let themselves in like that?

"Well, well. Look at you, duck!" she said as she came beaming through to the kitchen.

If ever there was a sight for sore eyes, it was Sylvie's beautiful smile lighting up the place. My troubles melted away in an instant. I hugged her so tight and for ever such a long time.

"Mind, need to get a bit more meat on you duck," Sylvie said after I'd let go of her. "Your clothes will be falling right off on their own accord if you're not careful."

She looked about the kitchen, taking in all the boiling pots and peeled veg and then rolled her up sleeves.

"Now, you go sit down and let me take over here."

I tried to protest, but she wouldn't have it. I told her it might make Mum mad if she found out.

"We just won't tell her then, duck. You any good at keeping secrets?" she said with a wink.

After dinner, Mum and Aunt Sylvie started getting ready to go out to the pictures just like old times. I was so used to going with Mum whenever she left the house, I started getting my coat and shoes on too.

"Well, I don't know where you think you're going," she said as she shut the door on me.

I was taken aback, but it wasn't quite enough to ruin my good mood. I went into the kitchen and sat at the table with Dad.

"Don't worry, love. You're better off here," he grunted from behind his paper.

"Mum never said Aunt Sylvie was coming to stay."

"Humph," he grunted again.

"How long's she staying?"

"She'll be gone by next Sunday night."

"I can't believe it. I've missed her so much," I said, more to myself.

He got up and stomped through to the lounge without another word.

On the Saturday, Mum and Sylvie were getting ready to go out after lunch. I was at the sink, as usual, and could hear them saying things in hushed voices.

"Rosemary," barked Mum. "Get yuh coat on."

I looked down at the half-done dishes and even though Mum herself had called me, I still dithered, unsure if I could leave the job half done.

"Come on, duck," came the more cheery voice of Sylvie.

I had no choice, I thought, and I could always finish them up after I come back from the woods. I hadn't been out with Mum since Sylvie had been there, so wasn't sure why I was suddenly needed. Sylvie had my coat held out, ready for me to slip my arms in. Then the three of us set off towards the bus stop. Mum and Sylvie nattered all the way and I listened. Once we got to the top of Almer Hill I wanted to at least say bye to Sylvie but thought better of it than to interrupt. I drifted towards the right-hand fork—as Mum didn't even bother to walk with me to my spot in the woods anymore.

"Oy. Where do you think you're going, you daft twit? Bus stop is this way," she called out, hands on hips. "Come on then."

I didn't react too quickly, less I made more of a fool of myself. But I judged her serious enough, so I ran back to them.

"Here," Sylvie said, offering her warm hand to hold for the short walk down to the bus stop.

The bus came and Mum paid for my ticket. And I actually got on it. But I still wasn't counting any chickens, as there was no shortage of other woods around for me to wait in.

Once we got into town, Mum arranged a time to meet Sylvie back at the bus stop and off she troshed.

I looked nervously up at Sylvie, still tightly clutching her hand. *Please don't let go*, I mouthed a silent prayer.

"Looks like it's just you and me then, duck. So what should we do with ourselves first?"

My eyes started watering, not cos I wanted to cry, but just from a sheer rush of emotion. My whole insides flushed with warmth, and if I didn't have her hand to hold on to, I think I would've fainted I felt so light-headed. I knew Sylvie wasn't going to abandon me—I really was going to town with her.

First, we went around the shops and Sylvie bought me a new ribbon, which she tied in my hair. Then we went for some cocoa and a scone in the teashop. We nattered away like nobody's business. She told me all about Blackpool and how different it was from Norfolk. They had all their own different words and things I'd never heard of. Then she told me all about the Blackpool pier and the arcades and fairs and shows and whatnot.

It weren't until we were eating our jam and cream scones that we paused for breath and I got thinking—did Sylvie know what Mum was really up to? I didn't know how I should ask, or even if I could. I felt it building up and my palms become clammy, but I knew it was all for nothing. Just like at the doctor's, there was no way I could actually say anything.

"You all right there, duck?"

I gripped my bottom lip with my teeth.

"Come on, out with it. What are you wanting to say?"

I told her it was nothing.

"Well, it don't matter to tell me then. So come on?" She spoke so friendly and normal, like nothing mattered, that everything was going to be fine.

"It's about... Mum."

"Okay," she nodded slowly. And waited.

"Where...? I mean, do you know...? Is she—"

"It's all right, duck," she said, putting her half-eaten scone down and dabbing at the corner of her mouth with a napkin. "I know."

"You... do?" I wasn't at all sure she did.

"Your mum's your mum, and that's all it is," she said with a slight shrug.

What on earth was that meant to mean? I finally did feel like crying.

"Oh dear," she said, reaching over and cupping my hand in both of hers. "There ain't no changing her. I guess she's always been like it, and always will."

"But... Dad?" and I still weren't certain we were singing from the same hymn sheet.

"Hmm... he's had his suspicions all right. Nearly caught us once back in the East Rudham days," she said with her cheeky smile.

Oh.

I don't know what I found more confusing or shocking, that it had been going on since we lived back at East Rudham, that she said 'us' or how open she was being about it.

"You see, this one time he come down to the picture house, and seeing our bikes outside decided to wait with them. Of course, we come down the road from the other way and there he was. I got a bit worried but quick as a flash your mum told him the projector had got snagged, so rather than wait, we'd gone off into town for a walk." Sylvie shook her head with a rueful smile at the memory, then took a sip of her cocoa. "After that, we made sure to get the soldiers to tell us about the films and who was in them and such, then we could sound like we had seen them, you see."

It was as if she was telling any old silly story of no importance, but as the words kept tumbling out so did the shocks. Soldiers? Which meant my mum... that they were both... at least that was what I was thinking, so I had to ask.

"You weren't...?" I was too dumbfounded to be shy with my questions now. Pandora's box wasn't just being tipped up, it was being shaken.

"What's that, duck?"

"I mean... soldiers? So...?"

"Yeah, the Yankee soldiers at the base. Ever such nice fellas they were," she said with a blissful smile.

"So that means...?"

"Well, duck, I don't how much detail you should really know."

"How many?"

"It wasn't like it was a different one each week or anything. We were generally true to one fella at a time. You see, they move them about a lot. Just as you were getting close to one fella, they'd whisk 'em away to some other corner of England or even Europe."

"But... were you... did they...?" Then I just said it, "Pay you?"

"Oh, duck. No, no, no, not like that. I mean, they always looked after us, giving us goodies. You know, the things we'd bring back for you, the comics and the food and such." Then she laughed to herself. "They always thought I was a funny bird when I asked if they had any of those American comic books you liked. They'd tease me rotten, saying they were for me."

I felt empty and stupid, but couldn't get angry. She was so kind and friendly that she almost made it sound normal and okay. I also felt some guilt for having enjoyed the chocolates and comics. Or had I got it all wrong? Was this what all adults did? Was this normal, and I was just finally at the age where you learn the truth?

The more you grow up, the more and more secrets you realise adults have been keeping from you—I mean, even outright lies. Not just the ones that all kids get told, like Father Christmas and the Easter Bunny, but they even make up new ones on the spot. I once asked my gran where honey came from. She made a big thing of telling me, like I was being let into a secret club.

"Well, my dear," she said, leaning in closer and lowering her voice. "First you take an empty jar, must be clean, mind. Then you take it outside and place it on the bird table. Then you must leave it there and let the busy bees do their work. You see, they'll come one at a time and keep coming until they've filled that jar right to the top with honey."

I spent a whole afternoon peeping out of the window at the empty jar, with Gran coming through every now and then asking if I'd seen any yet. A whole bloomin afternoon. That wasn't even the worst of it. I'd also stood up in front of the class bold as buttons and told everyone this is how it happened. Even the teacher laughed at me.

You're brought up to think adults are like gods, they know everything. They never make mistakes, they never lie, and they'll never do you no wrong. So it's difficult to know what to put your faith in once your gods crumble to dust.

Sunday dinner was such a different event with Sylvie there. The squabbling and sulking was replaced by laughter. Mum laughed as much as she ate. The boys were still messing about, but in a good-natured way. Dad, not having much to say, finished well before the rest of us and went out to the garden for a smoke. We carried on though, sat at the table talking over empty plates.

It was when Mum told me to clear the table that the tumbling in my belly started. I managed to keep from crying until after she left this time. I made her promise to come back sooner, but that really was the last time I saw her until that day as an old lady in Blackpool.

18

THE BLANKET

Things went back to normal again after Sylvie left—Mum gallivanting about at every given chance while I cooked, cleaned, and covered for her. Our meetings at the bus stop became more and more regular until eventually one night I was so tired I curled up and fell asleep in the woods. When I woke and realised the time, I ran the whole way down, but she was already there, clutching her picnic blanket.

"Where the hell have you been? I was worried something rotten. Anything could've happened."

"I'm sorry, I'm sorry," I panted.

"It's all right saying that now, but who'd look after all them kids if something had happened to me, eh?"

It wasn't like something snapped, as they often say, but something definitely pinged loose. For the first time, I felt my emotions stirring up a bit of anger. Just a little spark, mind, but it was there. In truth, it may have first sprouted from my chat with Sylvie and finding out that it wasn't just one fella, but perhaps a string of them. Did it actually make a jot of difference how many there were? I guess if it was just one then you might think it was all for true love, and finding true love was a tricky thing—certainly more tricky than suddenly discovering yourself in the family way and having your decision about love made for you.

The next night I told her I wasn't going with her, that I needed some rest because I'd been nodding off at school. She was having none of it until I also told her the school were thinking of sending Mr Dimsdale round again, and that was enough to get me the odd night off once in a while. Did this mark the first time I'd brazenly lied to her? At the time, it didn't feel like it to be honest—after all, it was possibly true. Also, I was in too much of a constant dazed state to think about it with any clarity.

She still went out, of course, just not with her walking alibi. At first, I was wracked with guilt in case something happened to her. However, my overbearing need for sleep was often greater.

On the nights I did go with her, my first job was to smuggle in the blanket as soon as we got home. Straight up the stairs I'd go to stow it away, then back down to nod in agreement as Mum talked about all the fun we'd supposedly had.

Even on my nights off, she still managed to involve me.

Tap

I'd get out of bed.

Tap, Tap

I'd pick my way through the dark to the window.

Tap

I'd open the curtain, then the window and look down at her with her impatient frown, a handful of little stones, and that dreaded blanket hanging limp in the crook of her arm. Nothing would be said as she tossed it up to me.

I hated that blanket. It always stunk of her distinctive perfume. I could barely bring myself to touch it most of the time, so I'd leave it slumped on the bedroom floor, wallowing in the gloom like some fat wrinkled monster. I didn't even like to look at it. I would tuck my bedcovers over my head and face the other way, and still couldn't help but to imagine the horrid heap trying to drag itself across the floor, slowly humping its way towards me, hauling itself up onto my bed, then over my face as it tried to smother me.

In the morning I would kick it into the corner behind the door, then at some point later in the day it would disappear, perhaps crawling shamefully back into its lair.

The first time, she gave me what for. "You pick that up and fold it neat. What, you think this is a pigsty?"

I stood with my head bowed and shook it.

"Pick it up then."

I stayed with my eyes fixed on the threadbare grey carpet.

"It's a belting you want then, is it?"

I glanced over at the horrid pile of cloth and took a deep breath.

"Okay," I said.

"Well... come on then."

Still, I didn't move.

"I said come on. It ent gonna fold itself, is it?"

"I meant, okay, I'll have the belt."

The silence was smouldering, her eyes burning into me. I hadn't intended it as an act of rebellion, but out of the two options I just decided I really would rather have the belt.

"Oh dear, oh dear," she said slowly as she bent down and picked it up. "Don't start thinking you're clever," she whispered between her teeth.

She left the room with the blanket under her arm, then came back without it. I remained on the spot, not moving. She went over to the drawers and yanked them open. She pulled out an armful of my clothes. I thought she was gonna take them away as a punishment, but instead she threw them on the floor. She kept going until the drawers were empty. Then she left.

And still, I stood there waiting. I heard her clomp down the stairs. I could have quickly picked the clothes up and put them back, but I didn't.

I heard her barking at my dad, telling him I was refusing to clean up the room, that I needed a good belting.

"Give the girl a break," came his quieter, weary reply. "She does more than plenty cleaning round this house. Belt her yourself if that's what you want."

It was a rare occurrence—him standing up to her, and even rarer on someone else's account. Even after everything she put him through, he idolised her, and it was like that right up until his death. It was as though he was addicted to her, couldn't give her up. And the problem was, she knew it.

The next day, there was nothing doing and nothing said about it. These small victories gave me some crumbs of confidence, made me realise for the first time that maybe she wasn't a saint, that maybe I wasn't the bad apple, that I wasn't an island, and I wasn't alone.

19

THE UNEXPECTED VISITOR

A week later, I was given a chance for a lay-in on the Saturday. This was because Dad had to go into work extra early, as a new load of cattle had arrived at Rawlins. So Mum said she'd get his breakfast and I could do the rest of them at whatever time they all got up. But being so used to early mornings, I couldn't sleep in and thought I might as well get things ready before the rabble rose.

The house was quiet and still, so I stayed in my nightgown as I made my way downstairs. Wiping the sleep from my eyes, I walked into the kitchen and then jumped right out of my skin. Thinking the downstairs was empty, the last thing I'd been expecting was to see the two silent figures by the sink. I say *silent,* only cos they weren't talking, but that's not to say there wasn't noise being made from what they were doing to each other. Locked together at the mouth in full embrace.

After the fright slipped away, it was anger's turn.

After all, right there.

In *our* kitchen.

Our house.

Mum and young Ray from the hardware store, slopping away like teenagers behind a bus stop.

Young Ray was young all right, probably twenty years her junior, and married himself. It was so shocking it didn't seem real to me. It was like I was watching the pictures. Then the screaming started...

"Get out!" came the first shriek, followed by, "Get out of here now!" I continued bellowing as loud as my puny lungs would allow. I don't know where it came from. It was the first time I'd ever lost it like that with anyone. The first time I'd heard myself scream even. It just happened, it just came out. And I was beyond caring what I said to her.

"Get him out of here. Now."

Just for a brief second, a brief moment it seemed my mum looked afraid.

"What if it weren't me?" I continued. "What if it had been one of the others? One of the little'uns? Seeing you... like... this."

They let go of each other. She was still lost for words, but her fear was fading and I could see her own anger beginning to build like dark storm clouds.

Then I locked on to Ray. "You. Get out of our house."

Ray took a backward step. He looked to my mum. "I ent going. I ent going 'til your mother tells me to go."

Ray's efforts at making a stand seemed to snap her fully back to her senses. "He ent going anywhere," she said, straightening up to her full height and puffing up with a deep breath. "This is *my* house," she said, prodding at her chest.

I wasn't going to crumble, not like usual, I was too mad—I was beyond mad. I fixed on Ray and waited a moment. Then real calm and real slow I said, "If you don't get out *now*, I - will - tell - my - dad."

"Huh. Huh," she said much louder and began to laugh. "Tell your dad, will you? Tell... *your* dad? *Your*... dad?" Her eyes narrowed like a snake ready to strike. "Let me tell you, it's only a wise child that knows who her father is. And you, my gel, you ent ever been close to being wise."

A cold, feverish shiver rattled through my body. I felt sick. I could taste it in my mouth, like I actually wanted to throw up.

She was just saying it, just saying anything to be cruel, anything to get the upper hand, to get me down... but... but I could see it in her knowing smile, and in her eyes. They were possessed by some sort of gleeful sparkle of pure energy, as if she'd been waiting my whole life for the best time to drop this bomb. And finally, the time had come. Fourteen years worth of built-up resentment was being released in one enormous blow. She could finally sit back and find out just how much damage the bomb she'd been holding onto for so long could wreak.

"What's the matter? Got no wind in your sails now have yuh?"

I took a long breath. A thousand thoughts crashing through my head, but I pushed them aside. Another long breath—a breeze beginning to stir and gather itself again. I wasn't sure what I really thought, but I couldn't let her win. I had to deny her this moment she'd craved for so long.

My voice came out unbroken, each word slow and clear. "He - is - my - dad. I know him as *my* dad, and he loves me like a dad. And so he will always be *my* - dad."

"Huh." She turned to share her wicked smile with Ray, but the pale-faced Ray was shrinking further and further away, looking to take shelter.

Still, I stood firm.

"So what then?" she began again. "You want to tell him? That's what you want to do, do yuh? Fine, you tell him. And you know what will happen—I'll be gone. I'll just bugger off, leaving you to look after all these kids for the rest of your life. That's what you want is it?"

I so badly wanted to say *yes*. I wanted to tell her to go, but I couldn't. It wouldn't really have changed things that much for me. However, the little'uns and... my father—they'd be the ones who'd suffer.

In all honesty, I thought she was bluffing, but there was something inside me that made me think she secretly wanted it to happen. Did she want to get caught? I mean, it would account for her ever-growing boldness and outright lies. It would give her the escape route she'd perhaps always been looking for, but never quite had the courage to take.

Finally, it was all too much for me and all too confusing to sort out in my head. I couldn't hold back the tears. "Please," I sobbed. "Just tell him to get out."

"He was going anyway," she said as she picked up their tea mugs and put them in the sink.

Ray stood there fidgeting with his hands, looking like a scolded schoolboy.

"Well, go on then," she said, motioning with her head. "I'll come see you later."

Ray risked a quick glance in my direction before looking back to her as though he was waiting for something—a goodbye kiss? He went to speak, but it came out as mumble, then he made for the door.

I couldn't stand to be in the same room as her and wanted to make sure he was definitely going, so I shepherded Ray to the entrance. He paused and turned back.

"Y'know I love her. I do. I... really do."

He looked sad and pathetic, so much so I almost felt sorry for him. My mum was a pretty lady, but she was also a very large lady and nearly fifty—and from my point of view, not a particularly nice person. How those two come together, I'll never guess.

I opened the door. "Just get out. Go home to your family, why don't you."

20

MOVING OUT

The next day I moved out.

I moved out, but not away. I followed my older brothers and started living in a caravan in the garden. They'd both passed up the gypsy caravan, on account of it being too small and full of junk, and instead decided to share the regular one.

The gypsy caravan sat on crumbling cinder blocks, the rotting wooden wheels having not survived the move from East Rudham. Even before the moss and lichen had taken a fancy to it, the big curved canopy had been green. It arched over dark wooden panels that, although fading, still bore wonderful painted swirls and flourishes.

I didn't bother wasting my energy by asking if I could move into it, I just got busy doing it. I knew it wasn't going to be an easy job, but when I wanted to be, I could be a right determined little so-and-so.

He came out for a smoke as I set about emptying the last of the boxes of old magazines and clothes. I was ferrying them over to the growing bonfire pile. He watched me, without a word. Then when he eventually acknowledged me with a simple nod of the head, my heart went into a nervous flutter. I took a breath. *He's your dad, Rosie. He's your dad no matter what,* I said to myself. But I still couldn't bring myself to look him in the eye, and so paid him no mind as I concentrated only on my mission.

Surprisingly, it was him who spoke first. “What you up to? Running away to join the circus?”

“I'm gonna sleep here now.” I stopped and waited.

“What you wanna do that for?”

“I'm fourteen.”

He nodded. “It'll be cold.”

“I know.”

He started to roll another cigarette.

I went into the house to fetch my bedding. When I returned he was gone. A few minutes later, though, he came back with some wood and nails. “Might want a shelf in there I s'pose.”

I finally looked him in the eye. And as I feared, it was no good.

“Oh Rosie, what is it?”

“I love you. Dad,” I said through the tears and threw myself into his arms.

He wasn’t really one for affection and he didn’t really know what to do with me, but I squeezed him tight, savouring the heady smell of mothballs, oil and tobacco—a smell I’d known ever since I could first make and keep memories.

Even completely cleared out, it was a tiny old thing. It reminded me of a doll's house, with its miniature cupboards and a fireplace painted on the asbestos walls. There was only one window, a little latticed bay on the back. Dad brought in a tilley lamp and we worked in silence together—me making it homely with blankets, ribbons, and some of Karl's paintings he'd given me for birthdays gone by, my Dad plugging holes, fixing the door, and oiling the hinges. The two of us, working away together—father and daughter.

She never said a word. Didn’t even acknowledge I'd moved out. I still set the table and made the dinner and such, while she pretended it was her doing, but I never did go out with her in an evening again.

Instead, I got to see the other side of the penny, sitting at home with my father and seeing what we'd been putting him through all that time. Sometimes, he'd be all agitated, never settling. He'd get up and start doing one thing, then stop halfway through and sit down, only to get up to start doing something else.

Sometimes he'd ask questions.

"Why she need to go out so much?"

"What's wrong with staying at home with your family?"

"We're not good enough for her time? Is that what it is?"

I never answered them, nor did he expect me to.

The evenings were long and quiet, but at least I had time to myself at last, and I wasn't worried sick waiting in those dark woods. I gotta admit I did still worry about her, it's just in my nature, but so did my father. Therefore, it was a problem shared—a problem halved. We didn't talk about it, but I could see it in his eyes and actions, and that was enough sharing for me.

"Why d'you no longer go out with her anymore?" he asked one night. But this one, he did expect to be answered.

I was at a complete loss. Was I to say it was because she didn't make me no more? Was I to say it was cos I didn't want to and never had? But both answers would've of stirred up more difficulties.

"I thought I just asked you a question," he said, his voice rising.

My lip began to tremble and then the crying came on again.

He watched me sob for a moment, not doing anything. I was getting ready to up and leave for my caravan, but then he came over to my side of the table. He reached down and put his big calloused hand on my shoulder and gave it a squeeze.

"I'm sorry," he said, barely loud enough to hear. "I dint mean to make you cry."

"It's not you," I said, wiping away the tears on the back of my arm.

"What is it then?"

I looked up at him, a quiet, tough man of simple pleasures, and I opened my mouth ready to speak. I felt so sorry for him. I knew how much she meant to him and how he'd probably never love another.

His eyes closed slowly. His face grimaced as if bracing himself to have a tooth pulled.

"I saw her one time," I began. "Here... in our kitchen. One

morning when I come down." The words came easier than I'd thought, but I imagined what was gonna happen next would be the difficult bit. I expected an explosion. I expected that anger of his to erupt, the air to be turned blue, something to get broken.

He didn't move. Just stayed with his hand on my shoulder, his eyes closed and his face scrunched, sorrowful and pained.

"I'm sorry... I didn't..." I didn't know what to say. I stared down at the table and felt his hand slip off my shoulder.

He walked back to his seat, sat down and sunk his head into his hands.

I wanted to go over to him and put my arm around him, like he had for me. But I didn't. I could hear him breathing deeply in and out through his nose.

We sat there saying nothing. Eventually, I asked if he wanted a cup of tea. He didn't answer. I got up and made a pot. I poured him a cup, but he didn't even look at it. I sat back down. A cold and complete silence. The kitchen no longer felt like a place I was familiar or comfortable with anymore. It looked the same—kind of, but it didn't feel how it once had.

His cup of tea was long cold when the front door latch rattled. Still, he didn't move, but his eyes opened like a dragon guarding treasure. He didn't look towards the door. Stared straight, just over my head. I don't think he was looking at anything, more listening. Listening to her familiar bumbling as she sorted herself out in the hall. Grunting and oomphing as she hung up her coat.

"Phew, blimey," came her voice.

Dad's throat moved as he swallowed.

"Good to be home," she called as she went up the stairs.

We waited a minute, then she came back down.

"Well, what's been going on here? Sounds like a bloomin funeral," she said all bright and breezily as she entered the kitchen. Then she stopped. She craned her head trying to see my dad's face.

"Well, come on then, who's died?"

"Where you been?" he said, his voice hoarse and dry, still staring at the wall.

"You know full well where I been," she said, doing her best to sound offended. "What you got cloth in your ears? I told you I was at Deidre's helping her with the cross-stitch blanket for the new baby."

"I remember where you *told me* you were going, but I asked where *have you* been?"

She hid it well, but I could see the edge of panic in her eyes. She wasn't in control. She didn't know what he knew. Had he been round to Deidre's to check? Had someone seen her in another place? Or did she suspect I'd finally broken my vow of secrecy? After a while, she realised something had to be said to break the guilty silence.

"Now c'mon, what is this silliness?"

Her usual tactic. Fight fire with fire. Make the other person feel like they're in the wrong.

"You look at me, Trevor Page."

"I'm not looking you in the face 'til you stop your lying."

"I don't know what you think you know, or where you're getting your silly ideas from, but it stops this minute, you hear me?"

Then he wavered, just for a second. He doubted what he thought, what he knew.

"Well, Trevor Page. What you got to say for yourself?"

Dad's mouth opened. He turned towards her ever so slightly, as if being pulled by a kite string. The fixed-stare was gone; his eyes went soft and my heart sank. I felt so sorry for him, so sad. I could see his strength to stand and fight just wasn't there, cos he knew, either way it went, he'd end up being the loser.

His eyes flicked to me for just a second. I wanted to help, I really did, but I just didn't know how.

Her hawkish gaze had followed the path of his sight, and found me, sat quietly watching. She locked onto me. Her chin tightened. Her chest slowly rose. Then stopped.

"YOOOU," she boomed. "You. Isn't it? You evil - little - BITCH."

I'd never been so a-taken back. I literally jumped and had to clench my legs together to stop from wetting myself. I'd heard her use bad words before, but never with so much venom and never at me, or anybody for that matter.

My dad looked equally petrified. "No, Shirley, you... you leave her... just leave her out of this," he managed to say in a broken voice.

But he wasn't there anymore; she only had eyes for me. "You and your stupid little make-believe stories."

"Leave her be Shirley," my dad tried again, but his words were lost under hers.

"This is your doing, isn't it? I warned you, didn't I? I told you, but you wouldn't listen. And now look what you've done."

I couldn't even speak, even if I knew what to say my throat wasn't working. Then came the crying from upstairs.

She raised her eyebrows and fixed me with that smug, self-satisfied grin of hers. "See what you're doing to this family? Well, I hope you're happy now."

"Muuuummy," Valerie's voice rang out.

She shook her head slowly and turned away from us and walked out the kitchen. She calmly plucked her coat from the peg and went out of the backdoor, not even bothering to close it. And was gone.

That night I slept in the house. I went up and comforted Valerie. She kept crying and asking questions I didn't know how to answer. The boys were quiet and just watched, all wide-eyed and pale-faced. I didn't get to sleep until gone four in the morning, and by that time I hadn't heard Dad come up the stairs. When I woke he wasn't there. No one was.

I got all the children up and breakfasted; I dropped the little'uns off at Keith and Elaine's, the boys at school, and then finally myself too. The day passed me by. If you asked me now, I couldn't remember a single detail about it.

I got the dinner on when I got home. Then at quarter past five, the door sounded. Two voices—familiar voices. And then in they come. It was like nothing had ever happened. Like everything was the same. Like they'd just come back from their honeymoon. The other kids sensed it and were all jiggling about with excitement. Neither she nor my dad were able to meet my eye, though.

After dinner, Billy came and helped me with the dishes. He didn't say anything, but gave me a look, a look to say that he wanted to speak about something. Later we sat in his caravan and he told me he'd heard the shouting the night before. Said he was about to come in when he saw her go storming down the garden path. I told him everything, and he just nodded, said he'd as good as known most of it. It was such a weight off my shoulders, having someone else I could talk to about it all. But he said it was up to Dad if he wanted to do anything.

"We just gotta do our best to keep it from the others and do our best to keep the family right."

Then he told me he was moving away to be with the girl, Carroll, he'd been going steady with for the last few months. Said that they were in love. My heart was broken.

He said they'd been planning it for a while, and although her parents were less than pleased, it was what they were going to do. He said he was sorry and knew it was bad timing and all, but he couldn't risk losing it. I could understand and could never begrudge it.

We played happy families for a week, but it wasn't long before she returned to her old tricks with a vengeance.

Me telling my dad about her had only made things worse. I suppose, if I had the mind, I should've blamed him for forgiving her so easily, because all that did was hand her the permission slip to do whatever she wished. Absolute power. There was nothing doing. Now she really was invincible.

Some nights, she wouldn't be back until gone four in the morning. Dad would be stomping and clomping around the house, shouting and smashing things, the little'uns would be screaming their lungs inside out. I don't think they knew exactly what was going on, but they knew all was not rosy in our garden. However, the following morning, when she'd come back, Dad would be all meek and mild and nothing would be said about it.

The week before Billy left, Dad sent him out with a torch at three o'clock in the morning to find her. And find her he did. He said she was crawling on her hands and knees along a neighbour's hedge.

If she did return before Dad went to bed, he'd be so relieved that she was okay and had come back to him that he was almost apologetic.

PART II

THE WORKING GIRL

21

THE TERRIER

AGED 15 (1960)

Back in my day, you could leave secondary school as soon as you reached 15, and so that's exactly what I did. The day after my fifteenth birthday, I got a job working at the local hospital as a trainee nurse.

Work-life was a welcome change from school, as there weren't so many cliques and as much pressure to fit in. There was more a feeling of everyone working together for the same reasons, and that people just wanted to make friends and get along. It helped that there were several of us around the same age starting at the same time. Unlike the hodgepodge of kids thrown together at a school, we all shared at least one main interest too—wanting to help people.

The training itself was tough and a lot was expected of us, but that only further helped to bring us closer together. Not everyone survived the rigours of the training, mind you. However, me—well, I took to it like a duck to water. I don't mean to sound like a braggart, but I guess it was a perfect fit. I'd spent my whole life caring for other people, putting their needs before my own. A lot of the other trainees struggled, what with being ordered to do things under great pressure and then getting very little in the way of thanks.

I soon became good friends with another trainee, Wendy, who was a year older than me and started the week before. She lived in

Hempstead, only a few miles from our house. She was ever so nice, a really delicate and kind girl. She had beautiful light-brown wavy hair that bounced around her shoulders whenever she got excited—which was all the time. She was one of those people with so much natural happiness it overflowed and was contagious. I loved just being in the same room as her, didn't even matter if we were talking or not.

There was also two other girls who had already started before me. They came from Kings Lynn and stuck together like glue, so were most often known as the Lynn Girls. It was too far for them to travel in daily, so they lived at the hospital and shared a room.

Usually, the trainees would answer directly to a ward sister, but in our little country-hospital the matron took on those responsibilities too. Things were often a bit more relaxed in the countryside, but not with this matron, who—make no mistake about it—ran a tight ship.

She was a small, wiry Scottish lady, as tough as old leather. She wore big flat-heeled shoes, so you could always hear her coming with a dreaded *clip-clop, clip-clop* echoing down the ward. The problem was, she walked at such a pace that you never got enough warning, as soon as you heard the clip-clopping she was on you like a ratter. She spoke just as fast too and never accepted any excuses. She quickly became known as the Scottish Terrier—feared by all. You could feel the change in the air when she entered the room. Wendy's hands would actually shake whenever the Terrier was near, and her voice would shrink into an almost high-pitched squeal. In fact, I don't think the matron ever heard Wendy's real voice.

She had a sharp angular nose jutting out between her narrow sunken eyes.

"No one's ever seen her blink, y'know," the Lynn Girls told us once.

Although she looked more like a hawk than a terrier, she marshalled the ward like a dog—the patients her sheep, the ward her territory. I couldn't believe it when I even saw senior doctors sometimes asking permission before entering her realm.

I did my best, as usual, to keep my head down and do whatever was asked of me without fuss. But strangely, she didn't hold the same fear over me as she did with the others. Of course, very soon the other girls started teasing me, saying I was her favourite.

"Well, you think the Terrier's bad? You should meet my mum," I'd say, and the girls would all giggle thinking I was making a joke.

The Terrier was more than our boss, she also acted as our guardian, especially for the Lynn Girls who stayed in the nurse houses. She kept a firm grip on the old-fashioned ways, despite it being the dawn of the liberal 1960s. There were strict curfews, and in some cases we were told whom we could and couldn't be friends with, and even whom we were allowed to be courting. Sometimes, can you believe it, we were also told how we should dress in our free time.

During work hours, our uniforms were under constant scrutiny from her piercing eyes. Wrinkles the enemy and stains unforgiven. Your cap worn straight at all times, your apron brilliant white, your shoes perfectly polished and the hem of your skirt no more than twelve inches from the floor.

As strict as she was, I thought she got hard done by with her reputation. She had a heck of a lot of responsibilities, and she only wanted the best for her patients. Mind you, she could be equally strict with them too. She didn't take any messing from anyone, no matter who they were.

Us trainees always had a good relationship with the patients, as most of them stayed awhile. At times, they'd stand up for us, and even cover for us if they knew we were in danger of getting savaged by the Terrier. Though, to start with, we didn't have all that much to do with the patients, because after the war, and a few years before I started, the General Nursing Council brought in new measures for training up nurses. This meant more learning from the textbooks and more classroom practice. Even so, our jobs were mostly cleaning, laundry and ferrying out the meals.

Each of us were given a little wooden box in which we kept our cleaning stuff, like our dusters, scrubbing brushes, bottle of Dettol, and Vim scouring powder. Twice a day we had to make sure the ward was spotless. We'd damp dust under the beds, on top of the lockers, envelope corner all the sheets and smooth out the counterpanes. We even had to turn all the bed castors so they were facing inwards.

"It seems silly to me," Wendy had said. "Why she makes us do this, d'you reckon?"

"Well, I guess it's so no one trips and falls on them," I replied.

"Ah, I see," she said, thinking about it for a moment. Then with her brilliant smile. "And I see why you're *Mummy's* favourite too."

It made me blush when they teased me so, but secretly it gave me a thrill and a buzz that would tingle inside my chest for minutes afterwards. I'd often make some excuse to turn away to hide my reddening cheeks and let out a quick smile too.

When we finally got to start practising the real stuff, it was a case of learning as we went. Watching and listening and having to think on our feet. This was mostly done by shadowing the proper nurses, hovering close by without being a nuisance. Again, something I was already well versed at. After watching them doing the basics a few times, like taking temperatures and cleaning bedpans, we were eventually allowed to do our first 'real' nursing duties.

The day Wendy had to take her first temperature, she was unlucky enough to have the Terrier lurking beside her. Poor Wendy's hands were shaking so much she dropped the thermometer, smashing it on the floor. Wendy screamed and turned to await her fate. But the Terrier didn't shout—as we'd all expected her to. She just stared at her. You could see it in Wendy's face, the silence was too much to bear; she was begging to be put out of her misery. It was actually the patient who spoke next.

"I think she wants you to get a dustpan and brush," the old lady whispered loudly.

The Terrier didn't move a muscle until Wendy had cleaned it all up. She didn't even move her feet out of the way of the brush. But I guess it was so she didn't step on the broken glass and make more of a mess.

"That's a one 'n sixpence you owe Carruthers," she finally said, once she was satisfied the floor was clean. Then she walked off and didn't speak to Wendy for the rest of the day.

Without instruction, Wendy didn't know what to do with herself. She was convinced this meant she'd got the sack. I told her to try and find stuff to clean, anything and everything, even if it was already done. Just get busy and get your mind off it.

22

FRESH MEAT

After a few weeks, we were introduced to a new member of our group. She went by the name of Bessie and was a sorry thing all right, dressed in awful old-fashioned clothes that smelled like sour cheese. She wasn't much of a looker either. She had the gormless stare of an old cod, thick strawy hair and a grimy face. None of us liked her much and did our best to not even touch her unless it was our turn. And if we thought we had it bad, it was nothing compared to what pitiful old Bessie went through in the classroom. She was always having leeches put on her, and she was given so many injections, enemas and blanket baths that you almost felt sorry for her. Then at the end of each lesson, she was shoved back into the cupboard with all the other practice equipment until the next time. However, being stored in the cupboard did mean Bessie escaped one of the hardest day's training we ever had.

There was a real buzz of excitement amongst us girls when we were told we were going offsite for an educational visit. That morning we all took extra care in making sure our uniforms were in tiptop condition. Leaving the hospital grounds meant people on the outside would be seeing us in all our nursing finery. And who knows, we thought, they might even think we were proper nurses.

Well, our faces were a picture and no mistake when the minibus dropped us off at the muddy yard. We were dumbfounded; we couldn't understand it.

"Why on earth have they brought us here?" we muttered to each other as we looked up at the wrought-iron gates of the slaughterhouse.

"You girls want to be nurses, is that right?" clipped Matron.

We nodded uncertainly.

"I see you all got nicely dolled-up this morning. So you think nursing is glamorous, do you?"

No one answered.

"Nursing is about trying our utmost to make people better or ease them in their final moments. They'll be times when you will see things you wished you'd never, times when you'll see things that no human should ever. And that - is why - we are here - today."

Strangely it wasn't the blood and guts that got us, or the poor souls getting the bolt gun to the head, it was the cattle and sheep penned up, waiting their turn.

Even though I'd been brought up around farms my whole life, I'd never given it any thought before. And I don't care what anybody says, those animals knew. They knew why they were there and they knew what was coming, and worse yet, there wasn't nothing they could do to change things. They'd found themselves in a hopeless situation with no way out, that was for sure.

They huddled together in the holding pens, unable to keep their feet still, jostling restlessly against each other. You could see the fear in their eyes as they looked into yours. You could hear it in the sheep's pleading baas.

"HelllIllllllllp."

"Pleeeeeease," they were saying.

When it came to the bullocks, they had to pretend they were about to transport them somewhere, then once they got them up onto the transport float they'd deal them a shot with the stun gun so they could get them inside the slaughterhouse.

At the end of the day we all made a spit-pact to be vegetarians. "Til the day we die," we all swore (although we just pretended to spit, what with us being proper young ladies and all).

The next day, as we cleaned the ward ready for inspection, the Lynn Girls were unusually quiet.

"Looks like yisty really shook them up some, don't it?" Wendy whispered to me.

Later in the bowl room, while we were warming the bedpans, I asked if they were okay and told them it was best to keep busy and not think about it, just shut it out of their mind and pretend it didn't even happen. *There was no slaughterhouse.*

"Oh... it's okay, it's not about yesterday," said Tracey

"But... it is a bit," the other Lynn Girl said.

"You see..."

"This morning..."

"Well... we..."

"It just smelled sooo good though."

"We couldn't help ourselves." They each gave an uneasy smile.

"You've both completely lost me, what on earth are we talking about?"

"Just tell her," Tracey said.

"Why me? You tell her. Oh okay, I'll tell her then. We... both of us, that is... had... bacon for breakfast this morning."

"Oh," was all I could think to say.

"We're sooo sorry."

They stood looking at me like a couple of puppies who had widdled on the floor, waiting for me to scold them—as if I was the Terrier.

"Don't be silly. You don't need to apologise to me none."

"But, we all promised."

"Oh my goodness," Wendy suddenly blurted out, before trapping her open mouth with a hand.

We all turned to her.

"I'd clean forgotten. I had bacon too!" And we all laughed.

I don't know why it was funny when Wendy said it, just most things she said ended with us laughing.

"It's all right," I told them. "I mean... we didn't *actually* spit, so it don't count anyways." To this, we all agreed.

It was a whole fortnight before my mother noticed.

"It's cos I'm a vegetarian now," I told her.

Dad just shrugged.

"What?" she said. "I never heard nothing so daft in all my life. If we weren't meant to eat animals God would have made them out of rocks and sand. Daft twit aren't yuh."

But, even though we didn't actually spit on it, I never have eaten meat since that day.

It had really taken me by surprise that the Lynn Girls were so worried about breaking their promise. It made me realise I had actually made some proper friends who cared about my feelings and what I thought.

Getting that job and the timing of it couldn't have been better for me. My entire life, up to that point, had been all about trying to win over my mother, gain her love, measure myself by any crumb of respect I could glean from her, and though I can't say I still didn't crave it, I was at least starting to realise it wasn't a realistic dream anymore. But the nursing— that gave me a new horizon, gave me new hope, gave me something I was good at, and maybe even some real friends of my very own as well.

For the first few months, the only young people I saw were the girls I worked with. However, I never dared ask anyone round my house, heaven knows what they might have witnessed or what bitchery my mother would've conjured up. Also, there was never any chance of visiting Wendy or even meeting up with the girls outside of work. My mother made sure she knew my schedule, and when she saw I had a day off she would be up and out of the house extra early, leaving me stranded at home looking after Valerie and Daniel.

Occasionally, if we got the ward scrubbed down in good time and the Terrier was pleased with our work, she'd let us go half an hour earlier. Knowing that she'd still be busy, meant we could all sneak off to the Lynn Girls' room where we would try on their clothes and practice putting on make-up. I wasn't that fussed about make-up in the beginning, as it was a reminder of my mother and what she got up to.

Because I never had the chance to see them, unless at work, at times I felt like I was on the outside of our little group. It felt like they were changing and growing up together while I was staying as boring 15-year-old Rosie. So one day, I finally gave in and asked them to make me up... and it was wonderful! I felt like a proper little lady —gosh, even a movie star. Now, I'm no more vain than anyone else, but those first few times I couldn't stop looking at myself in the mirror. It was like looking at a different person, a new me. This feeling would only last for twenty minutes though, because I had to scrub it off and cycle home before my pushbike turned into a pumpkin, the glass slippers into my clumpy work shoes and I returned to being plain old Rose busy mopping floors and boiling nappies.

It was always a bit of an event for me when Wendy and I cycled home together. It was something to look forward to at the end of a busy day because it was the only free time we really had together.

After both Karl and Billy left home, the family pushbike pretty much became mine, and I soon set about making it my own. I tied long ribbons around the handlebars and short ones along the crossbar. I never told anyone the reason why, but it was to make it look like it was a horse's mane.

Wendy and me, only shared the first ten minutes of the journey home (if we went slow enough, that is). However, we always stopped for one last chinwag when we reached the point that we had to go our separate ways. These were often my favourite chats. Sometimes we talked about personal things and shared secrets and such, just like proper best friends.

"We could buy some of our very own make-up, couldn't we?" Wendy had said one time.

"Yeah, though I never have a reason to wear it. And Matron would never let us wear it at work."

"You could come to youth club with me one time, we could wear it then?"

"Nah, that ent for me."

Thinking about things such as youth club or any gathering of lots of young people made my stomach feel a bit queer. I knew it'd be just like school all over again.

"Have you got a fella... if you don't mind me asking?"

"A fella?" I'd never really had time to think about boys before. I shook my head. "You?"

"Well... there is this fella Philip at youth club I like," she said, her cheeks pinking.

"Does he like you?"

"I think so. He even looked right at me last time. That's a good sign, right?"

"I guess. I never had a boyfriend."

"Hent yuh?" she paused. "Me neither, actually. Apart from at school one time, but we was too shy to even speak to each other."

"I don't really know if I want one. Seems a whole lot of trouble."

"You think? But don't they take you out and buy you things? And some of them even have cars and that."

"Well, I ent got the time to be going out, anyway."

Wendy went quiet. I'd already told her bits and bobs about my home life. I'd have told her more, but she always started to squirm on her saddle and not have much to say for once. I didn't blame her none though.

"Why don't you speak to this fella next time," I said—if only to shoo away the silence.

"I can't do that! Can I?"

"Why ever not?"

"Cos I'm a girl, silly."

I knew enough that it was generally the fellas who had to make the moves, but I was sure it'd be okay to just speak to them.

"So what you going to do then?"

"I dunno. Wear some make-up. See if he talks to me. What do you think?"

"And if he don't?"

She shrugged.

After another dawdling silence, Wendy spoke again. "If you come to youth club, you might find a fella too? Then we'd both have one, wouldn't we?"

"Sorry, it just ent my thing, really. Anyway, I better be getting back now. More floors to scrub for me," I said with a half-smile.

"Oh. You going home then?"

"Yep, gotta get the dinner on as well."

"Oh, okay." She looked glumly down at her pedal and re-positioned it with her foot.

I smiled properly this time, but she didn't notice as she was looking at anything but me. "Yeah, well, I better get off now, Wendy. Cor I tell you what though, it's gonna be reeeal dark soon," I said almost giggling to myself.

She nodded and squinted up at the sky. "Yeah."

"So, see you at work tomorrow I reckon?" I hopped onto my seat.

She nodded again and took her time as she got onto her bike.

"Rose...?"

"Yeah...?"

"Do you think...?"

"Do I think what?"

"Urm. Oh, nothing really."

"Wendy...?"

"Yeah...?"

"Do you want me to bike you home again?"

She gave a coy smile. "Would you mind? I'm so sorry."

"Course not. But come on, we need to get going though."

As the autumn nights began to draw in, this soon became a regular thing. I'd have to bike with her down past the Felbrigg Lakes, through the dark woods and all the way down to Hempstead Mill to where she lived. I'd then have to turn around and bike all the way back home again. Truth be told, I didn't mind one bit—cos it also meant we got more time to natter. And going home alone meant I could get a bit of a speed going. And when I was sure there was nobody about, I'd pretend I was riding my horse, *yaaring* and geeing her up as we galloped through the countryside, her mane flowing through the breeze.

23

CINDERELLA SHALL GO TO THE BALL

For the first time in my life I actually had my own money. It weren't much mind you—just a trainee's pay. However, because the only time I ever needed to use it was to pay board to my parents, I soon became quite wealthy for a girl my age.

The other trainees would spend theirs during their holidays—going on shopping trips and buying their own tea and cakes in cafes and stuff. For a sheltered country girl like me, that seemed like the most glamorous thing I could imagine. I'd listen to their stories in absolute wonder as they told me all about their outings.

The Lynn Girls kept a little tick chart to countdown the days until a long weekend or a holiday. Once the last day was ticked off, their mums would come and pick them up, come and fuss over them, tell them how pretty they were, or how proud everyone back home was. Again, I would stand transfixed, staring at the happy commotion being whirred up, a big smile plastered on my face. But afterwards, after they'd left and the kerfuffle had settled down, all that remained was me sniffling up my tears before I went and hid myself away.

Because the Lynn Girls were allowed to have their holidays together, so were Wendy and me—not that it mattered a dot, thanks to my mother. Just like with my days off, she'd arrange her own little trips, knowing that good old Rosemary would be there to take care of everything at home. Most often, she said she was going to the seaside with Aunty Fran. Whether she really did, I don't know and didn't care.

Wendy also had very few friends outside of our job, so she was just as upset that we were denied our chance to go on trips together. We were a good pair, Wendy and me, good for each other in our own ways. She always said she felt safe when she was with me, that just being in my company made her feel braver. Where she got this notion from I didn't have a clue. If I didn't know better, I would've sworn she was having me on, but she weren't the dishonest type. Well... I say that, but one of the things I liked about Wendy was, that even though she was this sweet innocent girl and never wanted to get into a sniff of trouble, at times she could come up with the most devious of thoughts and sneaky ideas that would've never occurred to me.

"Why don't you just tell your mum you got to work after all. Then make as if you're going in each day, but instead just come meet me?" She said it in such an easy and offhanded way that it reminded me of Aunt Sylvie.

To suggest this, she really must have believed I was the brave type. But in truth... just hearing her say such a thing made my hands clammy, and just the thought of trying to lie to my mother made my heart skip triple.

"Okay," I blew out hard, "I'll do it," I found myself saying. I was so surprised, I almost looked round to see whose mouth it had really come from.

I guess I'd never had anyone who looked up to me before (even with Perry, it was only because he *had* to follow me rather than because he wanted to). This was new, and I liked it. I liked it enough that I didn't want to lose it, even if it meant doing things outside my reckoning.

If I thought I felt nervous when Wendy suggested it, I felt like my insides were going to explode when I actually told my mother that my holiday had been cancelled.

"They can't do that! Dint you say something? I already made my plans, I can't change 'em now."

"I'm sorry but..."

"Sorry? You should be standing up for yourself. Who do they think they are, taking advantage of timid little girls like that? If I could give 'em a piece of my mind..."

As it turned out, fake-Rosemary was no match for my mother. And as she stomped about the kitchen huffing and puffing, I was already thinking how I could backtrack on what I'd said. I'll wait until tomorrow, I thought. I can tell her that I stood up for myself, and I don't have to work after all. Maybe it would actually be a good thing. I mean, I wouldn't get my holiday, but I might get her respect, is what I was thinking.

It did shame me, standing there in the kitchen, knowing that even after everything, I still craved any little crumbs that might fall my way from her table. I felt pathetic, but she was my mother. After all was said and done, she was the one who brought me into this world and we shared the same blood.

"Well... maybe... I could ask, or could see and..."

But she wasn't listening, she was rummaging through the old bureau muttering and cursing to herself, so I left her to it and went and made a start on the dinner.

The next day at the hospital couldn't finish soon enough. I was desperate to get home and tell her it was all okay, that a mistake had been made, that Cinderella could go to the ball—or Margate in this case. It felt like, that for every minute she had bad thoughts about me, her hate-meter would tick round further and further, putting me in ever-growing debt that I could never hope to pay off, no matter how many dishes I washed and floors I scrubbed. The best I could ever hope for was to slow it down from time to time, but I couldn't even do that until I got home.

All day I worked like a madman, hoping the time would go by quicker. Then finally the Terrier gave us the nod that meant we'd done a good job and were allowed to leave off twenty minutes early. This also meant it wasn't quite dark, so maybe Wendy wouldn't mind cycling on her own. Everything was working out until...

"Page, let me have your ear a minute."

My mind was on other things, so she caught me off guard.

"What d'you look so worried about, Rose?" whispered Jenny. "You know she's only going to praise you again for making us lot look so slow."

"Maybe she forgot to bring an apple for her today," said Tracey, as the other girls funnelled out of the ward in a giggling gaggle.

I turned back towards the matron. She beckoned me into a corner —out of earshot of the patients. On the odd occasion she gave me praise, it never worried her who heard, and sometimes I think it was more for the other's ears, anyway.

"I had an unexpected visitor come see me today," she said, raising her eyebrows as if she'd asked a question.

Well... my brain was all over the shop. I didn't have a clue what she was on about. Then, as she spoke again, my heart slipped its moorings and sank deep into my body.

"Yes. I had your ma come see me." And then that look with the raised eyebrows.

I felt hollow, as though my insides had drained away, through my legs, through my feet and through the floor. I'd gone and ruined it again. All the training, all the good work I'd done—gone. I was devastated. Even the blasting I was sure to get from my mother, later on, didn't seem as bad compared to losing the matron's respect, my confidence, and maybe even my job.

"What's the matter, Rosie?" said the matron, her keen hawk-eyes narrowing.

The one time I tell a lie—I get caught. I remember thinking that maybe I didn't share any of my mother's blood after all.

"It's all right, deary, nothing bad has happened, everyone is okay," she continued. "Just a bit of confusion we had to straighten out. She thought you weren't allowed to have your holiday, but it's all fine, I set her straight."

I was fighting the rising lump in my throat. I couldn't speak and had already started to snivel. All I could do was nod.

"Whatever is the matter, deary. Dinnae you hear—you can have your holiday, it's all fine."

I was staring down at my shoes, trying to get myself together so I could thank her and leave.

"Do you... *not* want to go on holiday with your ma?"

I raised my head enough for her to see my eyes.

"Why ever not? Come on. Speak up. God gave you a voice for a reason."

"Well... because... *I* won't be going anywhere."

"No, no, dear. She told me she was taking you down to Margate for the week."

I shook my head.

"They were her own words. I heard them. Be nice, won't it? You deserve it too. A break from this old place."

"I won't be going. Only her." I felt ever so guilty, as if I was reporting her to the police.

"Only her? By herself?"

"Well, yeah. Someone's gotta look after the kids and such."

"So you won't go... so why...? So she just wants you to... ohhh. I see."

I nodded. It didn't really seem to matter; I was sliding down a slope with no hope of making it back it up, so I confessed it all—that I'd lied to my mother, that I'd been planning to deceive her all week, that I was going to be sneaking about while she thought I was hard at work. I'd accepted my fate. I was fully deserving of whatever was in store for me.

I felt Matron's cold bony knuckle pressing lightly under my chin. I didn't resist as she lifted my head. She looked at me long and hard, as though she was trying to figure out some difficult sum.

"I see. I'm sorry, deary but I told her everything was okay. Even showed her the diary. Oh deary. I'm so sorry. I didnae realise."

I swallowed the lump in my throat and couldn't quite believe it. I wanted to give her a big hug. She seemed ever so upset with herself. Then I wanted to tell her it didn't matter, that I'd known my plans would never come to anything, that I was used to the constant disappointment, that it was the natural way in my life.

"Hmm... so what about your half days and days off and such?"

I shook my head.

"I see." She had that edge in her voice, like when she asked us if we'd dusted on top of the doorframes.

We stood in silence for a moment—the matron slowly shaking her head from side to side. “I'll tell you what we’ll do, deary, next time you get a half-day or day off, we'll make sure not to tell your ma. How does that sound?” She paused again and started talking as if to herself. “But we can't have you traipsing around town in your uniform.”

“It's all right, it don't matter none—” I started to say, but she wasn't listening.

“So what your ginnae do, is bring a bag of clothes and keep them in the wardrobe in the cellar. I'll have to clear out a few of the cloaks, but I've been meaning to do that for some time now, anyway. You can give it a good clean, of course. So, yes, that's what we'll do. Yes, yes, indeed.”

This time I did hug her.

“Oh my!”

It certainly wasn't like hugging my mother, there were bits of her poking out all over the place, but I didn’t care.

From that day forth she was always as good as gold to me, and I never called her The Terrier behind her back again or even joined in when the other girls complained about her.

As much as I enjoyed my job, actually having time to myself was something else, something special, something I always looked forward to and treasured. Wendy and me would stroll about town, go out for lunch or cocoa, sit in the park and do each other’s hair, shop for clothes, or whatever took our fancy on the day. However, if I bought new clothes, I had to be careful and keep them in my secret cellar at work. The main reason was to not give the game away by bringing them home, but the other was to stop my mother from ruining them. She was always borrowing my jumpers, and because of her size she'd stretch them, leaving them as good as useless—unless I was in need of a woolly tent to go camping in, of course.

I remember the first thing I bought was a hat, a big white thing that came down around my head like a lampshade. It took several trips before Wendy finally plucked up the courage to tell me that it looked as though I'd walked out of the hairdressers with the dryer still stuck on my head.

I was able to laugh with her, mainly because I hadn't bought it for fashion reasons. I'd chosen it because I thought it made a good disguise (when in truth it made me stand out like a bloomin sore thumb).

I was so afraid I'd bump into my mother while she was out and about doing whatever she was doing, but luckily I never did—which meant I spent all that time going around looking like a right twonk for no good reason.

This newfound freedom meant I finally started to feel like I was my own person with a future that was worthy of imagining. Whether Matron had noticed the change too, I don't know, but it was shortly after that she gathered us up after work one time so she could *have our ears*.

The hospital had received one of its regular invitations for the nurses to go to the dance at the army base out at Weybourne.

"And since you trainees have worked so hard and are all good sensible girls," she said, the hawk eyes roving closely over our faces, "I've decided to extend the invite to include you."

Well my giddy aunt. All of us were too stunned to speak, and I think we all grew up at least three years in that very moment.

Matron certainly laid down the ground rules about appropriate dress and behaviour. She told us that we were not just representing ourselves but also the hospital and, with so many American soldiers still knocking about, even our country.

When the night finally came, we were ever so excited as we got ourselves ready in the Lynn Girls' room. We'd all bought new dresses, Wendy and me finally bought ourselves our own make-up, and the Lynn Girls even got some perfume.

"Do you think the army men will be in their uniforms?" said Wendy as she did a twirl in front of the mirror. "Just think, we might be about to meet our future husbands tonight, do you reckon?"

We spent the best part of an hour getting ourselves ready, but as the clock ticked ever closer to the bus-catching time, I started getting that tingling feeling deep inside my chest. This was a big thing for all of us, but maybe more so for me. I was ready though, this wasn't going to be school kids and all that silliness, this was a proper adult affair. It felt like the beginning of a new chapter, the opening up of a new world.

"Do you two want to try some perfume?" Tracey asked. "I can show you how to use it. My mum bought it for me, says it's ever such a popular one, you know." She stood in front of us as we sat on the bed.

"Now, with the lid still on, of course, you tip it upside down. Then you take the lid and you dab it on the under-bit of your wrist," she explained, "then rub it against the other, like this... cos then it gets into your pulse and is sent all around your body making all of you smell nice," she finished with a big smile. "Oh, but don't forget to put some extra on your neck, just here."

"That's for when you're dancing up close, you see," Jenny chipped in with a mischievous smile.

It was all so new and exciting for me, having never been to a dance before, let alone going out wearing make-up and perfume.

Tracey came over to me with the bottle as I sat on the bed straightening the ribbon in my hair.

"Hold out your arms now, Rosie."

I stood up and turned over my hands for her, and she daubed my left wrist. Then, as she had explained, I rubbed them together before wiping them on the side of my neck. But as I did so, I was gripped by a strange and sudden reaction. The strong whiff of the perfume and suddenly seeing myself in the mirror as Tracey stepped out of the way gave me the fright of my life. All at once the blood drained from my face, goose pimples dominoed up my arms and I stumbled backwards knocking into Tracey and almost falling over the bed.

"My goodness," gasped Tracey, juggling with the perfume bottle. Wendy let out a surprised yelp. And I ended up sitting on the bed, wiping desperately at my neck with my hands.

"You... okay?" asked Jenny.

I realised all three of them were staring at me. I looked around at their confused faces and I managed to gather a smile. "I'm sorry. I'm so sorry. I just got a fright. I forgot about the mirror and saw myself... and just made myself jump was all."

"Blimey, Rosie, you give me a right shock," Wendy giggled nervously. "You're not tellun fibs now are yuh? You sure it weren't my old mug that gave you the fright?"

Tracey was still staring at me, perfume bottle in hand. She looked down at it and replaced the lid.

"I'm sorry, Tracey. I dint make you spill none, did I?"

"No, no, it's okay." Her face softened. "Some people don't like perfume. I... guess?"

"No, it's just I remembered... I got... funny skin and sometimes get a rash from things. I'm so silly, I'm so sorry."

"It's all right," Tracey smiled. "I thought it might have hurt you or something."

"No, I promise. It's just me being silly."

We all stood in silence for a moment until Jenny spoke. "Well. That was exciting, at any rate," she said, sitting next to me and putting a hand to my shoulder.

"You can say that again," said Wendy. "I thought you'd seen a ghost, dint I?" And we all laughed.

But triggered by the sudden whiff of that all too familiar perfume, it wasn't a ghost that I saw when I caught myself in the mirror—all dolled-up and ready to go—it was someone far more frightening.

"I guess we oughta being making moves for the bus soon if we don't want to miss it," said Jenny.

I had my eyes closed and could hear the others wittering away but wasn't taking in their words.

"I'm so sorry," I said almost in a whisper as I opened them again.

"Stop apologising, Rosie. It's fine."

"No." I took a breath. "I'm mean, I'm sorry... I can't go to the dance tonight." This was met by silence. All eyes on me again. "I just got a bit spooked and feel a bit funny now." I rubbed at my belly.

I'd never felt so rotten in all my life, as none of us ended up going to the dance that night. As much as I pleaded with the others to go without me, there was nothing doing and they wouldn't listen. Eventually, I started crying. I begged them to go. I even said I'd go with them and wait outside, if only it meant they'd go. But of course, to them, the idea of a young girl waiting outside by herself all night was the craziest thing they'd ever heard of. Fancy that, huh.

Instead, we spent the entire evening in the Lynn Girls' room, all dolled-up, chatting the night away. I felt ever so selfish and even worse because they were all so nice to me and kept fussing even though it was my fault and I hadn't really told them the truth. However, looking back at it, it was a really good night and one I always remember fondly. I think we all had fun, talking and being silly. I remember Wendy covering the mirror with a blanket and giving it a good telling off, which made us all fall about. Every now and then the blanket would slide off and she'd get up, march over with her hands on her hips and start wagging her finger at it, scolding it again like she was the matron.

The following evening, I baked them all some buns to say sorry and thank you. My mum came into the kitchen while I was up to my elbows in flour and butter and asked what I was up to.

"Oh, I'm just making buns for Wendy's birthday," I lied.

24

BED NUMBER 9

Matron soon found out we hadn't gone to the dance, and although most people thought she had cold rivers running through her rather than veins, I couldn't help but to think she seemed upset by the news. I told her it was my fault, that I'd had a dicky belly. I managed to not count that as a lie, deciding it was close enough to the truth.

"That's one of the downsides of working with the sick. You'll get used to it though," she said, before clip-clopping away.

The girls said they didn't mind, but I knew they must've been resenting me a bit for making them miss the dance, especially since those who went wouldn't stop harking on about it.

For a couple of days after, I tried to work extra hard and did my best not to stop for chats. When there was a natural pause in the workday, I'd mumble my excuses and try and find something to do. But my self-punishment was short-lived because as soon as the next new exciting thing came along, it was all forgotten about.

"...I know. He's so funny too," said Wendy as I entered the steamy bowl room. "Mind... I dint really get all the jokes, but the other patients were all laughing, weren't they?"

"Did he say how he did it?" asked Jenny.

"Fell off the back of his friend's motorbike," said Tracey.

"He's got a motorbike?"

"Well... he said it was his friend's."

"He's so brave. Do you think?"

"Which bed is he in?" Jenny peeped out of the bowl room and down the ward.

"Bed nine," said Tracey, peering over her shoulder.

I didn't ask what they were getting their knickers in a twist about. I just left them to it and went to give out the clean bedpans. However, I found out anyway during the lunch service.

"Bloody hell! They keep get'n prettier and prettier." He smiled at me, bold as buttons and as if we'd known each other all our lives.

Well, blow me. I couldn't quite believe what he'd just said. I couldn't believe he'd come out with something like that to a person he'd never met before, and in front of all them patients too. Just like that—he'd sworn out loud.

Then... after a moment... I realised what else he'd said.

Surely he wasn't talking about me, I reassured myself. The only people who'd said I was pretty before were Sylvie and the photographer, and as nice as it was to hear, I always knew they were both just trying to be kind. Other patients had said it on occasion too, but they said it to all of us trainees. And it was generally the old ladies who couldn't tell one trainee from the next, so that didn't count neither.

But this patient... this patient was young—and a fella. I wanted to check over my shoulder to see who he was actually talking to. But his deep, dark eyes, that seemed to sparkle, just wouldn't let me go. He just kept on looking at me with that big daft smile. I tried to carry on, be all professional, but he'd got me in a fluster and I found myself hurrying away, food tray still in hand.

I hid around the corner, my back to the wall, and cursed myself for being so silly. As my heartbeat began to settle, I started thinking clearly again. He'd probably said the same to all the nurses and was just being nice like the other patients, so I should go back in and say that I ran off with his food because *I forgot the cutlery, so here's your meal, please enjoy it.*

"What are you up to, Rosie?" said Tracey, coming through from the kitchen area.

"Oh. Urm... Which bed is that for?" I said, nodding at her tray.

"Mr Wardle, bed seventeen. Why's that?"

"I thought you might want to swap, this is for the fella in bed nine you girls all seem to like."

"Teddy?" Her eyes lit up.

"Is that his name, is it? ...Teddy."

"My goodness. Urm... okay. How's my hair, is my cap straight?" she said as she flicked her head.

"You look fine. They're eating the same thing, aren't they? No need to swap then. Thanks, Tracey."

She gave me a funny smile. "No, thank you."

As I propped Mr Wardle up with a pillow to eat his dinner, he interrupted me.

"Sorry, dear. I think Nurse Hall wants you over there."

I turned to see that Tracey had returned to the ward entrance, still holding her food tray. I could only think she'd got stage fright too. She beckoned me over with a nod.

"Looks like it's your lucky day."

"What's that?"

"Only Teddy saying he won't take his meal unless the *pretty* nurse serves it to him."

"I don't know where the nurses are," I said, looking around. "I think it's just us doing lunch—"

"No, you. You prinny." She pushed the tray into my hands.

"But..."

"Well, go on then." She reached up and tucked a strand of my hair behind my ear and into my cap, stood back and smiled at me.

"I... I can't."

"Yes, you can." She took me by the shoulders and guided me around the corner into the ward, "Do your job, Nurse Page. Before that food gets cold," she said, doing her best Matron impression, and then with a giggle gave me a gentle shove to help me on my way.

I started walking, slowly, telling myself not to blush. I felt like I was walking onto the stage for the school nativity play. I felt like the whole ward was watching me—whole ward? More like whole world.

Just don't think, I was telling myself, just do your job.

But my mind kept turning things over and over. He'd... he'd actually told *someone else* he thought I was pretty, though. So... was he really fool enough to believe it? How hard did he bang his head when he came off the motorbike?

"Ah, here she is," he said, turning to Mr Sullivan in the bed next to him, "my favourite nurse."

I couldn't look him in the eye, but I knew he was watching me closely because his head moved every time I did. Be professional—pleasant, of course—but professional. He is a patient, after all, I told myself. Act like you would if it'd been Mr Sullivan who said you were pretty. Accept the compliment, be polite, smile and tell him you hope he enjoys his meal.

However, he didn't really give me a chance to say much as it was him who did all the talking.

"She's right quiet, do you think she'll tell me her name?" he said this as if to Mr Sullivan, but his eyes were fixed firmly on me. "Maybe she's one of them mutes, who can't say nothing. What d'you reckon, Douglas?"

I had to say something now. Don't try too hard, I reminded myself. Just normal and professional.

"There we go." I leant over and placed the tray on his lap.

As he reached forward to take it I felt the warmth of his hand as it slowly brushed mine. I don't know what came over me, but our bare skin touching for the first time sent a tingling up through my arms, before pooling around my shoulders causing me to give a little shudder. I found myself smiling uncontrollably, I actually wanted to giggle, or laugh out loud.

Compose yourself now, Rose. Be professional. I took a breath. "And I hope you have a pretty meal," I managed to say, risking another quick glance into those deep, dark eyes. I turned away, straightening my pinny, happy with a job well done. Then... then I heard my own words echoing in my head...

"Oh my goodness," I blurted out, shoving my hand over my stupid gob. All I could do next was turn-tail and flee.

As I scarpered away, I could hear him shouting loud as day, "If you won't tell me your name, I'll just have to call you Pretty Nurse." There couldn't have been a soul, live or dead—bless 'em—on that ward that didn't hear him. I'd never known anyone like it before, so carefree and confident. He didn't care a blot what others might be thinking of him.

It was downright embarrassing at first, but Teddy refused to take his meals unless it was me who delivered them. It was almost like he was playing the spoilt child, but with that smile and sparkle in his eyes, I think everyone was quite charmed by it.

His arm had been broken and was in a full plaster cast. He also had nasty grazes all down his legs that needed regular dressing changes. He was only with us for eight days but was never short of visitors. They brought him so many gifts we had to find an extra box just to store them. His mum came in every other day and seemed like ever such a nice lady, ever so caring, fussing over him the whole time.

It took me until the third day before I could control my blushing enough to start a conversation of my own accord. But I'd hardly a chance to say anything before he started asking me so many questions it made me dizzy. *Where did I live? What did my dad do? Who was my favourite singer? What was my favourite movie? Did I like being given flowers? Did my boyfriend give me flowers? Why on earth did a pretty girl like me not have no boyfriend? Would I like to have a boyfriend? If I did, what kind of flowers would I like him to give me?*

Having only just survived that whirlwind, I was buffeted from the other side as the girls didn't miss the chance to tease me something rotten.

"So, where you gonna go on your first date then?"

"And what you gonna wear?"

"Will you let him kiss you, do you think?"

"When are you gonna get married?"

"Where will you get married?"

"How about a summer wedding?"

"What d'you reckon you're gonna call your first baby?"

"How about Teddy Junior?"

It was a strange feeling. For so long in my life I'd been in the background, no more than a dull piece of furniture in an overcrowded room, and now I was the talk of the group. Not only the Terrier's 'number one hardest worker' but now the patients' and Teddy's favourite too.

I can't lie and say I didn't like it at times, it made me feel good, made me forget about what was still going on at home. But at the same time, I wasn't quite comfortable with it. I guess because I wasn't used to it. It'd all happened too fast and it was too good for me. So, of course, I knew how it would end and what was round the corner. It would be the same as always, just as it seemed something good was going for me, it would go tits up and be taken away, like a carpet whipped from beneath my feet. I always had that dread when times were good. I was always waiting for it to sneak up and bite me on the bum.

The only thing I never feared going wrong was my job. I knew I was good at it, and I knew the matron respected me. The patients liked me too and I had a good group of friends.

As for the Teddy situation, I didn't pay it much mind. I certainly enjoyed it, but never once gave thought to all those things the girls teased me about. I knew in a few days he'd been gone and that would be that—my short-lived fame over and soon forgotten.

25

A BAD IMPRESSION

In the end, that day came all too quickly. And it was odd actually, although I couldn't deny I was going to miss having him about, I did feel some relief in knowing things would go back to the way they were before, knowing I could go back to being normal old Rose again. I wouldn't have to worry what others thought or said about me, or if my hair looked greasy, or if I had any new pimples.

I took him his last meal—which was a breakfast of boiled egg, bacon, and bread and butter. When I went to fetch the tray from the hatch I was met by the other girls. They were all stood around giggling away.

"C'mon then. What are you lot up to?"

"Nothing."

"Show her. Show her."

"Jen, move out the way."

They stepped back so I could see the tray I was due to take to him. They'd put a little vase on it with a single pink flower and the food was arranged all funny.

"Tut, don't be silly, take that flower off."

"You gotta take it like that, you have to," said Tracey, holding her hands together as if in prayer.

"Then you can ask him out, can't you?" said Wendy.

"I can't ask him out, he's a fella."

"You said to me that shouldn't matter, dint yuh?"

"And why is the food all funny? What you done to it?"

"It's a heart, a love heart," Tracey explained.

"The bacon, look," said Jenny, pointing to the rashers.

"That was my idea, weren't it?" said Wendy.

I told them I wasn't going to take it, and I definitely wasn't going to ask him out. They pestered me so much, in the end, I said I'd take the flower if they let me put the bacon right. Then, on my way down to the ward, I stopped and left the flower in the bowl room—after all, I said I'd take it but nothing about giving it to him.

"Humph. My last day today, y'know."

I nodded.

"I bet you're sad?"

"Maybe. Maybe only a little bit though," I said, setting the tray down and trying not to smile.

"Well, why the hell you smiling then?"

"Cos you make me laugh."

"I knew it! I knew you must like me."

"Now why would you think something as daft as that?" I said, hands on hips.

"Let's see, for a start, you don't let no one else bring my food out."

"Huh! That's not true."

"I don't mind none. In fact, I got you a present to say thank you for looking after me so good."

I'd noticed he'd been sitting differently, more upright than usual, as though he had extra pillows. He reached behind his back and pulled out a bunch of red roses.

"My goodness."

"I thought you'd like 'em. Roses for Rosie. You see?" he said, ever so pleased with himself.

"Thank you. They're... so pretty."

"It's funny you say that, cos they've been right worried."

"You what? Who have?"

"The flowers, of course. Said they were all jealous cos they weren't as pretty as you."

"Oh, stop being silly." I brought them up to my face as if I was smelling them, but in truth, it was to cover my blush.

"That's what they said to me, honest."

"Where did you get them from, anyway?"

"I got my mum to bring 'em in."

"Well, that's very nice, please say thanks to her."

He clutched at his heart in mock pain. "It was still *my* idea, y'know."

"Well... thank *you* too."

"*You're* more than welcome," he said with a wink. "So then, there's just one thing left really..."

I knew better than to ask. In fact, all I wanted to do at that moment was leave. But I didn't, and so he continued.

"...which is—what time shall I pick you up to go to the pictures next Friday?"

"Urm... I'm sorry... I can't really—"

"I'll tell you something for nothing, there ent no way I'm leaving this bed 'til you say yes."

But he did, and I didn't.

I told him I had to look after my family, that I was too busy, that my mum would never let me, anyway.

"Don't worry, I'll just come round and pick you up anyway, set your mum straight. Fancy keeping a beauty like you locked away from the world."

"It's a brave man who'd even try."

"You don't truly know me yet. I'd do it y'know."

"I can't, I'm so sorry." I started walking backwards, smelling the roses again. "But thank you so much for the flowers. And I'm sorry, I am, I really am."

I expected him to call out like he'd done so many times before, but he didn't. It was the first time I'd seen him without his smile. He looked really upset. His face was always an instant giveaway of his feelings; he was never able to hide his true emotions. He almost looked as if he would cry, and it was almost enough to send me the same way.

Again, I was the victim of the girls' teasing.

"You're a hard girl to please all right."

"Did you not like him then?" Jenny asked me.

"He was all right. I dunno."

"Not your type, I guess."

"Maybe not."

"What is your type then? A bloomin prince," said Wendy.

I shrugged. "I dunno, maybe I just ent into boys. Not everyone is."

There was a long embarrassed silence, and all but Wendy made to be looking at something else. I couldn't work it out. What was so wrong with that? I could see Wendy was desperately searching her head for something to say.

"Oh, but I think you do like him really," she said to the Lynn Girls. "Cos she was always laughing with him and spoon-feeding him, weren't you?"

"Only cos I had to. He had his arm in plaster," I said.

The following day, that lonely, empty feeling I sometimes got, found its way back to me. Just knowing that him and that beaming great smile of his weren't gonna be waiting for me, made going to work a lot less exciting than usual. Things were awkward with the Lynn Girls too, and I couldn't understand it. It wasn't supposed to be like that. I hadn't gone out with him, so why were things still going bad for me. It wasn't how it was meant to go at all. It wasn't right and it wasn't fair.

I realised my confidence was such a brittle thing that could be cracked so easily. I felt like the Lynn Girls didn't have any time for me no more. Wendy was lovely as usual and kept asking if I was okay, but she too wasn't her bubbly self. It made me think, was it just Teddy who made me feel good? That without him I was nothing? Was it just him who made me interesting, made me fun and popular?

I'd thought the other girls would be happier, would like me more after he was gone. I'd always feared they'd been a bit jealous of all the attention I'd been getting. I realised I needed to do something to show them I was my own person, to remind them I was still Rose, that I could still be fun, that nothing had changed.

The next day, Wendy and me were damp dusting under the beds when Mrs Longswick mentioned we'd missed a bit.

"Leave it out, Mrs L. You sound just like The Terrier, don't she?" said Wendy.

We both knew Mrs Longswick wasn't being fussy but just looking out for us, worried we might get wrong. And Wendy was just trying to be upbeat. Mrs Longswick laughed and wagged her finger at us.

"That's not right," said Wendy. Then she put one hand on her hip and shook her finger sharply back at Mrs Longswick. "See, that's how she does it, ent it, Rosie?"

I smiled. "You've got to do the walk as well," I said. "No... not like that. Let me show you."

Taking lots of quick tiny steps and making sure my shoes clopped noisily on the floor, I marched over to the next bed and pretended to look at a chart.

"How are you, Mrs Wilkins?"

Mrs Wilkins had been listening and so played along.

"Ah yeah, improving, Matron, but I do—"

"Excellent. Very Good." And with that, I marched onto the next bed and looked at the imaginary chart again.

"Mrs Housen. How are you?"

"I'm—"

"Excellent. Very good." And off I marched again. Everyone was laughing at this point and I could see the Lynn Girls, who'd started cleaning from the other end, looking and laughing too.

"And you, Mrs Loughton?"

But Mrs Loughton didn't know what to say.

"Come on, speak up. How are you? I haven't got all day."

"I... ur... I'm okay... *Rose*," she said very deliberately.

"Rose?" I said. "It's Matron to you, I'll have you know."

Mrs Loughton seemed a bit distant, almost confused, and that's when I realised—she wasn't even looking at me anymore. She was looking past me. I didn't need to turn around to check, I knew. The quiet after the merriment just moments before was painful. I stood waiting, my neck on the executioner's block, waiting for the axe to fall, waiting for it to be all over.

"I think you're getting a bit ahead of yourself there, young Page," came the chop of the axe in her unmistakable clipped tone. "You think you're good enough to be the matron now, do you?"

I felt my head shrinking into my shoulders and wanted to crawl under Mrs Loughton's bed.

"Looks like someone has just volunteered to clean out Mr Walker's sputum pot for the entirety of his stay," still measured. Then came the eruption, "Now *get* back to work. *All* of you!"

I couldn't even look at her as I scurried away to my damp duster.

"She don't mean no harm," I heard Mrs Loughton protesting.

"Oh be quiet, you!"

Matron was often firm with patients, but this was the first time any of us had heard her scold one.

Later that day, Tracey gave me a sympathetic smile and put her hand on my shoulder as she passed.

The next day, when we were cleaning the lockers, the girls were all having a good giggle as they acted out the moment I got caught. I couldn't help thinking how strange life was, just like a seesaw. The point when both sides are balanced only lasts a second or two, the rest seems to be constant topsy turvy ups and downs which you can never predict. Sometimes you plant something good and it all turns rotten, other times you sow a bad seed and only positives sprout from it.

I thought about going to apologise to Matron, tell her I didn't mean nothing by it, that I was just showing off and should've known better. But every time she came near me, I couldn't help moving as far away as possible. Nothing more was said of it, and a few days later things seemed as normal as you could figure. It was a rare day when Matron spoke to us in any way but her curt tone—whether a compliment or a ticking off.

"Yep, very good as usual, Rose," she said after overseeing me do an injection for the first time, and then off she clopped.

26

MOVING ON

I was sterilising the rubber tubes by boiling them up in a big pan of water when I heard his familiar voice ringing through the corridors.

I stuck my head out of the bowl room and listened. Then I followed it all the way to the plaster room. I stood outside wondering whether I should go in and if I did what my excuse should be.

"You're a sort aren't yuh, Teddy. What we gonna do with you." This was a female voice that I guessed was his mother. "Right then, I'm going to the ladies if you're gonna be like that."

I was too late in gathering my wits, and so she nearly knocked me off my feet as she came bustling out.

"Blimey you give me a fright," she said holding a hand to her chest. She then broke out in a smile. "Well, blow me down with a summer's breeze. Look who it is..."

I smiled, too embarrassed to say anything.

"Oy. Teddy," she called out.

"What you want now, woman?"

"I got a surprise for you, my boy." And with that, she grabbed my arm and dragged me into the plaster room. She stood beaming. "I only gone and found that nurse you like so much. Now, I really must get to the toilet. So I'll leave you to it," she said with a wink before leaving.

“Hello,” I said meekly, and then waved to him for some bizarre reason.

“Ha. I knew you wouldn't be able to keep away from me. I'd wave back if I could,” he said, nodding down at his plaster cast. “Getting it off today.”

“If you don't keep still, I'll be having your arm off too,” said Nurse Davidson who was busy with the big plaster scissors.

“How you been? Missing me, of course?”

“Urm...?” I looked at Nurse Davidson.

“Obviously not then,” he rolled his eyes. “It's okay, I ent gonna waste no more time asking you out again.” Then, after a pause. “And it’s probably not even worth tellin you that I go down to the youth club in Holt on the odd occasion.”

“Aren't you a bit old for youth club?” said Nurse Davidson. “And if you don't stop moving, I'm just gonna leave this on.”

Still, I had nothing to say.

He looked up at me. “I do wanna say thanks for your help though.”

“Just doing my job,” said Nurse Davidson.

“Gawd, I weren't talking to you, was I.”

I tried to stifle my chuckle, but she was a good sort, so it didn’t matter. It never stopped amazing me how direct he was, and also the effect he had on other people. He made everyone feel as though they'd known him all his life, as though they were instantly his best friend.

“What you two love birds up to then?” said his mum as she came back in, tucking her curled hair back under her green felt hat.

“Nothin. Go away, Mum.”

“Blimey, he's a right charmer ent he?” she said giving me a burly nudge. His mother was taller than average, and whilst in no way overweight, she seemed very solidly put together and moved in a very deliberate, meaningful way in whatever she did.

“I... I really should be gettin back to my work.” I straightened my cap, even though it wasn’t even on the huh. “Just wanted to check you're all right... and say... hello.”

“Yeah, well, we did that,” he said pulling at the frayed edge of his plaster cast. “S’pose it was good seeing you once more though.”

"Yeah. Thank you. Urm... bye then I guess." And with that, I hurried out, cursing myself for being such a coward.

I started thinking of all the things I could or should've said, then realised I needed to forget about it, clear my mind, get it back on to work matters. I was worried it'd been noticed that I'd been gone a while, so I scurried away hoping to find another trainee that I could ask if I needed an excuse at the ready for the matron.

As I rounded the corner I was met by a god-awful smell. It wasn't like a patient smell, such as the thick sour smell of a gammy dressing, or the mouldy pong of a badly cleaned bedpan—those smells I was used to. This one was different, an unnatural smell, almost like something burning and also a bit chemically. In fact, it was so bad I had to hold my nose and blink my eyes. I started to worry that something terrible and unimaginable had happened and I hadn't been there to help.

I turned into the corridor; the ward came into view, but all seemed calm. However, the stench had got so thick I could swear I could taste it, and it tasted like melting plastic maybe. But it wasn't that. There was definitely something familiar in it, I thought. Something that I knew, not plastic but perhaps more like... and then it clicked... rubber.

Clamping the end of my nose with one hand, I wafted away the beginnings of smoke with the other and peered into the pan of boiling water that I'd left the tubes in. Trouble was, there wasn't any water in it anymore. All that was left was a crawling, bubbling mess of once-red rubber.

After I turned off the gas burner, I stood with the pan in my hand not knowing what to do. It was still too hot to shove in the bin and there was no hiding the smell.

"Page? What on earth have you been doing?" came Matron's voice from behind me.

I spun around and froze. She pinned me good with that stare of hers, catching me red-handed.

I felt terrible; it was just one thing after another with me at that time. I thought about saying that my mum had been getting on to me bad and that's why I was making so many mistakes recently.

"I... forgot about them," I said, offering her a look in the pan.

She peered in but said nothing.

"I... was just... I put them on the boil and then I went to..."

"Hmm. Well, as long as you weren't thinking of eating that mess." Her tone and face were still so serious, I couldn't be sure if she was joking or not. She gave a weary sigh. "Go on," she said and motioned with her head. "Don't think I haven't done the same thing myself. It can happen when you're trying to do too much at one time. But open the window at least."

"I'm very, very sorry."

"It's all right, I know you've been trying hard recently. It's nee bother." She went to leave, then stopped. "Tell me, how are things at home?"

"Urm... okay. I s'pose. Well, no worse than usual."

"I see. And... are you courting?"

"No," I said, shaking my head violently, hoping the more I shook the more she would believe me. I think given the choice, I'd have preferred her scolding me than starting a conversation about courting boys.

"Why not? You're a pretty young girl."

I shrugged.

"You know, kiddo, there's more to life than just working."

I nodded.

"Go on then, take that mess to the bins. And don't be forgetting about Mr Walker's sputum pot either," she called after me.

As we wheeled our bikes through the Hospital car park, I could tell the question was coming. I'd seen her take several curious glances at my bike as we pushed them round from the shed.

"You took the ribbons off, dint yuh?"

"Uh-huh."

"Why's that?"

"Dunno. Just... felt like it."

"Oh." She looked down at her bike. "I might... keep mine on still. If that's... okay?"

"Of course it is. You should always do what makes you happy, not other people."

"Oh, okay."

We hopped onto our saddles and biked down the Cromer Road towards Holt. Not much was said, I wasn't feeling much like chatting and Wendy was good at sensing my mood. When she didn't talk, she hummed real quiet instead. I think she was as afraid of silence as much as she was of the dark.

"I been thinking," I said eventually.

"What's that?"

"I was thinking, you know a while back, you said about us going to the youth club? Maybe we should do that one time."

"Really?" Her face lit up.

"Yeah. Just... maybe."

"Oh, we should. We should," she nodded. "I can't wait already!"

"Yeah, me too."

"But I guess—" she started before stopping herself. She bit her bottom lip and I could see that mischievous glint in her eye.

"What is it? Go on, say it."

"I guess... we just need to be sure we don't wear any... perfume is all." She cringed as she said it, but with her cheeky smile, she could tell me the world was ending and I'd find it funny.

What my mother would say to me about going out in the evening, I didn't know, so I decided to talk to Dad first.

He shrugged and grunted something that sounded like a yes.

"What'll Mum say, do you think?"

"Huh, you think she'll even notice?"

"So... should I not say then?"

"I won't."

"And...? I mean, should I get back early to put the little'uns to bed?"

"She can do it."

"What if she's..."

"What?"

"If she's... you know... out?"

This was met with silence. I thought he was gonna pretend I hadn't said anything.

"I suppose I'll have to do it then."

"Thanks, Dad."

All that night I felt the good tingly nerves. I tried to imagine what it would be like, but I wasn't very good at it as I kept picturing everyone in their school uniforms. Right, there's no use thinking about it. I decided I should just go and concentrate on having a good time with Wendy, and that is all.

We told the Lynn Girls, and to our relief, they wanted to join us. We got ready in their room and this time nobody wore *that* perfume, let alone mentioned it, which made me feel a tad bit guilty. But this time we managed to get to where we were going, at least.

It was a bit daunting at first, so loud and busy, so many unknown faces. I hadn't been around that many young people all in one place for a good while—if ever. Wendy clutched at my arm and wouldn't let go. At times, she was almost hiding behind me, even when we were walking. But mostly, we stood at a table in the corner.

With my make-up and nice clothes on and Wendy being so nervous it made me feel braver, and I soon got used to all the noise and people.

"Have you lost something?" Tracey said to me. "You can't keep your head still."

I told her I was just seeing if there were any people I recognised from school.

"Ahh, I see. Well, I haven't seen him yet, but if I do, I'll let you know," she said with a smile.

And sure enough, he turned up shortly after that. And sure enough, I became a bag of nerves. I was really worried that he might actually come and say hello and then I'd have to say some stuff too. However, he didn't notice me for a time—seeing as he was king of the room; all the boys and girls hanging around him, laughing away. When he did eventually notice me, all he did was give a casual nod. I smiled, but my insides felt like they were dissolving and draining away. And so I realised, of course, it had all been a bit of teasing after all. I felt so stupid.

I knew I couldn't ask the girls if we could leave already, they'd never speak to me again if I made a habit of ruining nights out. I was too upset to even talk, but I desperately needed to pass the time. In the end, all I could think to do was my old trick of reciting nursery rhymes in my head.

...when the pie was opened the birds began to sing, wasn't that a dainty dish to serve before the—

"Come on then," he said, appearing from nowhere. He took hold of my arm and pulled me up from my chair. "You coming outside with me or what?"

"What?"

"Well, I'm guessing you don't want me to kiss you in front of all these people, right?"

"Certainly not." I gave him a soft clip on the shoulder. "That's certainly not gonna happen."

He sighed and I felt his grip soften on my arm. He made an effort at a smile and went to turn away.

"No," I said a bit louder and more sudden than I meant to, and this time it was me doing the arm grabbing.

He turned back.

"I mean... you gotta take me out properly if that's... if you want to... I mean if we're going to... if you want to take me out, that is."

27

PARTNERS IN CRIME

And so that was that. The next Friday he took me to the pictures, we saw a movie, and I kissed a boy for the first time in my life. I won't go into all the slushy details, as it's nothing we don't know already.

Even though I still had to work for the house, the little'uns weren't so little anymore, so free time was easier to come by. Of course, I daren't tell my parents I was courting. Instead of telling lies, the first time I didn't say anything, just put my coat on and got ready to leave. I heard Dad lowering the paper behind me. I turned. He looked me up and down and knew I wasn't just nipping out to the loo.

"Where you off to, Rose?"

"Going to meet a friend."

"Friend?" My mother jumped in.

"Wendy."

She looked at me blankly.

"I work with her. We pushbike home together—every day."

"Well, if you see her every day, then why you need to see her at night?"

My parents never had a problem with me cycling home from work and youth club in the dark. I guess the only difference now was that I was doing it in a nice dress and make-up.

“We want to go to the cinema together.”

Her eyes narrowed, she went to speak but then stopped herself before saying, “Why are you suddenly so interested in going to the pictures then?”

“Well... you know how much I used to enjoy going to the pictures with you...” I felt bad for my dad having to be there, but he did at least have his paper shield up. “And... since you don't take me no more...”

She bristled like a disgruntled, craggy old cat, the corner of her top lip twitching. My heart was beating so fast, but not just through fear—I have to say, I was also getting a bit of a thrill out of it too. So much so, I foolishly jabbed again. “And I guess I'm old enough to be out there all by myself now.” I couldn't help it, but instantly realised I'd pushed too far and given her something to jump on, and she never missed a chance to pounce.

“No. I won't have it. Not going out by yourself,” she said, crossing her arms and raising her chin defiantly. “It's not safe. A young girl like you traipsing around, all alone in the dark.”

All I could do was watch as she performed her little theatre piece, not once coming out of character. “Anything could happen,” she continued. “I'd be worried sick. It'd send me to an early grave it would.”

I don’t know whose sake she was performing for. Sometimes, I thought it might just even be for her own benefit, trying to convince herself she had a real heart. But most probably, it was just cos she enjoyed it—she was a born performer who longed for the return of the excitement and the popularity of her pub singer days down in the big city.

Anyway, the obvious answer which I should’ve seen coming, was for the terrible twosome to be reunited. We stood silently in the kitchen looking at each other, neither best pleased about it. I wanted to complain; I wanted to argue my case, but I knew it was better to take something, rather than end up with nothing.

“So... guess we better get our coats then,” I said.

Perry made some harrumphing and grunting noises as he followed me out to the shed. We stood in silence, looking down at the bike. I took the handlebars and hopped my leg over and waited. Perry sighed, then sat himself on the saddle and rested his toes on the back spindle. "At least you've took them stupid ribbons off," was his only comment.

Nothing more was said until we got to town. I spent the whole ride thinking about what I could do with him. What would Teddy say if I turned up with my kid-brother in tow? It'd also mean Perry knowing about him, and then I'd only be a silly sibling argument away from my parents finding out.

As we hid the bike in the bushes behind the bus stop on the edge of town, I looked over at a small copse of trees... then shook the thought out of my head. It would've been impossible anyway—Perry was too fidgety to stay in one place for too long, plus he was still scared of the dark.

"Well? What do you want to do then?"

"I dunno." He kicked at a stone. It skipped twice across the road before crashing into the hedge on the other side.

"Did you want to stay at home?"

He shrugged. "Did I have a choice?"

"Haven't you got no friends in town?"

"Yeah. Course I have."

"Well, what do they do with themselves of an evening?"

"I dunno. Some of 'em muck about at the old pump house."

"Yeah?"

He nodded.

"Hmm. Do you know how to tell the time?"

"Course I do."

"Good." I passed him the old, rusty pocket-watch. "So, I'll tell you what, if you promise not to be get'n in any mischief, I'll let you go muck about with your friends as long as you're back here by ten past ten."

"Really?" He looked a little nervous.

"If you want to be with your friends that is?"

"Yeah, course."

"But that's all you do, mind. You stay with them and no getting wrong off anybody, otherwise you'll ruin it for the both of us, you see?"

"Yeah, I geddit."

"Ten past ten though. No later. You got me?"

"Yeah, I got it the first time."

"And if I ent here by then, best you hide behind the bus stop 'til I come along. After all, we can't have no one seeing you, can we?"

And sure enough, he was there on time. And sure enough, this became our regular routine—always arriving home together, making sure we had the same story about something funny Wendy had said and what movie we'd seen.

I was still 15 at this time, and Teddy was older than me by seven years, but in those days this wasn't such a big thing. He had his own car, so he'd take me to the pictures or Sheringham seafront or sometimes to youth club or sometimes just out for a drive.

His parents were certainly doing all right for money, not that they were posh, the family just owned a lot of bits and bobs of land and property that had been in the family for years. Mostly, they themselves worked at their shop-come post office. They were ever so kind, and just like Teddy, after knowing them for five minutes, you felt like you'd known them all your life. Mind you, his grandparents on his mum's side were a different story. They were a little bit funny, maybe puritans I think, as they wouldn't let their children wear perfume or even use soap that smelled too nice.

Teddy had two sisters and a brother. Mary and Jack were lovely people just like their parents, however the youngest sister, Karen, now she was a bit of a rum'un and had somewhat of a temper on her. Usually, I only bore witness to it through tales from Teddy, but there was one time, shortly after Teddy and I had started courting, when we popped into the house so he could pick up a jacket. While I waited in the hall, I could hear Karen's raised voice and then the quieter one of her father—who she was shrieking over. The door was ajar, but I still couldn't see them and knew better than to go peeking. When Teddy came down with his coat, he didn't seem to notice the row blazing away in the next room.

"Well, come on then, are we going or what?" he said as he shrugged his jacket up onto his shoulders.

"Is everything... okay?" I said, nodding toward the lounge.

"Ahhh, she's always like that. Come on." He ushered me towards the front door—and just in time to.

"Why don't you piss off and leave me alone!" Karen shouted, before an almighty crash and an upturned chair came tumbling through the door right where I'd been standing mere moments before.

"Woo-hoo!" whooped Teddy as he skipped out of the house, dragging me along. "I told yuh!"

Whilst he actually seemed excited by it, I looked down at my hand to see it shaking uncontrollably as we sped out of the driveway.

Nothing seemed to faze Fun-Time Teddy; he was always in a good mood, always having a good time. He didn't have a care in the world or take anything too serious. I ent no psychologist, but it's easy to imagine that because of his mum's strict upbringing, she must've decided to do things differently with her own kids.

I remember his other sister, Mary, telling me how when they were little, their mother would take them on the train to Sheringham for music lessons. Mary was learning the flute and Teddy the recorder, and every week they'd take that same train. She told me how one time, for no real reason, Teddy just threw his recorder out of the train window right in front of their mother. Well, apparently all the other kids fell about laughing, but not a word in anger was said about it by his mum. She just went out the next day and bought him a new recorder. Of course, the following week, not wanting to disappoint his expecting audience, the brand new recorder also took a flying lesson. I'd never heard anything like it. If I'd done that, the next thing going out of that window would've been me—and headfirst, at that.

28

THE FIRST TIME

On the days I was due to see Teddy, work always seemed to drag on. I still enjoyed my job but just the thought of seeing him made everything else seem dull and almost pointless. The day didn't really begin until I saw his beaming face and heard that rascal voice of his.

One Friday, Teddy had promised me a special romantic evening. Not wanting the bother of dealing with Perry, I got my alibi in quick and told my parents I was staying the night at Wendy's.

That morning, I got to work early because I needed to replace my going-out clothes that I kept in the basement. On my way down, I bumped into Matron, who asked if I wouldn't mind taking down a box of beakers since I was going that way. The box wasn't heavy but was big enough that I couldn't see my own feet, and miscounting the steps, thinking there to be one more than there was, I got caught off balance. First I pitched forward, then in an effort not to throw the beakers across the basement, I lent back. But this caused me to stumble and my heel to finally find the mysterious missing bottom step. And down I went.

Desperate not to drop the boxes I'd been entrusted with, I forgot to break my fall with my hands and I managed to bump the back of my head on the edge of one step and my spine on another two. I lay there for a while, waiting for the pain to ease enough so I could decide whether I should swear, scream, cry or do all three at once.

My eyes were wet, but I wasn't sobbing as I gathered myself. I managed to put the beakers back in the box and stacked it in the corner, but then I had to stop for a long moment before I could take on the stairs. Every upward step sent a spasm through my lower back as though my spine had been entangled in an electric fence.

Matron was understanding, if not feeling unnecessarily guilty. She made me rest up in the Lynn Girl's room and gave me some painkillers that didn't do too much.

Just before lunch she came to check on me and said she'd call my mother to see if she could come by and take me home.

"Actually, I think it's feeling all right now. I think I'll probably be okay," I told her as I gritted my teeth and tried not to move.

She looked at me for a long, measured second. She said she'd come check on me after lunch, and if I still couldn't move without flinching, she was definitely calling my mother.

I gave myself a ten minute rest before forcing myself off the bed and gingerly making my way back to the ward. I spent the rest of the afternoon grimacing and groaning as I hobbled around.

"Cor, are you all right, love? You sound like you're having a baby," Mrs Davies said to me as I bent down to collect her bedpan.

"A real trooper, that one," Mrs Hollis nodded to Mrs Davies.

I smiled, but not for long—because even that hurt.

As I was leaving, Matron caught up with me and gave me a telling off. She said I should have gone home, and told me I didn't have to come in the following day.

I was so relieved to finally finish work, but my heart sank when I realised I still had the long bike ride home.

"I wish I could do something for yuh," Wendy said as she saw me struggling just to get my leg over.

"I'll be all right."

"I can walk with you if you want? We don't have to bike, you know."

"I'll be fine once we get going." I found that when I got into the rhythm of pedalling, the pain settled to a constant ache rather than the occasional hot electric jolt.

"You're so brave. I would have just gone home when Matron said, wouldn't I?"

"Well, the worse is yet to come. I gotta go home and pretend I ent hurt at all now."

"What on earth for?"

"Teddy's taking me out tonight and there's no way Mum will let me go if she knows I'm hurt."

"Ahh, well least it's nice to know she cares though, ent it?"

"Yeah, right."

After a short period of silence, she spoke again. "You don't have to bike me home, if you don't want. It don't get dark so much now."

I biked her home anyway. But regretted it coming up the hill after.

Before going into the house, I had to prepare myself with several deep breaths. I felt like an old woman but no one seemed to notice my slow crooked walk. I reminded my parents of the story about staying at Wendy's. Maybe because my mind was focussed on the pain, the lying came a lot easier this time. However, I did also realise I hadn't really thought it through properly, because after Teddy dropped me off I'd have to come back home. I figured if I was quiet enough, I could sneak into my caravan without anyone noticing, then as long as I didn't use the tilley lamp they wouldn't know anyone was in there.

After dinner, I got myself ready, hobbled out to the shed, biked to the bus stop, hid the bike in the bushes and caught the bus the rest of the way into town.

Teddy met me by the old pump house. He was dressed all dapper in what I guessed was his dad's best suit. He'd even combed his hair for the first time since I'd known him.

"Well, don't you look a pretty sight," he beamed. "How's my luck, eh? Prettiest girl in all of Norfolk, and I get to take her out."

I still got embarrassed by his compliments, but it was more than worth it for the tingling rush they caused, and already I'd started to forget about my pain.

"If the lady would like to take my arm, I'll escort yuh to the car."

"Where we going then?" I said, linking my arm in his. I was

thinking maybe we were headed for the Theatre Royal in Norwich and suddenly felt underdressed.

"For a romantic evening for two, my dear."

"Stop talking all funny," I said, batting his shoulder.

"Anything for you, madam."

"Stop it," I laughed, causing a surge of pain.

When we got to his car, I caught a glimpse of a bottle of his dad's homemade wine and a blanket on the backseat—so probably not the theatre after all.

Teddy drove with the radio turned up as loud as it would go, though still not enough to drown out his bad singing. He always drove as fast as his car—or the roads would allow. The first couple of times I drove with him, I was scared out of my wits.

"My car only has one speed," Teddy told me, "and that's flat out!" Then he'd stomp down hard on the pedal.

I never dared ask him to slow down, thinking he was just showing off and it would pass. I eventually got used to it. To be honest, I always felt safe with Teddy, it was just the way he was. He made me feel like there wasn't a care or trouble in the world, that everything would always be okay with him.

I couldn't quite be sure where we were going as we whizzed through the dark country lanes. The roads were so narrow and the hedges so high it was like we were racing through a never-ending tunnel, as if we were burrowing deeper and deeper into the earth. Eventually, the car slowed. We turned into the small car park at the rear of Blickling Lake. I felt the tumbling tingle inside my chest as we pulled in. The last pieces of the jigsaw were now starting to show the whole picture. Suddenly it all seemed so obvious and I felt foolish for not having realised earlier.

There were two other cars in the car park. The cars dark, but their windows pale with breath. He parked a polite distance away from them.

He stopped the engine. He turned and smiled at me. My heart was already racing and my leg jiggering uncontrollably. His arms came over towards me. I managed to wipe my palms on my sides before he took them in his hands.

"Could I interest the lady in a moonlit walk around the lake?"

"Yes," I said, already going for the door handle. "I mean... that'd be nice."

He reached over into the back. I thought he was going for the blanket, but he grabbed the bottle of wine.

"You ever had wine before?"

"Yeah. Of course."

Then he stopped. "Oh, bugger it." He turned back. "I didn't bring no glasses."

There was a nip in the air, so I clutched tight against him for warmth as we walked through the small copse that separated the car park from the lake.

"Afraid of the dark, are yuh? Don't worry, I'll take good care of you."

As we came out from the cover of trees, there was a few dull wisps of cloud that did little to hide the modesty of the huge spread of stars. The lake stretched out in front of us. Long and thin before eventually bending out of sight as it reached all the way to the grand old Jacobean hall. Its surface was no more than a ripple as it lapped gently against the bank.

We walked round to a small bay where the path slipped into the shallows. Teddy set down his coat under a small willow, having forgotten to bring the blanket.

"Oh, shit it."

"What now?"

"I dint bring no bottle opener neither."

"I guess we're lucky you remembered the wine at least."

Teddy flashed me a sarcastic smile before picking up a stone from the shallows. He began to rap the bottle's neck with it. The ting of stone on glass seemed so loud as it echoed across the water.

"Mind you don't cut yourself."

Finally, there came a deep crack as he knocked half the neck off.

"There we go," he said proudly.

I asked if he was going to leave the broken bit on the floor, worried a dog or a swan might step on it, so he picked it up and threw it into the middle of the lake with a splosh.

"There, it's gonna have to be one hell of a long-legged swan that'll step on that," he said, making me giggle.

He came and sat down next to me again.

"I'm sorry that I forgot the glasses. I'd usually say ladies first but I best check it ent gonna cut us."

I'd tried wine before, but never much more than the odd sip. I found it quite sharp and I don't think Teddy enjoyed it much either as we didn't finish it. It was enough to make me feel lightheaded and dreamy as we sat in the darkness; my head nestled into his shoulder.

We had a kiss and fumble, but when his hands started exploring too far beneath my clothing I sat up and told him I was starting to feel the cold. He didn't seem to mind too much.

"I could get the blanket from the car?" he said, getting to his feet.

"No, it's okay."

"What do you want to do then? Go for a swim?"

"Don't be silly."

"I'm not, come on," he said and took off his jacket.

"It's cold and dark, I ent going in there."

"Well, I am. I'm gonna swim right up to the hall and back to prove how much I love yuh." He started to lift up his jumper.

"Teddy, stop being silly."

"How else am I gonna prove I love yuh?"

"Certainly not by getting yourself drowned."

He paused, looking out at the lake. "Yeah, you're right. And besides, I don't know how to swim anyhow. I'll just have to think of another way."

"Just sayin it, is good enough for me." And it was. They weren't words I'd heard much before, if at all. It was a strange feeling, knowing someone liked me that much. I found it difficult to believe. I couldn't think of what I had to offer, what I had that was so good, that would make someone say it to me. At times I found myself wondering if I was stuck in a really long dream. It seemed the only way a less-than-ordinary girl like me could have ended up going with Fun-Time Teddy, the king of youth club, a guy popular with everyone he ever met.

"Come on, let's get you back to the car then."

I felt a tension wash away as he took my hand and we walked the short distance back to the car park. The strange thing of it was, I only realised I'd been holding that tension once it was gone.

Another car had pulled up, its windows already pale.

Teddy went to the back seat, spread out the blanket and invited me for a cuddle. I was hesitant, but couldn't think of anything to say, so I let him lead me in.

He kissed me briefly, then got on top of me.

I didn't feel at all comfortable because the seat was so cramped and my mind was on my back once again—not to mention the blanket. I knew where it was going, where he wanted it to go, something I wasn't so keen on. After all, I only knew of it as a thing that brought trouble, that did nothing but caused people pain. It made people lie to each other. It made people get married for the wrong reasons. It broke up families. It caused people to do things they would never otherwise dream of—such as throwing a broken man in a field and leaving him there to die.

I wanted to say no as he began to remove my clothes. I wanted to tell him my back hurt, but I hadn't mentioned it before, so I was worried he'd think I was only making excuses. As much as I didn't want to do it, I also didn't want to upset the one person who cared for me, the one person who showed me real love. I also didn't want to make a drama, because maybe then he would start to think about finding some other girl less likely to make a fuss.

One thing I couldn't hide was the pain, it was just too much.

"It's okay, it always hurts to start with," he said, banishing any doubt that it was not the first time for him.

His lips brushed close to my ear.

I groaned again.

"It's okay, it's okay," he whispered.

After a short time, it was the pain in my back that was the worst. I bit down on my lip and felt water filling the bottom of my eyes.

When it was over, I was nearly crying. Teddy was ever so apologetic, saying it would get better the next time, and that I'd come to enjoy it more than anything else in the world.

I nodded.

He held me for a while—and that was nice. But soon the weight on top of me was pressing my back into the seat too much.

My whole life, I've had a strange relationship with sex. In fact, I can't say it has ever been that special thing that most people seem to lose their head over. That night, afterwards, I felt like I was being pushed down a path I didn't want to follow, almost as if I had been tricked into taking it—not tricked by Teddy, but by... I dunno—life? It felt as if it had already been fated, that it didn't matter what I thought or even what I did, I was going to become something I hated. Or probably more accurately, someone I... I didn't want to be.

As we drove back, I promised myself I wasn't gonna tell any more lies, even if it meant taking the brunt of my mother's wrath or getting wrong with Matron or upsetting my friends from time to time.

Teddy dropped me off at the bus stop so I could pick up the bike. I insisted on taking the blanket so I could wash it—after all, it was my blood. He gave me a kiss and roared off into the darkness. I walked most of the way; I wasn't in any rush.

I hid the bike behind a hedge, covered it over, and crept down the lane toward the house. I carefully lifted the latch, then slowly pushed the gate open. As I did so the un-oiled rusted hinges let out a pained groan. I froze, looking up at the house. Nothing stirred. On my second go, I lifted the gate up slightly. It worked a treat as I managed to open it with hardly a sound.

Once on the other side, I quietly closed it again and lowered the latch. Then... I sensed something... a bustle or a breath? I stopped to listen, putting my ear to the wind.

I heard it again and knew it was drawing closer. I stayed stock-still, eyes straining into the darkness until I could finally make out a shadowy figure hugging the hedgerow and heading my way.

29

SHE'S NOT AFRAID OF THE DARK

I held my nerve, thinking it would pass me by if I didn't move. But the figure kept coming, kept growing until I realised it was heading towards our house. As it came to the gate, it must have finally picked out my outline. It stopped, suddenly alert, like a fox raiding the bins.

"Who's that?" came the sharp whisper.

"It's... me."

She took the final two steps to the gate and craned forward. "You?" she said, as she gathered the blanket that was trying to escape from the crook of her arm.

My mind scrambled for an excuse, but nothing was coming. Then I remembered—no more lies. You got caught Rose, now you're gonna have to accept what that brings.

"What then, he sent you out looking for me again, did he?" she said defiantly.

And then I realised—it wasn't as I thought, neither of us was the hunter. We were both playing hunted.

"No, I..." Was it okay to lie to *her*? I was thinking. I mean, *only* her —since she was the queen of the liars. Perhaps I should play the hunter to give myself the upper ground.

But then I saw her look down towards my arm.

Even in the half-light, I could make out the smugness spreading into her grin, "Bit late for a picnic, ent it?"

Then it hit me.

Like a train.

Full pelt.

I felt sick to the very pit of my stomach. I was at a complete loss for words as we stood either side of the gate. The occasional glimpses and distorted flashes in the grotesque mirror had finally settled to reveal one clear picture.

"What was it you said you were doing t'night...?" she started up again. "Oh... that's right, going to see that little wet rag of a friend of yours. Staying at her house, wasn't it? Or am I mistaken—you little trollop."

"No, I'm not staying at Wendy's tonight. I decided to come back—to my family," I said flatly.

"Is that so? Well... I suppose *most of them* are your family," she said, her grin widening. "Well, I'm going inside now, so you better totter off to your little dolls house." She eased the gate up, taking the pressure off the hinge, and swiftly opened it without a noise.

The scent of fried bacon and *that* perfume trailed behind her as she crept towards the house, checking up at the dark windows as she went. I watched her skirt around the edge of the gravelled area by the backdoor. Next, she stepped along the edging until she could take a long stride, cutting the corner onto the doorstep. She took another glance at the upstairs windows and carefully began to turn the door handle.

I was determined not to let her words get to me. I shook them from my mind and started across the lawn to my gypsy van. But... not before I let go of the gate, letting it swing shut with a groaning yawn and a jarring clunk of the metal latch that rang through the cold silence of the night.

I didn't check back to see her angry scowl—I'd seen it enough times to picture it, and that was good enough.

With everything that had gone on that day, I was so exhausted I collapsed into a deep sleep as soon as my head hit the pillow.

The next morning I woke early, all in a panic because my alarm didn't sound, but then remembered Matron had given me the day off, and so I was able to find sleep again quickly.

I'm not sure how much time passed before I was roused the second time. This time it was by a flood of sunlight pouring in from the caravan door being opened. I curled the blanket over my head to shut it out, before hearing her voice.

Still not fully in the land of the living, I couldn't quite make out what she was saying. I was expecting her to start barking at me, saying if I was at home I should be cleaning or making myself useful, but her tone was softer, quieter—kinder even, would you believe.

My bed was at the far end, so I felt it rise up as she stepped onto the entrance. She began to poke her head inside with a grunt. "Bloomin heck," she grunted. "Well, come on then, give me a hand."

The sleep fog was starting to clear, but I was still confuddled by what was going on.

"No, just hold the door open, you gret nana," she continued in a playful tease.

And then I realised. She wasn't speaking to me.

Next came the male voice. Unfamiliar. Too young to be my father. Too soft to be my brothers. I sat up, shielding my eyes against the shards of light that had managed to squeeze past her hefty frame.

As my eyes began to adjust, I could make out more and more. She was gathering up her skirt and trying to crawl fully inside, but clearly being pestered somehow from behind. "Get out of it, you. That's not helping is it," she laughed.

This was until she looked up.

For the second time in twelve hours, the sudden appearance of her bleary-eyed daughter stopped her in her tracks. She wriggled backwards desperately scrabbling for the doorframe.

"Careful there," came Ray's muffled voice. "You nearly stepped on me foot."

Her lips moved up and down looking for words that weren't coming, then she shook her eyes as if she thought they were seeing things.

I didn't say anything, instead reached up and rubbed tiredly at my face.

Then, as if backing away from a rabid dog, she tried to bustle out, pushing her way down, rocking the caravan wildly from side to side.

"Woh, easy gel. What you—"

"Shut your row!" she hissed. "Get out. Get out. Quick."

"Whatever are yu—"

"Ray! I said shut it, dint I." And with that she was gone. The door pushed shut, leaving me in darkness once again.

Their muffled bickering faded as I lay back down.

It was never brought up by either of us. But the next day I washed my bedsheets twice and then asked Dad to fit a lock.

When I returned to work, Wendy was all excited and asking me lots of questions, wanting to know every detail of my romantic evening. I wasn't giving much away, but when I finally told her we ended up at Blickling Lake, her questions stopped and I realised she obviously wasn't as naïve as I'd been.

"Oh. I see. So what... urm... did you...?"

"We just went for a walk. Sat down and had some wine."

"Oh. And... was it... romantic and that?"

"Yeah, he was very sweet," I said, busying myself by stacking up the bedpans.

"And... well... did you...?"

"Yeah, it was a very nice evening. Come on then, we better get these out."

"Yeah. Good idea. We had better get them out, hadn't we?"

Most people make such a fuss, but I didn't feel any different. I was still the same old Rosemary I'd always been. Some people feel excited, as if it marks a big change in their life, like they've become an adult or at least started a new chapter. I guess the fact I did things all topsy-turvy, confused matters for me. I'd already raised three kids before ever doing the deed that was needed to make them. Also, with having gone through all the things that her antics caused, I only had bad associations with it, and that never really seemed to leave me.

For the first few times, it always felt like I was betraying myself or poisoning myself if that makes any sense. And maybe that's why I couldn't really let myself enjoy it.

I knew that the first time wasn't always meant to be pleasant, and that apparently it would get better. I also knew that Teddy would be expecting it all the time now, and no matter how much of a gentleman Teddy was, the chances are he would up and leave me if I didn't let him.

I wasn't afraid of love and affection; I liked nothing more than when Teddy hugged me, held my hand or put his on my thigh while we were driving. Even when his leg brushed against mine while we were at the pictures, it would sometimes be enough for me to have that same reaction as when we first touched in the hospital.

30

THE UNWELCOME VISITOR

The following Monday, I was in my caravan getting changed out of my work clothes when I heard a car engine roaring down the lane. I paused to listen, thinking it couldn't be. Next, came tyres skidding on gravel. The engine stopped. A split second later, a slamming door.

I pushed aside the curtain just in time to see Teddy stroll past. I couldn't believe it—what on earth was he doing. I'd told him to never come to the house, that she'd cause us big problems given any chance. But it was too late. He'd reached the backdoor. I could only hope he'd have enough wits about him to make up some lie if *she* answered. Tell her he'd got the wrong house or that he was a Jehovah's witness or... just anything.

I peered through the window but the angle was so tight I couldn't see. I could only catch a part of his back and shoulder. The shoulder moved.

Knock. Knock. Knock.

Then a few seconds later, "Hello there," he boomed. Even from the caravan, I could hear him clear as day. "I've come to pick up Rosie."

I couldn't hear the other end of the conversation, but by the way he spoke I guessed that it must've been Perry or Valerie. I thought I might just have enough time to get to him before they fetched her. I pulled on my cardigan.

"And who exactly might you be?"

Too late.

"Teddy, of course."

"Teddy? Teddy who?"

"Just Teddy to you. She in then?"

"No, she ent. And I won't have you coming round here trespassing."

"I'll wait 'til she gets back then."

"No you won't. You'll get out of my garden and you will leave before I call the police."

"Tell her I'll be waiting in my car then."

"Have you got cloth in your ears? Git out of it! Go on, scarper."

"Well, there's no need to be rude. In fact, I don't think I'll leave until you can ask me politely."

I'd told Teddy some stuff about her, not everything, just hinted that she wasn't that keen on me, and how she made me work so hard, and at times had a temper like thunder. However, her anger didn't shake him for a moment. It was as if he didn't hear the venom in her voice. The whole time he remained carefree and pleasant, as though he was popping round to borrow the lawnmower.

"You want me to call the police then?" I heard her say again.

"If you like. What, are you lonely or something? I'll talk to yuh if you are, save you a phone call."

I knew I had to do something, tell him to go, and then try explain things later. If I didn't, they'd likely be there until the moon come up... or worse, until Dad came home. This last thought was worrying enough for me to finally act.

I opened the door and stood on the caravan step clutching at my cardy. They both turned towards me.

"Ahhh. There she is," Teddy said with a broad smile. Turning his back to my mother, he started to stroll over.

"Rose. Get back in your van."

I saw his brow beginning to darken just before he turned to face her again. "Don't you tell her what to do," he said. A slight crack showing in his upbeat manner for the first time.

Her jaw hung open, and no reply came.

Teddy smiled at me, and I shut my mouth. It was as though all he'd done was bat away a pesky fly.

"Do you... do you know this... *boy*?" she spat.

"Boy? Boy? I'm twenty-two, I'll have you know." Then to me, "Come on Rosie, are you ready? I'm taking you out. Let's go."

"You ent going nowhere."

"Give it a rest will yuh. Yuh giving me a lug ache," he said as he reached the caravan.

"How dare you! Who do you think you are?"

"I told you already," he said over his shoulder. "I'm Teddy." And then to me, but loud enough for all to hear, "I think she must be the one with cloth in her ears."

He held out his hand for me, his dark eyes alive and sparkling. For a second, I forget all about her as she smouldered on the doorstep, as I let him lead me away.

But then, like a moth to a tilley lamp, my eyes were drawn back to her.

"You get in here at once! You've got your jobs to do."

"Do 'em yourself why don't yuh," Teddy said throwing up an arm, his smile gone. "How do put up with this ol' lug ache? Come on, let's go before I start getting really angry."

I found myself hunching my shoulders as if I was expecting something to be thrown at us.

"If you walk out that gate..." she started, but Teddy continued talking to me, drowning out the rest of her words.

I had to fight the urge to run to the car as soon as I saw it.

Although my hands were shaking, I felt safe once inside with the doors shut.

Teddy turned to me. "You all right?"

I nodded quickly and stared out the windscreen so he wouldn't talk anymore. I just wanted to get some distance between us and her as soon as possible.

He started the engine and gave it a big ol' rev. He turned to me. "I see what you mean though, she's a right ol' cow, ent she."

This was enough to burst my tension bubble and cause me to giggle.

Teddy smiled back, stood on the accelerator and we roared away, spraying stones and a cloud of dust behind us.

I felt like I'd been drinking that wine again, my head all warm and floaty. I was smiling so hard it hurt my face. It almost felt as though *I'd* said those things, as though he'd read my mind and said the words that had been stuck in my throat for the last seven years. I'd never seen anything like it; he didn't bat an eyelid the whole time. He never seemed worried that he was talking to an adult like she was a 10-year-old; it had been nothing to him.

We drove about for a while, going nowhere in particular, just whizzing about the lanes. We ended up in town and bought a fish and chip supper and walked about for a bit. Teddy was also on a real high, even happier than usual—if that was possible.

When it got dark, we drove out to the lake. It wasn't until after we'd finished in the back of his car that I realised... I still had to go home to face her. I hadn't had the belt for a good year and wondered if I was too old for it now.

I got Teddy to drop me off down the lane. As always, he offered to walk me to the house, and as always, I denied him.

I could see a light was still on in the kitchen, but I headed straight for the caravan. Come the morning, I got up extra early, set the table for breakfast and was out before anyone else stirred. When I come home that afternoon, I kept my eyes to the floor as I went into the kitchen and started on the dinner.

She just watched me, leaning against the sink, arms crossed, not saying a word. All I could hear was the *tick, tick, ticking* of the kitchen clock. I did all I could without having to go near her until I got the potatoes out. I shuffled up to the sink and finally spoke.

"I need to... can I use the—"

"You're not to see him again."

I caught myself about to nod, then looked up at her and told myself to be strong. "I'm sorry he was rude to you, but you can't stop me seeing him, he's... he's my boyfriend."

"And you're my daughter, and you do what I say. You're not to have boyfriends," she said. "What'd he'd want with you at any rate, huh?" And then almost to herself, "Only one thing. And I doubt that's even worth his while."

I turned away and felt my face beginning to burn up.

"Humph, and just you wait 'til your dad gets home. You think he'll be letting you have a boyfriend, do yuh?"

When dad came home, nothing was said other than a mumbled hello before he reached for the paper as usual.

"I'm going out with Belinda tonight, so Rose is staying here," she said as we sat down to eat.

Dad took no notice.

"Trevor. I'm talking to yuh."

Dad shrugged. "She don't need to."

"Everyone needs to do their bit to keep things running round here, you know that."

"She's fifteen, she's got her own job." He raised the paper again.

"Which is too young to be gallivanting around at all hours. She's not been helping around the house enough of late, and the hospital say it's been affecting her work."

This stopped me in my tracks and my stomach began to turn over. I had to hand it to her, she always knew the most effective place to hit me. But it couldn't be right, I thought. Matron would have said something to me, surely. But I also knew there was some truth in it—with all the excitement of going out with Teddy, my job had taken a slight back seat.

Mum's eyes were fixed on me, arms still folded, wearing that smug self-satisfied grin. And then... I had a moment of realisation. She'd given it away. I could see it in that smile I knew all too well. I could see how clever she *thought* she was. How she was *trying* to get at me, but she wasn't a mind reader. She was only making guesses, all based on herself and what she did, based on *her* world, on everything *she knew* of the lying and sneaking-about game. So, why hadn't she told Dad about

Teddy yet? Why was she holding back from dropping her bomb again? Because she was a cat with a shrew, and what fun is a dead shrew.

"Dad," I said rather too suddenly. "Dad, I've got a boyfriend."

He didn't react. I checked and saw it had at least cured her sickly grin though.

Next, we both looked nervously to him, waiting to see whether it was enough to whip up one of his famous storms...

"You have?" he said, eventually.

"His name's Teddy and he's twenty-two, and he came here and picked me up in his car."

His eyes narrowed. "Aren't you too young for boyfriends?"

"Karl and Billy had girlfriends at my age."

Dad thought about this for a moment. "It's different for boys."

"Yeah, so we don't want you seeing him again," she said with finality.

I had so many things I wanted to say, so many confusing thoughts, so many ways to explain how it wasn't fair. I wanted to tell them how Teddy was the best and most positive thing to ever happen in my life, made me the happiest I'd ever remembered being. But was that something you could say to your parents? To the people who spent fifteen years of their life raising you?

I managed to control my breathing, but that was all I could do to hold back my emotions. I didn't want to storm out like some kid, but there was no way I could stay there and hold it all in. As calmly as I could, I made it to the backdoor, closing it quietly on them, before running the rest of the way to my caravan.

The next evening, again came the roar of the car engine. And again he came strolling through the back garden as if he was lord of the manor. This time I had my wits about me and managed to get to the door.

"Teddy. What are you doing?" I hissed, glancing nervously back to the kitchen.

"Gonna take you out is what?"

"Shhh. My dad's in."

"I guess we might be able to squeeze him in the back if he wants to come too."

Then, coming from within the house, *"That's him. That's the one. The foul-mouthed rat."*

We both turned to listen but couldn't hear the reply.

"Go out there and stop 'em is what?" Then shortly after, *"Call yourself the man of the house? Pathetic is what you are."*

Teddy shrugged. "Looks like we're good to go."

I didn't reply. I grabbed his arm and started pulling him away. I felt horrid. I didn't like causing my poor father trouble and then leaving him to face the storm I stirred up. However, as we drove away, I started to realise that she didn't have so much power over me anymore—at least not the power to physically stop me doing things. She did still have somewhat of a hold over my mind and emotions, though. But with Teddy supporting me, I found I could even stand against this at times. I just had to learn how to handle all the bad feelings it caused.

Of course, it still upset me. My own mother—who for most people is the one person you should be able to trust and rely on for love no matter what—seemingly despised me. In fact, it appeared it ran deeper than that. It seemed she actually enjoyed making my life a misery, went out of her way to do it. And no matter how much I tried to dismiss it or blame her, it hurt deeply, made me feel worthless and alone. The only cure that came close to making things feel normal was being with Teddy. In the beginning, there was always the usual row whenever he came to pick me up, but because it was a fight she never got anything from, she soon started making herself scarce whenever we heard his car.

31

FAMILY WAYS

I can't pretend I didn't know about those things—how it happened and the like. But at the time, I never gave it any thought. Maybe I was too shy to bring it up. Teddy never said anything about it either, and so I followed his lead. I trusted him. He was older. He was a man. He was always in control and knew what he was doing—or at least knew what he *wanted* to do. And so, the trips to the car park soon caught up with me and I found myself in the family way just shy of my sixteenth birthday.

When I missed my first period, I told myself it might just be coming late, but I knew. Of course I was scared and worried about what my parents would say and what other people would think. Abortion wasn't legal back then, and even if it was, it wasn't something I would have ever given the time of day to think about.

Everything felt right between Teddy and me, but I was sure he'd up and leave me once I told him the news. I always seemed to have a feeling of waiting... waiting for it to all go wrong. Nothing as good as Teddy had ever happened to me before, so it made sense that I'd lose him, that my parents would never forgive me, that I'd lose my job, that everyone in town would be talking about me, that I'd go back to my old life of being the Little Mother of High Kelling. Maybe I'd have to move away, I thought. Maybe to London with Billy, but what would he think? Would he be ashamed of me too and not want anything to do with me?

The actual thought of having a baby held no fear for me since I'd already brought up two in the shape of Valerie and little Daniel. In fact, the thought of having my own child stirred up a strange feeling. Even if I was to be abandoned to bring it up myself, I would still have a family member who I knew was real, who was a part of me. And unlike myself and my mum, we'd be starting off on an even keel—mother and daughter, just as it should be.

Knowing that I had an actual human life growing inside me, made me feel like I wasn't so alone in the world anymore. And I promised myself I would do everything in my power to make sure it also grew up feeling the same. That it would be happy and healthy, no matter what life chose to throw at us.

But before all that, I needed to face my fears and find out how Teddy was going to take the news. I had no choice of course, I had to tell him even if it meant the end. I decided to tell Wendy first though, as a way of practising, I guess. I knew she'd be as surprised as anyone, but she was the one person who might not think so badly of me (plus she had a bad habit of smiling whenever she was told shocking news).

The two of us had booked a half-day and gone into town for lunch. Afterwards, we sat on a bench and I told her I hadn't had my period yet.

"Yeah, mine's all over the place too, the stress of work or something. Really annoying ent it?"

"Actually, mine's always regular."

"That's good then, right?" And then, "Oh..."

I nodded.

"Nooo," she said, the beginnings of her smile appearing in the corners of her mouth.

"Yep."

"Oh my goodness! Rosemary! So you've... you and Teddy?"

Again, I nodded.

"I knew it! I knew you was... you know. And you really are...?" she said, nodding at my belly. "So what are you gonna do, Rose? Have you told him yet? Oh my god, have you told your parents yet? What do you think they'll say? What do you think *he'll* say?"

"Calm down, you're making my head spin."

"You're right, I shouldn't be getting you excited in your state, should I?" she said as she placed her hand on my belly.

"Don't be silly, it's still very early yet," I said placing it back on her lap.

"Can you feel it?"

"What? No. Well, yes, kind of. I can't feel anything inside, but *I* feel different if that makes any kind of sense."

"Well... I guess. So what you gonna do?"

"I'm not sure."

"What's he said?"

"Nothing."

"Oh."

"I haven't told him yet."

"Oh. Oh! So... I'm the first to know?"

"Yes, you are."

She gave me a great big hug and squeezed me tight. "Oh my. Sorry... I forgot again."

"It's fine, stop being so silly." I found myself smiling and was glad I'd decided to speak to Wendy first. "Well, what do you think I should do?"

"Me? I dunno. What do you think?"

I shrugged.

"Do you love him?"

"Yeah, I think so. I'm mean, of course I do."

"And do you think he loves you?"

"Well... he says he does all the time."

"I guess maybe you tell him and see what he does. I mean... see what he says, right? That's all you can do, really."

The next time I saw Teddy, I couldn't bring myself to say it. He was so happy I didn't want to spoil it. But he was always happy, and surely telling him when he wasn't happy, would be a worse idea. I was so confused.

When he dropped me off he asked why I'd been so quiet.

"Is it that old witch of yours? Want me to go sort her out? I will you know?"

"No, it's fine, silly." I was going to tell him that something at work had upset me, *but no more lies,* I remembered. And I knew he'd pester me until I told him what it was, and then he'd want to sort it out. "I'm just tired is all."

I walked down the lane; the night was cool and fresh. I leant against the front of my caravan and found myself smiling. I couldn't imagine Teddy being angry at me, he seemed to care so much. I thought if he was okay about it, and if he would stand by me, then everything would be fine no matter what others thought and said. I promised myself I'd tell him the next time. I had to be a proper adult now, make proper decisions and face any difficulties, not pretend they weren't there and hope they'd go away.

Two nights later he picked me up and we ended up at the lake again. I wasn't sure whether to tell him before or after. In the end, I decided before was best.

32

A NEW START

He looked at me blankly for a moment, maybe only a second, but it seemed like forever. I remember folding my thumb under my fingers and gripping it tightly. I remember hearing blood pumping in my ears. Dull, soft thuds, *budum, budum, budum,* and then I remember his face relaxing, and he spoke.

"Well, it better be mine."

"Teddy! Of course it is you fool."

"Fool? How can I be a fool if the prettiest girl in England is having my baby?"

"Really? You really mean that?"

"Okay, okay. Prettiest girl in the world!"

"No, I mean you ent mad? This is okay, right?"

"Of course. In fact, I think we shouldn't waste any time and should get in the back seat to celebrate, see if we can't make another."

While driving back, Teddy went quiet and I started to worry he was thinking differently now he'd had a chance to mull it over. I daren't say anything, so I waited. Finally, he turned the radio down and said, "I guess we're gonna have to get married now then?"

The mere mention of the word quickened my breathing. Why this had more of an effect on me than finding out I was pregnant, I don't know.

"Are you... are you asking me to marry you?"

"Well... I guess we'll have to, really."

"No. Only if that's what you want. Only ask me that, if that's what you *really* want."

He'd slowed the car right down.

"Well, yeah. You've got one in the oven, so we'd better make ourselves a family, I reckon."

"What if I weren't?"

"But you're sure, right?"

"Pretty sure."

"Then there's no problem," he shrugged.

"What if it... I don't know... it doesn't happen?"

He turned to me. The car came to a stop.

"Rosemary... er, Bethany? No, Dorothy? Gertrude? Mildred? Page. Do you even have a middle name?"

I smirked as I shook my head.

"Well, just Rosemary Page then. Now, I don't have a ring to give yuh, but I do have a lot of love, a half packet of cigars, and er... this?" He passed me his favourite mottled tan comb, which had a tooth missing. "So the question is, will you accept all these things and me, and be my awfully wedded wife—or whatever it is they say."

"Oh Teddy," I said, clutching the comb.

"Yeah?"

"I don't know... I need to think about it a bit."

His brow furrowed. "What? What do you mean?" he said, his voice growing higher.

"I need to ask my parents. Let me speak to them first."

He looked away and started the car again.

I put my hand on his thigh, but his leg moved as he pushed down on the clutch.

I knew we didn't have any other choice than to get married, but I couldn't have him doing it for the wrong reason.

I knew how the charade had to play out. There was to be no mention of being in the family way 'til at least a few weeks after dropping the bombshell of the marriage proposal. No one would be fooled by it, of course, but it was the unspoken way things should be done, and also helped keep the gossiping to a minimum.

I was at the sink cutting sprouts off a long stalk, while she was sitting at the table resting her feet on a chair and complaining about her aching calves. I told myself that I had to just blurt it out by the time I got to the end of the stalk.

"What's up with you? Some of us want to eat before our next birthday, you know."

The last sprout sploshed into the pan of salted water. And so I turned and told her.

She laughed. Laughed out loud. "You? You getting married? Don't talk so daft."

I told her we loved each other.

"You're not getting married. You think Billy will ever talk to you again? And your father, well, he will go up the bloody wall."

I had to battle hard to keep it together. Don't listen to her lies, I told myself, don't give her the pleasure of seeing you cry, that's all she wants. She always used the same old tired threat of my angry father, but recently he seemed to be growing weary of her... well, everything. She kept pedalling it though, cos she knew how to affect me, how to press my buttons. But not this time, I promised myself.

"Where do you get these ideas from, huh? Don't you think you're a bit old for making up stories? Married? You? Huh."

"I'm going to say yes."

"Look at you. You can't even have a conversation without crying and you think you're cut out for marriage. I knew that boy was wrong in the head. What on earth would he want with you?" she laughed again. "Just look at yuh," she said, shaking her head.

"He loves me, and we're gonna get married," I managed to snivel.

"And never see your brother again?"

"That's not true." I concentrated on breathing regular.

"Go ask your dad then. Go on, see what he says. See if I ent telling you the truth. Go on little miss, off you go, go make a fool of yourself yet again."

I wiped my eyes and nose.

"He's in the garden digging up the spuds, see what he has to say about it, then you can come back in and peel them."

~

I stood next to Dad, my finger playing along the teeth of Freddy's comb in my apron pocket.

"Dinner ready?"

I shook my head.

He stood the garden fork into the ground, pushed down on the handle, pulled it back and turned over the soil. A great clod broke around the fork, releasing a shiny black beetle. The beetle was flipped onto its back, its tiny fragile legs running hopelessly in the air for a few frantic seconds until my father gave it a nudge with a fork prong. Righting itself, it scurried straight into the very broken clod it had escaped from. Dad pushed the fork into the soil once again.

"Dad..."

He paused and looked up. "Rose," he nodded.

"Can I talk to you?"

He dusted off his hands on the side of his thighs, reached into his pocket and took out his rolling tobacco. I waited until he'd finished and lit it up, and then I told him.

"That's right, is it?"

I nodded.

"That boy who picks you up?"

"Yeah."

He nodded.

"And what did you say?" He took a long drag on his rolly.

"I haven't yet. I didn't think you'd let me."

"Not let you?" His eyes narrowed and he cocked his head. "Why d'you think that?"

"I dunno. Just Mum..."

"Is that what your mum said?"

"Yeah."

"Not let you? You think I'd stand in your way?" He let out a great cloud of smoke that swirled around his head for a moment before getting caught by the breeze. It whooshed up into the darkening evening sky where it gradually disappeared. "If you say yes, that'll be the best day's work you ever did, my gel."

The tears came again.

He sighed. "Don't think I don't know what's been going on here all these years. Don't think I don't know what you've been through. You say yes to that young man and you get outta here. I ent gonna stand in your bloody way."

It felt like my heart was melting and a massive tangled knot inside my chest was finally loosened. He hugged me for the first time I could remember. He held me tight, his big hands gripping my shoulders. I could feel his chest judder, I heard him sniffle and then felt the wetness from his eyes on my cheek.

"Look at me," he said, "I'm getting your clothes all dirty."

"I don't care, Daddy."

"You go to the young man and you tell him yes."

"Yes," I said, wiping at my own eyes.

"Now, get yourself out of here for good. And who knows, maybe *she'll* have to keep her backside at home for a change."

I told Teddy I'd say yes, but only if he asked me properly and made sure it was more romantic than the first time—and there weren't any broken combs involved.

He took me to our bay at Blickling Lake where we'd drunk the wine before, and this time he remembered the glasses and the bottle opener. We sat on a blanket, huddled together getting tipsy from the wine, listening to the gentle rustle of the reeds, watching the reflection of the half-moon shimmering on the lake's surface, and he asked me.

I made him get down on one knee, then we kissed, then we made love—right there in the open. Afterwards, Teddy fell asleep with his head nestled into my neck. I let him slumber as I looked up at the tree above, watching the stars winking at me between the gently swaying branches. And perhaps for the first time in my life I felt complete. Felt happy. Truly happy.

33

MY MARVELLOUS HUSBAND

AGED 16 (1961)

And so we got married. It was a wedding like most others. To be honest, I can't remember the details all that clearly. The whole day seemed to whirl me up and carry me along. My memory of it no more than a blur of smiling faces, drunken laughter, toasts and speeches and all the trimmings, young'uns dressed to the nines chasing each other in and out of the marquee—can you believe, which back then was no ordinary affair. It must've cost his parents an arm and leg, but they insisted on only the best for their boy.

Back in those days, it was rare to have a movie of it made or hundreds of photographs taken. We did hire a photographer, but of the ten or so photos he took, most were given away to close relatives. We kept one of Teddy and me outside the church door and then another of both families.

Teddy looked ever so handsome and smart in his suit, my dad too. It was lovely to have the whole family together again—all my brothers and their girlfriends, even my aunts and their American husbands, who timed their annual "vacation" as they'd say, so they could come all the way from California just to be there. The only noticeable absence was Aunt Sylvie, she'd just got a new job, so she wasn't able to get the time off, unfortunately.

Considering my mother was usually the loudest person at an event, she was surprisingly quiet. I don't know whether she felt outshone by Teddy and his mum's efforts. Teddy's mum did make moves to speak with my parents, but getting more than two sentences out of my dad was like getting change out of a penny. And it was clear from the very start that my mum was going to be barely polite at best. Afterwards, I remember her muttering and complaining about how it was all a bit much, all a bit over the top and they were just wanting to show off their money. Then she complained how loud his mum was, and how she was always trying to make a fuss just so everyone noticed her.

After we were married and just as I was beginning to show, we moved into Teddy's grandfather's old bungalow. Although it was already set up to live in, we decided to redecorate it and make it our own. What with the decorating and my ever-growing belly, I had to finish my training at the hospital.

On my final day, Matron said to me one of the nicest things I'd ever heard. She said she was very sad I was leaving, and it was an even sadder day for the nursing world to lose me, but she also said she was sure I would make a fine mother. Wendy, of course, was upset too, but at least she still had the Lynn Girls. Amongst the tears, they made a promise of arranging a girls' night out to properly send me on my way into married life.

I spent the next two weeks decorating the bungalow and doing the housekeeping in my breaks, while Teddy was busy at work. The housekeeping wasn't much bother for me, and you may think I'm a rum'un, but at times I'd be finished by lunch and prowling around trying to find something else that needed sweeping, dusting or folding. My whole life I'd been used to looking after an entire family and household, only to find myself in a tiny bungalow with only two people to cater for. I couldn't help feeling a bit incomplete at times. Most days I was topping up the laundry pile with already clean clothes, and some days I'd end up washing the kitchen floor three times—once after every meal. Teddy certainly thought I was a rum'un and said I'd soon wear the floor down so much that we'd end up eating our supper in China.

Having our own place meant we no longer needed to go to the lake for privacy, so going down The Compass, our local pub, took up most of our evenings. Usually, I'd only go two or three nights a week—Teddy four or five.

I remember the first time he took me, just after we'd announced our engagement. I tell you, it was like we were a celebrity couple or something. Everyone seemed to be best friends with Teddy, slapping him on the back, each seeming to have their own particular joke they shared with him and everyone offering us drinks. He refused all offers and it was him who ended up buying a round for the whole pub.

What with being introduced to so many people, all the noise, the rosy cheeks of all those laughing, happy faces, glasses clinking and clunking, swirling smoke and even the odd dog swimming in and out of the forest of legs, it made me feel quite dizzy, like I was caught up in some kind of dream. I could hardly hear what anyone was saying and had no clue who they were. Only being a slight girl, I was getting knocked to and fro. At times, I had to grip onto Teddy's sleeve just to keep myself from being lost in the jostling sea of people. I didn't mind one bit though, to be honest. I was glad to be a part of the joyful goings-on and all that happiness in one small place.

It seemed everyone had kind words for Teddy.

"Yuh done well for yourself there, Teddy m'lad," one said.

"You weren't a-lying. She is a looker too," said another.

"Keep an eye on her or I'll be arter her before y'know it," laughed another old-boy.

The other times that we went down the pub weren't quite as crazy as that first, but what never changed was the greeting Teddy got. And it wasn't just from the younger crowd either, it was even the old-boys. Cos he was so full of life and always making people laugh with his cheeky humour, he was everybody's favourite and no mistake. There was also no denying he liked to have himself a drink or three. And of course, with that came all sorts of mischief.

One night, I was waiting up for him when a strange car came roaring into the driveway, nearly taking out the flower tubs. I went to the window, thinking something might have happened, that it was someone coming to tell me some terrible news. Nervously peeking out through the net curtain, I could see a person fumbling about inside the car. As I made up my mind to go see what was going on, the door finally opened and a more than squiffy Teddy come falling out.

"Teddy?" I called to him from the window. "You all right there?"

"What? What's that? I'm fine, couldn't find the door handle was all," he said as he picked himself up off the drive and squinted at the house, trying to work out which of the windows was talking to him.

"Teddy? Whose car is that? You ent crashed the Datsun have yuh?"

"What? Nah, nah, nah."

"Whose car is it then?"

"That's mine, you silly bugger."

"Teddy, I don't know what car that is, but I do know that it's not our Datsun."

He turned and squinted at it. "That's definitely my car all right."

"Well... it's not though, is it? It's not even the same colour."

"That's cos it's my new'un."

"What d'you mean, your new'un?"

"Well, I got us a new car, dint I."

"What? How? Why?"

"I swapped it with Albert for the Datsun. Or maybe it was Peter? Well... I must've swapped it with someone."

"Oh. Okay. What is it?"

"A caaar," he shouted as if I was stupid.

"I meant—what type?"

He paused and turned back to it. "Dunno, it's too dark." Stooping forward, he propped himself up with one hand on the bonnet and studied the car closely. "I think it's a blue one."

And that was Teddy, swapping his car on a whim.

I soon got used to it though, as it seemed we had a different car every six months or so. There never seemed no rhyme or reason for the swap each time, other than too many drinks. Sometimes it would be newer than last and sometimes older and more dented. Teddy never was too sharp with money. The way he saw it was, if the new car had more petrol in it than the old one, he'd got himself a bargain.

Even though I was still only 16 years old and five months pregnant, I sorted out all our finances and the running of the house. I didn't mind having to do this and it seemed Teddy didn't mind me taking this role on either, mainly cos I really don't think he'd have managed it himself. In a way, I think the car swapping was important to him; it gave him some responsibility—even though it was usually done when he was two-sheets to the wind in a dark pub car park. Sometimes he got so drunk he clean forgot, as one morning he came into the kitchen all suspicious, wanting to know why there was a strange car in our drive. The bloomin pillock.

Every week Teddy would give me five pounds to do the housekeeping on. With that amount, I not only had to buy all the household goods but also all of his clothes and shaving things and the like. The only thing he spent his money on was petrol, the twenty mini cigars he smoked a day, and of course his drinking (and most likely other people's too).

I often picked up household stuff from his parent's shop-come-post office. It wasn't the closest shop and didn't have all the stuff we needed, but I felt it was important to support their business now I was part of their family. It was also nice to be greeted with such warmth each time, and not to mention useful for them if they needed to pass a message on to Teddy.

Usually, it was his father manning the till during the afternoons. He was ever such a calm and well-mannered fella. He was quiet, but not like my father. He was quiet in the way he spoke—and did at least speak more than a few words each time.

I was chatting to him one afternoon as he packed my bag. After I'd paid, I noticed him fiddling awkwardly with the money, not putting it in the till. He was looking at me as if he had something else to say. At first, I thought he wanted to apologise for taking my money, but heavens, I never expected anything in life for free.

"Urm, Rosemary..." he said, concentrating on the coins he was pushing around the palm of his hand.

My next thought was had I not given him the right amount.

"Urm... Muriel's been saying recently, well... that maybe it's time... you know... you pay the rest of what you owe..."

"What I owe? I don't owe nobody nothing," I told him. I was ever so careful with the money. While maths wasn't my strongest point, I kept strict tabs on what I spent and always made sure we were never in debt.

"I know that you're family now and that, but you know..."

"No, I'm afraid I don't. Honestly, I don't owe nothing, I'm more than sure of that."

"You won't be able to say that to Muriel, you know." He looked up from his hand. "She says you owe on your bill and she knows exactly how much too."

"But... I don't even have a bill. I'll tell you what, I'll pop over and speak to her later, sort this out, cos there ent nothing I haven't paid for." I was trying to keep control of my voice. I was getting quite upset, even though I was sure it was just some silly misunderstanding. I hated the thought they'd been going around thinking I was taking advantage or something.

He smiled at me uncertainly. "It'd be easier to settle your account with me, I'd say." Again with a look that suggested there was more to his words than what I was hearing.

"But I don't even—" I stopped myself and took a breath.

"Look, Muriel thinks the world of you, you know that."

I nodded slowly.

"If she likes you," he continued, in a more measured way, "you'll be hard pushed to find a better ally. But..." he let it hang for a moment, "she ent the kinda person you want to get on the wrong side of."

I couldn't make head nor tail of it. I even wondered for a moment if he had a bit of the old dementia that I'd just never noticed before. Or maybe he'd mistaken me for someone else? Or was this some silly joke Teddy had put him up to? This last one being the only thing that made any kind of sense.

He continued looking at me, his eyes gentle and kind but as if he was waiting for a confession, as if he was trying to ease it out of me before he had to set the attack dog on me.

"Well... I still have no idea what this is about, so could you please tell me exactly what it is I am supposed to have not paid for? Is that possible?"

"Okay then." He tucked the pencil behind his ear, his movements quick and businesslike as he walked over to the back shelves. He pulled out a weary-looking book, brought it over and dropped it on the counter.

"The tab book," he announced.

"Urm... like I said, I don't even have a tab."

"Well, let's find out shall we..." he looked at me, waiting until I gave him a nod to go ahead. He opened the book. "Let's see..."

Even though I knew he wasn't gonna find anything, I'd never felt so nervous in all my life. I couldn't help but to peer forward as he fumbled through the pages and loose papers full of scrawl.

"Grimstead... Woodthorpe... Joseph H... yours is under your first name, I do know that. Seen it myself."

I found myself biting at my lip as I looked on.

"And... yep... here it is," he said, tapping the page firmly with his finger.

I was flabbergasted. It had to be another Rosemary.

"Rosemary. Your address too. So, your tab." He gave me a sympathetic smile as if I was some doddering old granny. "Just over... twelve pounds you owe."

"Twelve pounds! But I don't even have that much..." I started to worry whether it was actually me who had the dementia.

"Well, we don't expect you to pay it off all at once. Maybe you could—"

"No. I mean, it can't be mine because I would never spend money I didn't have."

"It's written right here," he said, tapping at it again. "I'm afraid in this day and age, you can't deny the truth of pencil and paper, my love. Look..."

I squinted at the book as he turned it around for me.

And sure enough, there it was at the top of the ledger. My name and address, followed by a long list of prices and dates. I read down the page. Boxes of matches, packets of biscuits, the odd hair comb, and many, many packets of cigars in a very familiar, almost childlike scrawl.

I looked up and smiled, "Well, yes that's under my name, but this certainly ent *my* shopping."

"Now look, Rosemary—"

"No, no, please look at the things..." I said, quickly running my finger down the list. "I don't even smoke. Look, it's nearly all cigars."

He turned it back and brought his head down closer to read the hand-scrawlings.

"Oh... right, I see. Yes, you don't smoke cigars, do you?"

"No, but I think we both know somebody who does, and I certainly recognise this handwriting. I think somebody has been a bit of a cheeky boy, don't you."

"Ah. I see. Oh my. I'm terribly sorry. He must've been coming in and helping himself I guess."

I told him it was fine; I was just glad we'd got to the bottom of it. I told him, since I only had five pounds a week, that I'd have to start paying off a little bit each time I came in until we cleared it all.

"No, no, don't you worry about it. I'm so sorry. You just forget about it. I'll sort this out. It won't happen again, hand over heart, I promise you that."

He couldn't apologise enough. In fact, he was still saying sorry as I walked out the door. What happened after that, I'm not sure. I have a feeling he paid it himself as neither Teddy nor Muriel ever mentioned a word about it.

I think this was one of the first times I realised there was so much more to my duties as Teddy's wife than I'd bargained for. Even though I was seven years his junior, I was the one who was going to have to keep an eye on everything and keep it all together.

I hadn't minded doing all the decorating and home repair, but I realised the main reason Teddy never offered was because he wouldn't have known where to start.

When we first moved in, the sink had been blocked and Teddy's answer to this was to ram a straightened coat hanger down the plughole, and when that didn't work he started kicking and swearing at it, which unsurprisingly didn't work either. Luckily, I heard the racket and stopped him before he kicked it right off the wall. I then opened up the cupboards beneath and unscrewed the cap at the bottom of the u-bend with a bucket ready underneath and fished out the blockage. I didn't feel embarrassed that my husband had been clueless. In fact, it made me feel good, feel useful. And Teddy had no ill feelings about it neither; he was ever so proud of me.

"Well, look at that! Bloody marvellous, you are," he said, after a big lump of grey gunk came out and the sink gave a burp. "I knew I married yuh for a good reason," he finished, as we watched the built up water drain away freely once more.

34

MY MARRIED LIFE

It marked a huge change in my life once we were married and living together. I finally felt I had some control, that I was my own person. I could choose what I did and when I did it—which, admittedly, mostly came down to choosing what order I did the housework in. I did also have time for myself every now and then, but soon found this was a bit overrated. There were occasions when I actually felt a bit lost and lonely when I had nothing to do.

I tried to keep in touch with Wendy and the Lynn Girls. But because I no longer worked at the hospital, I no longer belonged to their daily world, and once again I found myself on the outside of a gang that had once been such a big part of me. Anyway, with the baby on the way, I'd started to make my very own gang, one that I would always be a part of.

The girls did come good on their promise to give me a proper send-off, though. Just like old times, we were going to get dolled-up in the Lynn Girls' room, then go to the army camp dance. The thought of going to the dance didn't excite me, but I knew it would be nice to be together again, and I also felt like I owed them after the debacle of the last time.

I wasn't really sure what Teddy would say and thought maybe he'd even give me a good excuse not to go.

"Yeah, if that's what you wanna do," he shrugged.

"I don't really mind... it'll just be nice, they've been so good to me."

"Am I not good to yuh?"

"Of course. I just mean... before."

"Well, make sure they look after you is all," he said, nodding at my belly.

In an odd way, it wasn't what I'd expected... or... even wanted? Sometimes a bit of jealously is a good thing, makes you feel valued. Makes you believe it when people say things like, "You're the prettiest girl in all of Norfolk." Makes you think they aren't just saying it to be nice, or saying it to just get what they want.

I took the bus to the hospital, and then we got ready in the Lynn Girls' room. I'm not sure whose idea it had been to include a fifth member to our gang. To be honest, it started off as no more than a joke. But once we'd got her dressed up and plastered in make-up, we found it so funny, there was no way we were gonna leave the old practice doll, Bessie, behind. A couple of weeks before, Wendy had been told to take her down to the basement as she'd been replaced by a newer model, so it was also a farewell night for Bessie too. I think in the end we spent more time getting her ready than we did ourselves. Jenny was convinced that someone at the dance would see us with her and tell Matron and they'd all get the sack.

"Oh don't worry about it, just blame it all on me if she does," I said, but secretly prayed that wouldn't happen. I would've been mortified too if Matron got wind of it.

I felt a bit funny all made-up and in my nice dress with my little pregnant belly beginning to show. I couldn't help but to keep stroking it, as if I might flatten it a bit.

"Don't worry, Rosie," Wendy said with that mischievous glint in her eye, "we'll just tell everyone it's cos you've been eating lots of cakes recently."

In the end, Tracey lent me a fur collar that reached down my front and covered it.

The hall was a throng of happy faces, and all the soldiers looked dapper in their uniforms. However, I didn't really feel much like dancing, so I kindly said no to all the young servicemen who asked. After declining one particular nice soldier, he asked if he could dance with my friend instead. I looked about, but the others were already busy on the floor. Following his eyes, I realised he was talking about Bessie who was propped up in a chair keeping me company. I laughed, but he was deadly serious and so off he went with her. They danced together for two entire songs and soon pretty much the whole hall was clapping them on and laughing as he whirled her about.

The other girls were also having a great time, up and down like yo-yos they were. Though, they kept coming back to take turns sitting with me for a bit until the next fella come and whisked them away.

At the end of the night, the girls joked they weren't sure who got more attention—me or Bessie, but it was definitely Bessie who was the belle of the ball.

Even though I didn't dance, it was so much fun that I regretted not ever going before. We giggled all the way home, retelling stories of Bessie's antics, of poor Wendy slipping over in front of a jeering table of fellas, of Tracey letting a soldier kiss her on the lips!

I'd only had one gin, but being not much used to it I was smiling all the way home on the bus. I walked the last stretch and as I did I got thinking about how it was a shame I had to leave the hospital. I was damn good at my job, and would never know where that path could've taken me, what kind of career I might've had. But anyway, it'd still been an important step in my life, given me many things, and of course, it was where I met Teddy. Maybe life had taken me in a different direction to what I first imagined when I took the job, but it'd led to better things and that was what I had to remember.

There were no lights on when I got in, but Teddy's car was in the drive. The house was so quiet it was a welcome relief after the raucous hubbub of the dance.

Teddy was sat in the lounge with only a small lamp barely lighting his lap, leaving his face in darkness.

"I'm home," I said, taking off my coat. "Oh it was so much fun, I haven't laughed that much in ages." I waited for a reply, but he didn't even look up. I guessed he'd fallen asleep. I crept over to him and placed my hand softly on his shoulder. As soon as I touched him, he flinched, as if waking with a start.

"Sorry, didn't mean to wake you."

"I wasn't asleep." His voice flat and measured. "Where you been?"

"Sorry?"

"You heard."

"Well, the dance of course."

"And...?"

He still wouldn't look at me.

"And what?" I tried to peer towards him to get a clearer look at his face.

"Don't avoid the question. What happened?"

"Nothing..." I walked around into his line of sight only for him to turn away. "Teddy?"

"Nothing, you say?"

"Nothing much. I didn't even really dance. All the fellas—"

"Liar."

"I'm... not, I promise. I didn't dance with no one."

"So no one asked you? You're say'n, that in a dance hall full of men not one of 'em asked yuh?"

"Well, yeah people asked me but I just said no. I didn't really want to, was all."

He looked up slowly. His eyes hard and fierce.

"Oh Teddy, are you sure you okay," I said, again reaching a hand toward his shoulder.

"No. I'm not." He stood up, forcing me to take a step backwards. "I never said I was okay. Should I be okay while *my* wife goes out flaunting herself at the dance?"

"But I wasn't."

He took a step forward. "Stop lying." I felt tiny bits of spit flick on my face as he spoke and could smell whisky and cigar smoke on his breath. "Look at you, all done up. You weren't looking like that when you left."

"I... I got ready at the hospital, was all."

"Why? Why d'you need to do that?"

"It's nice... getting ready together. That's just what we usually do," I heard the tremble in my own voice.

"So you do it all the time then?"

"No. Teddy, I'm here with you all the time. Why are you being so silly?"

He stepped forward again and gripped my arm, pulling me so our faces were all but touching.

"Silly? Is that what you think of me?"

"No, of course not."

"Think you can lie to me, do yuh?"

"No."

"Think I'm too stupid to realise?"

All I could do is whimper as his thumb dug deeper into the soft flesh of my arm.

"Well, I bloody ent." He spun us around and pushed me into his chair. He gripped my neck just under my chin and pushed my head back.

"Teddy..." I managed to gasp...

"Shut up. Just shut up with your lies."

"I'm not," I struggled to say. "I'm not."

And then he hit me.

35

~

He struck a hammer blow to my upper arm with the base of his fist. It shocked me so much I didn't feel the pain at first, even though it was hard enough to bruise.

Then there was a brief moment... a pause, a momentary softening of his furrowed brow. I thought he'd realised what he'd done. I thought he was going to repent. Or maybe I had just imagined it—hoped for it. Instead, he struck the same blow, but this time on my thigh, and this time I did scream. The scream was still more from shock and fear than pain. He did it again, and then again, maybe three or four times. I crossed my arms protectively over my belly. I screamed with every blow. Every blow a powerful, jarring thud meant to cause me pain. He shouted at me above my own screams. His whole frame trembling. His face grimacing with rage. His forehead sweating.

After the last blow, he shoved my head back against the chair, turned and kicked out at the little table. The lamp fell on its side. He pounced on it, flinging it against the wall and smashing us into darkness.

I pulled my knees up and hugged them to my chest, and only then did I realise I had wet myself. I tried to stay quiet and still as the pain pulsed through my thigh. In between my sobs, I could hear his breathing—deep and slow. Then I heard him shuffling. Looking up, I saw his dark shapeless form coming towards me. I turned my face away and shut him out with my eyes.

"Rose?" came his broken voice. "Rosie... I'm sorry. I didn't mean you no harm. You know that."

I drew my legs up further as I felt his touch on my ankle.

"I'm sorry... I didn't mean it." Again his hand touched gently at my leg. "Please...?"

His other hand reached out for my shoulder. He pressed himself against me. I could feel the wetness of his cheek on mine. We huddle together on the chair, crying. I didn't move. I didn't say anything. He told me it wouldn't happen again, that he didn't know what had come over him. He told me that he loved me.

Come the morning, he cradled my head and kissed it, promising he'd look after me, telling me how much he loved me, and it only happened *because* he loved me so much.

I told him it was okay and that he should've just said something because I hadn't wanted to go to that dance, anyway.

Then he went to work, and I washed my clothes and the chair cushions.

36

~

I'd never known a person to wear their heart on their sleeve as much as him. I'd never known a person so unable to hide from their emotions as him. I'd never met anyone whose feelings were as intense and as raw as his. And I had never met anyone who could show me as much love as what Teddy could.

I didn't need telling that what he'd done was wrong, but I knew it had to be a mistake, that something... somehow... had made him do what he did. And I also saw where I was to blame in it too.

As soon as the girls had invited me, I'd felt it, felt it was wrong for me—a married and pregnant girl—to be going to a dance like that. And so we forgave each other for what happened that night.

We talked about it. I told him again—if only he'd said from the start he didn't want me to go, I wouldn't have, and that would've been fine. He said he didn't realise how he felt until after I left, and then it was too late, and all he could do was keep stewing on it while he waited for me to come back to him.

Maybe you're now thinking I'm daft or soft, but it melted my heart hearing him say that, knowing that he cared so much about me, and knowing that was the only reason why he did what he did. So please forgive me for what I'm about to say next—but at that time I remember thinking, it was almost worth being hit just to hear him say those words like that, so honestly and purely felt—not just saying them as part of a joke or a tease or anything else.

I also thought it wouldn't be a problem, as it was something I could control. It wouldn't have happened if I'd done the right things. If I'd told him I was going to get ready with the girls. Or if I'd just listened to my heart and not gone to the dance in the first place. Or if I'd been more sensitive when I came home instead of blabbing away about what a good time I'd had while he'd been at home alone worrying. I thought of my father, how I'd seen him and his anger when he'd gone through the same situation with my mother. And I was determined that I was not going to be my mother.

Before we were wed, people were always telling me how living together can be a challenge at first.

"You have to learn each other's ways, good habits and bad," they'd say. Well, we'd certainly learnt a hard lesson early on, but we had learnt it and survived. And so it was something that we could make sure never happened again.

37

A NEW MOTHER

Hazel was born on Wednesday the 16th of November 1961, and I'd never been happier or loved someone so much in all my life. I could just stare at her for hours on end. It may sound strange, but even at a few months old she was my best friend. There was nothing greater than when she'd reach out for me as I went to pick her up after a nap, or the warmth spreading through my chest when I felt the light grip of her tiny hands on my blouse as I fed her.

People often asked how I was managing, if it was difficult being such a young mother. I guess they didn't know that I was already an old hand at it.

I remembered the promise I made when I'd first found out I was in the family way, and I repeated it to myself on a regular basis. I would do everything I could to make sure Hazel had a happy childhood and that she would always be loved—no matter what. Of course, I knew I mustn't overdo it either, that there's a danger of spoiling a child too.

Teddy was good with her, except when she cried. She was no more of a crier than any other baby, but when she did, it seemed to flick the switch in him. Whether he'd been drinking or not, the mysterious anger would well up. He'd tell me to make her stop; he couldn't understand why she wouldn't, why I couldn't make her stop. He couldn't accept that at times a baby will cry for seemingly no reason, or that he may as well have been asking me to make the rain stop or the tide not to come in. In his mind, there always had to be a reason, and if there was a reason, there was a fix. If he wanted something, or something to happen, then he got it or it happened. The best I could do was get her clear of the storm, which wasn't always easy in a small bungalow.

It often whipped up so suddenly that I barely had enough time to drop whatever it was I was doing and get Hazel out of the way and myself in the way. And as usual, after the fury of the fists came the kindness of the kisses.

When it happened, it didn't seem like he was him no more. It was like someone or something else took control, that he didn't know what he was doing, that he wasn't of right mind at that time. However, he always struck me on the body. Never the face.

I didn't tell anyone. I didn't even think about telling. After all, it wasn't anyone else's business; it was between husband and wife. I guess it was also because I was embarrassed and ashamed. On the face of it, we were this happy couple that everyone liked and even envied in a well-meaning way, and I wanted that, I wanted to keep it.

As I've said before, it was like everything had a price or had to be balanced out. Good things didn't just happen for no reason, you always had to pay it off somehow.

Other times I thought it was something about me—that I was the problem. School, my brother, my mother and now my husband. It came from different places, but the only common thing amongst it all? Me.

38

TRIPS TO THE LAKE

AGED 18 (1963)

Hazel was 18 months and had just recently started walking when Teddy came home late from work one day and told us we were moving house. He was in a grump, so I didn't ask much about it; I just assumed his family were finally getting around to selling the place at last.

A week later, we'd packed up our stuff and were moving to a farm cottage almost twenty miles away. It may not sound that much nowadays, but to me back then it suddenly seemed like I was moving countries, far away from everyone and everything I ever knew.

Teddy started his new job on a farm and as part of the package, we got to live in one of the old cobblestone cottages there. The cottage was at the very end of a lonely, winding lane that had grass growing all the way along the centre of it—so seldom was it used. The farm itself was big and sprawling, spread across several fields, two roads and a little beck. The older couple who ran the place, John and Josephine, were the only company me and Hazel had for the first few months.

Teddy would go to the pub most nights while we stayed at home. With me hardly leaving the house, I'd say most folks in the area probably thought I was a bit of a cold fish. But it couldn't be helped, what with me being so busy. And also having to be mindful of what Teddy might think. Sometimes, he'd come back for lunch, but it was a rare event at best. Most times we wouldn't see him all day. Old John was our only visitor during the week; he would come by and sheepishly ask if Teddy was about, saying he hadn't got around to fencing off the cattle field or pulling up the seedy beet. Of course, I'd offer to do it and he'd say there was no need. But he always popped back at the end of the day to thank me for a job well done.

The weekends were generally our family days, so we'd either drive out to his parent's house or into town, but that wasn't always the way. Such as the Saturday afternoon Teddy had gone off to the pub. While he was out, one of his friends popped by to deliver a newspaper. He was ever such a pleasant chap, but from the off, I realised there was something a bit skew-whiff. It was in the way he spoke to me. Asking about my housework all the time. Though, it wasn't until he asked me whereabouts I lived that it finally came out.

"Well, here, of course."

He looked at me with a funny smile. "Oo err, what's he take it out of your wages then, eh?"

"What? My wages?" Hazel came to the door and wrapped her arms around my leg.

He looked down at Hazel and then back at me, clearly puzzled. "He said you were a good'un, but surely you don't work for free, does yuh?"

"Sorry? Who... who is it you think I am?"

"Ent you the housekeeper he's been tell'n us all about?"

"Housekeeper? Me?"

"That's what he..."

"That's what he said, is it?"

"Well... I urm..."

"This," I said, stroking Hazel's curly black hair, "is *our* daughter. And *I* am Teddy's *wife*."

"Oh..." His mouth hung slack like a pollock on the fishmonger's slab.

"He's married then?"

"Yes. To me."

"Oh my. I'm so sorry, I dint know... he said that... well, never mind. Cor, just you wait 'til I get hold of him," he said with a half-hearted laugh. “I dint mean no offence and that. He's a card all right, that Teddy, ent he,” he said shaking his head.

I was so angry I decided I was gonna have it out with him this time, regardless. Fancy going around telling people I was his housekeeper.

By the time he came home from the pub I'd worked myself right up, so much so I couldn't sit still. I was determined to say something, no matter what sort of mood he came through the door with.

“I'm late, I know,” he said, coming into the kitchen and giving me an excuse I didn't ask for. “I saw the bloody hay bales had come uncovered on my way past, had to get it done case it rains later.”

He didn’t seem in a terrible mood, so I thought it would be all right. I stood in the middle of the kitchen waiting for my practised words to come. He put his arms around me and grabbed my behind, lifting me clear off the ground. He gave me a big long kiss before putting me down again and going straight over to the table.

“Good to be home. So, what we got for dinner then? I'm bloody starving. I could eat a dead horse and the ground it was lying on.”

I just had to say it normally, not in an angry way, just ask him nice and calmly, I was thinking.

“What's up with you? You forget how to speak all of a sudden?”

“What...? No.”

“Well? What we got for dinner then?” he said with an edge creeping into his voice.

I knew the chance had been lost, the moment gone. I forgot about it and we enjoyed our dinner. He was happy rabbiting away, but then by pure coincidence another chance came my way. He'd been talking about how he'd stuffed a potato up his friend's motorbike exhaust the other day and mentioned his name—Jimmy. I weren't sure, but I thought I’d drop a hook and line down into the ice hole anyway...

“Jimmy? Is he the nice chap who dropped the paper off today?” I watched his eyes closely.

I saw him look over to it sitting on the table. “Yeah. That's him.”

“He’s a very jolly chap, ent he?”

“Yeah, that’s Jimmy all right.”

“But... a strange thing though...”

"What's that?"

I looked down at the frozen lake with no idea how thin the ice was today. "Well, he thought you said that I was... urm. That I was just the housekeeper here."

"He did? Jimmy said that?" He put a forkful of potato in his mouth.

"That's what he said," I waited for him to finish his mouthful. "I mean, where d'you suppose he got that idea from?" I finished, remembering to breathe again.

"Maybe he just guessed it and guessed wrong. Were you wearing your apron?"

"Actually... he said you said it to him."

"I did?" He pointed to his chest with the fork.

"Well, I'm pretty sure."

"Pretty sure?"

"Well... No. Maybe... definitely sure."

"That's what Jimmy said?" His eyebrows furrowed as he gave it thought. He then broke into a smile and begun nodding. "Yeah, you're right, I did say that."

"You did?"

"Yep."

"Well... why?" I said, testing the ice with just a toe.

"Let me finish and you just might find out," He said, his smile beginning to melt.

"I was only asking."

"And I was only *trying* to tell yuh."

"Okay... well?" One foot fully on the ice, now.

Creeeeak.

"It's cos I was pulling his plank, weren't I."

"You were?"

"Yeah, just joking about. You know what I'm like," he said with that big smile of his coming back with force.

"Ohhh. I see." A rush of relief flowed through me. The tension in my neck and shoulders crumbled away. I was so hoping there was an easy explanation, it was what I desperately wanted and so of course, I accepted it gratefully.

"Yeah, we're always doing that to each other. Seeing who can do it best."

"Right. But..." I couldn't help it, I had to check it would take my full weight, so I placed my other foot onto the lake's pale flat surface.

He looked at me. Go on, I dare you, the look said. You feeling brave enough to walk on it, are yuh?

"It was... Well..." I sighed. "It just didn't feel too good, hearing him say it like that. It was embarrassing, in fact."

He put down his fork.

Crck, crck, crck. Tiny cracks spread out from my heels.

"It weren't nothing against you." He pushed back his chair, causing me to flinch. He stood up and paused, just for a second. "I didn't mean it to embarrass you in any way, did I." He came over, bent down and cradled my face with his broad hand. He lifted my chin up and gave me a long kiss on my forehead. "I was just teasing him, making out I had more money than him, saying I had a housekeeper and all, you see? I even told him I had a butler too. Maybe that's who he thought Hazel was, huh?"

I felt horrid for thinking bad things about him, making him out to be worse than he was. There was no doubting how much he loved me, and if I went around making things up in my head, I knew it'd only cause more problems. I realised, in the future, it was probably best for me to stay away from the lake altogether. I felt better after our talk. Felt like I had some control over matters, over my own mind. All I had to do was keep my way of thinking in check, not be getting all paranoid and suspicious the whole time. But it was difficult not to get entangled in my own thoughts, seeing as I spent most of my time with only one other person who couldn't yet talk.

It certainly was a lonely existence at times, living in that cottage. But it did get better with the more I got to know John and Josephine. Between the four of us, we were always kept busy and worked hard for each other to keep that farm ticking along nicely.

A couple of months after we'd moved, John and Josephine bought a boarding house in Cromer. Seeing as I had a bit of experience working at the one before with my mum, I offered to help out. The place was in a bit of a state, so mostly it was cleaning and renovating. Me and Hazel would take the bus up there and I'd spend the day ripping out fireplaces, wallpapering, and unblocking sinks. Once it was ready, me and Hazel stayed on to run it for a bit. I made sure John knew it was only temporary until he found someone full-time. I thought it would be good giving Teddy a bit of space, make him realise how much he needed us, how much we meant to him.

I didn't ever doubt his love. Most days, he was eager to see us when he came back from work or the pub. It seemed it was only after being cooped up at home too long that the anger would come on. He was too used to his freedom to be kept in captivity, it seemed.

Hazel was growing fast and talking more than she was crying, which meant she was less likely to get his back up. The more she learnt to speak, the more time Teddy had for her. I'd hide around the corner listening to the pair of them babbling away sometimes, neither of them making all that much sense, but it was lovely to hear.

As promised, John found a local couple from Cromer to run the boarding house, and so we were able to return to the farm. With Hazel being able to toddle, it was a lot easier for me to help out John and Josephine and I was soon busy laying a new cow-yard with them.

Nearly a week had gone by before things calmed down enough for me to catch up on all the cleaning—which was quite something considering there'd only been one person living in the house while we were away. I believe it was a Friday, and come lunchtime, I'd done three baskets of washing, swept and dusted and was about to start the lunch before I mopped the floors when I heard a gentle knock on the door. I checked Hazel wasn't up to any mischief and went to answer it.

I opened it to a young girl I'd never seen before, maybe my age or a bit older. She'd been wearing a sweet smile and patting down her long, smooth brown hair as I opened it.

"Hello," I smiled back at her.

Her's faded slightly as she took me in.

"Urm..." She took a step back and looked the cottage up and down.

"Can I help you?" I asked, thinking she was lost or in need of directions.

"I thought this was Teddy's house?"

"...It is. Can I help you?"

"I come to see him," she peered past me into the entranceway. "Is he in?"

"Sorry... who are you?" I said as I moved to block her prying eyes.

"Is he not in then?"

"Urm... I asked who you are?"

"So he's not then?"

"I ent answering your questions until you answer mine."

"I didn't come to see you, I come to see Teddy. Well, if he ent in, I'll just come back after work then." She turned away, but not in time for me to catch her rolling her eyes as if I'd been the rude one. I watched as she made her way to the bike leaning against the fence. She picked it up and checked the house once more before riding off.

After shutting the door, I closed my eyes and took some deep breaths to calm my nerves.

Stay - away - from the lake - Rosemary.

Less than a week later, around lunchtime, two more girls come to the door asking for him. This time I was all polite and played the part of housekeeper, asking them where they'd come from. They said they were trainees at the hospital, which was just behind the east wing of the farm where Teddy worked most of the day.

"Well, I'm afraid Edward is out at the moment, but his wife is in if you wanna speak to her?"

"...His wife?"

"Yes, I can just go get her for you if you want?"

"Oh. Right. We probably need to get back. We're just on lunch break," said one of them.

"That's right," said the other, already turning away, "we shouldn't be late."

I stood smiling, watching them scuttle away, arms linked.

After shutting the door I let the tears roll free.

It wasn't even six months later when Teddy told me we moving again. Again, no reason given, and no reason asked for. However, this time I was more than glad for the chance of a new start. And so I swept everything under the carpet and left it in that little cobblestone farm cottage.

We started afresh, moving even further afield to the little village of

Burgate. But this only lasted four months, as Teddy was given the sack from the farm there. Again—none given, none asked.

So after that, it was full circle back to my parent's old house, would you believe. They'd got themselves a smaller place, what with the family shrinking. However, because they were selling the old place, we could only live in two rooms—the rest of it being left cleaned and emptied.

Moving house as regularly as we swapped cars had started to get to me, but living back in High Kelling was certainly a welcome move. I had my friends and family close by and I knew most of the people, and most of the people knew Teddy and me. And more importantly, knew I was his wife and not his bloomin housekeeper. Actually, with only having the two rooms, there wasn't all that much housekeeping that needed to be done anyway, so I got myself a job back at the hospital again. Keith and Elaine were only too happy to look after little Hazel, and refused to take any money for it.

39

FRESH MEAT

AGED 19 (1964)

Matron was delighted to have me back and made me feel ever so special. I felt almost like a celebrity when she introduced me to the new trainees.

"This here is Rosemary. She was one of the finest, hardworking, diligent trainees these four walls ever had the fortune to contain," she said to a group of new'uns. "And you'll do well to listen to anything she has to say to you. If you can measure up half as good as her, you will be on the right track to a long and successful career." This was met by a sea of wide-eyed stares. "All right, now stop gawking and back to work."

I wasn't that fussed whether the new'uns bought into her speech or not, but it sure as heck stirred up that wild tingling wave I got at times—all through my chest, spreading down into my arms and up into my cheeks. I felt like I was walking on clouds as we went down the ward together. However, as all the memories of how I'd started to grow into a confident young lady came flooding back to me, I couldn't help but to feel mournful for that young girl I once knew and had left behind.

After speaking with Matron, we decided there wasn't no point in me resuming my training, what with having Hazel and the possibility of more to come. Starting a family often meant the end of a nurse's career—thanks to the shift patterns and what have you. Instead, my official job was as the housemaid to the onsite nursing accommodation, but unofficially, it was looking after the pre-trainees who'd come and stay to get a feel for the place before committing. I'd help them settle in and teach them a few bits and bobs—though for the most part they were used as cleaners and porters.

I'd usually work three or four days a week. I'd feel bad about leaving Hazel all day, but the extra money made a difference to us, as the five pounds Teddy still gave me barely stretched to keep the house running. We were never penniless but at times I had to use my noggin just so we had dinner on the table. If we had any old potatoes that had started to sprout, I'd plant them in the garden. And we always had a couple of old chickens scratching around, so egg and chips was a regular meal in our household until I started back at the hospital.

It felt strange, at times, looking after these young girls who weren't really all that much younger than me. I was like a mother figure to them and sometimes felt guilty that I wasn't mothering my own daughter more. I'd tell myself, looking after these girls was good practice for me, for when Hazel was older.

I don't know what they really thought of me, whether it was as a mother, sister, superior or just gret ol' pain in the behind who does the cleaning. In the mornings, I'd be getting them out of bed for their training duties or after an army camp dance. For some of the lazier ones, I even used the wet flannel trick that I'd mastered years before on Billy and Karl.

I enjoyed my new position, but it was never the same as when I'd been a trainee—a time when we were always working for each other as an unofficial team, always had something to aim for. The sense of togetherness that kept us going through all that was so special. This time around, I had more power and respect, but it was a lonely role. Can you imagine it, surrounded by all those young girls every day and feeling lonely. I couldn't start to imagine how it must've been for Matron.

Things did begin to settle soon enough though—being back at home, back working at the hospital, back in familiar surroundings.

I was still getting knocked about by Teddy, but this had also become something familiar. Now, look—I don't in any way mean to say I didn't mind, or didn't care, or wasn't suffering from it, because I was, there ent no two ways about it. Most often it ended with the both of us exhausted and in tears.

The full-on beatings, the repeated hitting and kicking, were less common than the usual one-off thump. The beatings, I could see coming at times, whereas the thumps seemed to appear from nowhere. We could be sitting watching television and I'd take a bite out of an apple only for Teddy to hammer a blow into my thigh.

"Shhh!" he'd say. "Do you have to make all that noise."

I look back at it now and it seems clear there was something not right about him, that maybe he had some mental issues. Of course, his reactions were unreasonable, but at the time, I also heard the apple crunch, so I could at least recognise there was a trigger.

I was always worried about the effect it would have on Hazel. I once heard how young children brought up during the Blitz in London had never known a time when bombs weren't falling. And so, just like it sometimes rains, this was the normal way of life to them. They thought that it had always been and always would be like that—blackouts, sirens, air raids, and the odd house exploding into splinters and dust.

I'd have terrible imaginings of her reading out a school project in class, none the wiser.

When I get home from school, I help Mummy cook the dinner. Then Daddy comes home from work and we eat dinner. After we wash the dishes, then we watch television. Then after Daddy has beaten-up Mummy, we go and brush our teeth, wash our faces and go to bed. And if Mummy hasn't been beaten too badly, I even get a lullaby sung to me.

When it was time for a proper beating, I'd do my best to get her out of the way, then go back and face the music. She'd often cry as I suddenly swooped down and grabbed her out of the blue, whisking her off and shutting her away in a bedroom. Then before Teddy kicked the door down, I'd go out and try not to make too much noise while he bounced me about.

I didn't realise what it was doing to me, what was happening to me, how he was slowly but surely destroying everything I was, everything I'd struggled to be, everything I'd managed to salvage from my mother and my early teenage years.

As I said before, I'd had a small reminder of the old me when I returned to the hospital. Little things would bring back memories of the girl who once was, but she was becoming no more than a fading ghost, seemingly from a different lifetime.

It was always circles and false dawns—no horizon in sight. I could never so much as change course, so never got anywhere. I'd just go all the way around and eventually end up exactly where I started.

I'd gone back to the girl I'd been growing up under my mother's reign. I didn't laugh or even smile much anymore. I didn't see many people outside our families. I didn't do much for fun; I just did my jobs —kept my head down and got 'em done. The only good things I had were Hazel and Teddy's love.

Again, maybe you're gonna think badly of me for saying *Teddy's love*. But he did. I guess I was like a loyal pet dog. Teddy was my master, and all I wanted, all I lived for, was his love. I accepted everything with nothing being asked because I knew if I did this, there might be a pat on the head at the end of it. Like the times when he'd tell me how much he loved me, tell me while he held me in his arms on the kitchen floor, unashamedly sobbing.

I believed him and still do. It was a big thing for a man to cry, let alone in front of a woman or his wife. It was a big thing for men to even use the word love. And those moments meant everything to me, they were what I lived for—what I stayed for.

40

(MY) BIRTHDAY

AGED 21 (1966)

It didn't matter where we lived, Teddy was always the man about town and everybody's friend, while I began to shrink and fade away with every move. I guess at times this suited me, as I wasn't always keen on lots of attention.

I'd never been one to make a fuss of my birthdays, so even with my 21st around the corner, I'd given no thought to doing anything special. After all, it didn't feel like anything special. It wasn't marking anything important in my life, just another number.

I was thinking, if I could find the time and someone to look after Hazel, I'd just spend the day having tea and cakes in town with Wendy. However, once Teddy remembered I was going to be 21, he had other ideas.

"No expense spared!" he said. "Only the best and biggest party is good enough for the prettiest wife a bloke could ask for." He seemed more excited about it than me, as he started telling me what he wanted doing for it, while I kept trying to talk it down.

I took the Thursday and Friday off work so I could get everything ready—the food prepared, the furniture pushed to the side, the tin bath filled with water to keep the bottles cold, the glasses, the plates, the cutlery and napkins rowed out, the balloons blown up, and with Hazel's help the paper garlands made.

Teddy told me to make a big banner saying, *Happy 21st Rosemary*! To string up outside the front of the house. He said he wanted to do it but would only make a pig's ear of it. When it came to it though, I felt too stupid making it for myself, so I didn't bother.

Come Saturday night, Teddy was in his element—the centre of all attention. I didn't know half the people there; the only people I'd invited were Wendy, the Lynn Girls, and a small group of my pre-trainees who had been putting in good efforts—but really it was so it looked like I had some friends of my own.

My parents came but left after an hour when Mum and Teddy had a bit of a set to. I spent most of the night stood at the kitchen table with Hazel and Wendy. It'd been a couple of months since we'd last seen each other, so it was good to catch up. However, after an hour or so the conversation started to stutter a bit with a few too many silences. Wendy tried hard to fill them, and luckily Hazel was a good cause for us both to fuss over or giggle at when she said something funny. I felt really terrible, but the worse I felt, the more difficult things became. I blamed it on my mind being on other things. I felt responsible for my pre-trainees and was always making sure I kept tabs on them—how much they were drinking and who was talking to them.

I was also quietly keeping tabs on Teddy, which wasn't that hard as he was usually the loudest voice to be heard, and could easily be found by the laughter surrounding him. I'd hardly been able to say two words to him myself, but realised he was having fun with his friends.

I don't know if there were many people there who actually realised the party was for my birthday. In fact, there were so many new faces I felt like a stranger in my own house. Unfortunately, cos it was my house, there was no way of sneaking home early.

My brother Karl's wife made me a birthday cake, and I heard her telling people to move out the way and asking where I was. She managed to gee-up enough people to sing happy birthday before I blew out the candles. Whether out of guilt or goodwill, people I recognised, and those I didn't, came up and said their congratulations. However, I couldn't help noticing Teddy wasn't to be seen—or more accurately heard. I was too distracted to take much notice of what people were saying, and after quickly cutting the first slice of cake and then handing the knife to Wendy, I made the excuse that I was putting Hazel to bed.

We struggled through the crowded house—even though it had started to thin out a bit already. I told Hazel to get in her bedclothes and that I'd be back in a moment. I hadn't seen Teddy on the way, so I went outside where people were smoking and saying their goodbyes, but he wasn't to be found there either.

I'm not sure whether I heard the voice first, or whether it was the only other place left to look, or whether it was what I was expecting, but I made my way down the garden to the outhouse. As soon as I got there, I knew it was him inside. His voice loud and clear even though he was trying to be all quiet. And I knew he wasn't alone from the whispered giggles coming in reply.

I thought about standing outside and listening for a bit, but I didn't want to hear the things that I might, so I opened the door.

"Go away!" he said in an instant, his back to me. "It's busy. Use the garden." Then he reached behind and pulled the door shut.

I opened it once more and spoke this time. "Teddy," I said with remarkable calm.

He turned his head.

And me, still calm, "What are you doing?"

"Rose...? Is that... you? I can't see."

"Come on, get outta there now."

"I was just showing this girl where the toilet was."

It's hard to describe how I felt. I think, because I somehow knew before I even found him, I wasn't so shocked. I wasn't angry—but I was hurt. I was humiliated, and, worst of all... I was used to it.

"Weren't nothing happening," he said as he brushed past me, tucking in his shirttails.

"And you, come on," I said to the girl, who'd stayed silent.

...There was no movement, no sound.

"Come on. Out with you now," I said, with an edge creeping into my voice, usually only heard by the laziest of pre-trainees.

As she slowly emerged from the darkness, a feeling of nausea washed through me. I wanted to clout her, but that wasn't in my nature. I wanted her to feel the ache in my heart and what it's like to live with the overwhelming sadness that I was drenched in—but these were my everyday truths, my heavy burdens, no one else's.

"I... I didn't know, Rose. I promise," she said, sounding like she was close to tears.

41

A PROBLEM SHARED...

She claimed he really had just been showing her where the toilet was. She claimed she hadn't invited him in with her. She claimed they weren't doing anything saucy. And she claimed she was sorry. I told her not to worry, that I believed her. But from that day forth, I never did speak to Tracey again.

Of course, this meant the end of my friendship with Jenny too, as the Lynn Girls came as a pair. And so on my 21st birthday, Teddy's biggest gift was losing me two out of the only three close friends I ever made.

I was determined not to dwell on it, not to wallow in my self-pity for being the lowly wretch I was, and so under the carpet it went with everything else.

I still have to admit, I couldn't help feeling a bit sorry for Tracey, as I knew what Teddy was like. He had the gift of the gab; he was very charming and persuasive, and he always got what he wanted. I may even have been able to find it in me to be friends with her again, but to be honest, I just wanted her out of his way. If I had nothing to do with her, there was less chance of Teddy having a chance to finish what he started. At least it would be one less to worry about.

There was no apology from him, nothing even said about it. It was as if it never happened, which was maybe the way we both wanted it to be.

There was no man.

And so I returned to work on Monday and everything was back to normal.

A few weeks, maybe a month later, I was doing my rounds of waking up the bleary-eyed pre-trainees. Whilst I was shooing the girls out of their rooms, I noticed one girl lagging behind the others. As I poked my head back into her room, I saw her sit down on the bed.

"You all right there, Mary?"

She sighed, shoulders slumped.

"Come on, what is it?"

"If I told yuh," she said, "you wouldn't believe me."

"You wanting the day off? Cos I'm not buying it since you were out dancing last night," I said, adopting one of Matron's fist on the hip poses.

"No. It ent that."

"Well, what is it then? We've got work to do, y'know."

"It ent to do with work."

I shut the door and went over to her. "It's okay, you can tell me. Don't worry, I'm not one to judge. After all, a problem shared is a problem halved, don't they say?"

"It's not even 'bout me..." She looked up into my eyes.

"Okay... can I ask who it is about?"

After a pause, "You."

Work-Rosemary wilted away in that very instant, and in her place sat the real Rosemary, the timid fraud, the one who couldn't manage her own life, yet was here pretending she could help others with their doings.

In the moment's silence that followed, I tried to pull Work-Rosemary back—at least enough of her to try and bluff my way through.

I swallowed. "...Go on."

"It's just... I don't quite know how to say it to yuh. And you wouldn't believe me anyways."

I let my hands slip down to my side. "What is it? Am I... do you feel I'm too strict on you? Is that it?"

"Not work stuff. And though I said it's about you, it ent directly."

There was no use in me pretending I didn't know which station this train was heading for, so like pulling off a plaster real quick I just came out with it. "Is it Teddy?"

Her face crumpled and she sobbed. "Is that his... your husband's name? Teddy?"

"It's okay, you can tell me," I said, sitting down on the bed next to her.

"I weren't sure at first, but I remembered him from your party and then..."

"It's all right," I said, nodding for her to continue.

"I've seen him in North Walsham—where I live. And he was... you know... with a girl. And not just the one time." She wiped at her eyes.

I put my arm around her shoulder. "It's okay," I told her. "You certain though?"

She nodded. I pulled her close and stroked her hair as she sobbed into my shoulder. Staring out of the window, I looked through my own faint reflection and saw some trainees in their fresh white nurses' hats, bright in the morning sun, as they passed by. Jostling and joking as they made their way to the main hospital building, so young and free, not a care in the world.

"I'd like—" I cleared my throat. "I'd like it if you didn't tell no one else, please."

"Of course!" she said, lifting her head. "I hent told no one else. Well... 'cept Gloria, cos I dint know what to do and she said I should tell you, and she certainly won't tell no one else and I won't either, I promise that."

"Thank you. And thank you for telling me. I know it would've been easier to tell everyone else but me," I said as I pushed her hair behind her ear. "And don't worry, I will deal with it."

I always had the utmost respect for Mary from that day on. She was by no means the brightest button or the quickest learner, but full credit to her because I don't think I would've been brave enough to say something. Of course, it wasn't really news to me, but now it had come from the outside, it was getting harder to hide from.

I didn't want to get Mary involved; it was nothing to do with her, but I did get her to help me out one more time by finding out the girl's name and phone number. At the time, I wasn't sure what I was going to do with it—if anything. I guess I just wanted Mary to think I wasn't going to ignore it, that I was the strong woman I pretended to be at work.

However, once I had the name and number on a piece of paper in my hand, it became something more real. The dropped mitten had blown onto to the frozen lake, and so I had no choice but to follow it, to venture onto the ice, unless I forever wanted to be one mitten short of a pair.

One evening, when Teddy had gone to the pub, I phoned her. Her mum answered and I asked to speak to Dawn. I told her straight out that I was his wife and I knew about them. This was met by silence and I thought she was gonna hang up. Then she spoke.

She had a quiet and fragile voice, which surprised me. I'd been expecting a confident and cocky person—I mean, that's what you'd think they'd need to be like in order to be carrying on with a married man. But of course, it didn't work that way round usually. Hunter and the hunted.

Anyway, she claimed she didn't know he was married. I told her, he most certainly was, and then said if she wanted him she could have him, but she should know what he was like, what he was truly like, know what you got with Teddy. I told her he was a funny, friendly and loving man but she weren't the first and wouldn't be the last. I told her how he lost his temper all too quickly and told her how he liked to use his fists at times.

It felt good, almost like a confession. My shameful secret was finally being shared, even though the first person I told everything to was a girl I'd never met and who was carrying on with my husband behind my back.

I could hear her trying to hide her snivels. She begged for my forgiveness, said she didn't want him, pleaded for me not to do anything, said her parents would go up the wall if they found out.

After I put down the phone, I felt determined and strong. I'd kept my man. I'd beaten her. I'd won.

But as my emotions settled, I realised how quickly she'd agreed to leave him—how *ready* she was to leave him once she knew what he was truly like.

I'd only won my prize by telling her how terrible it was. And you know what, viewing it through someone else's eyes finally allowed me to see clearly. And so I decided that was it. I was leaving him.

42

LEAVING

The next day, I phoned his parents and told them.

"No. You can't," was the first thing Muriel said to me. Then she sighed. "I mean—please, don't."

"I've made up my mind and there ent no changing it."

"But you've been looking after him since you were fifteen, you can't give up on him now."

It didn't escape my attention that she hadn't asked the obvious first question of why I wanted to leave him.

"I thought you'd be able to change him," she went on.

"Change him? There's no changing him. He always does what he wants. His whole life he's had everything his own way." I didn't care what she thought of me for saying this.

"Bless him, he just wants to enjoy his life, is all."

"Hmph. Yeah, I know. I know all about the other girls too."

No reply.

"And I know about the girl he got into trouble before, right way back in Attleborough." This one, I wasn't sure about; I was just fishing on a hunch. In fact, this might have been the first time I'd even reeled this one up to the surface. I guess deep down I had always suspected this was the reason behind some of our moves.

Again, Muriel stayed silent.

"What'll he do without you?" she finally said. "He loves you ever so much, y'know."

"Well, he has a funny way of showing it."

She told me to think on it and not to do anything silly before she sent her husband round to speak to us both.

Teddy arrived with his dad, wearing a pitiful look as they walked into the kitchen. His dad made him sit down and then stood between us like the referee of a boxing match—but if it came to that we all knew there'd be only one winner.

"Rosie, listen," Teddy began to whine, "you gotta—"

His dad held up his palm. "What is this, Rose? What's going on?"

I told him that I knew Teddy had been messing around.

"That's not true, it's not," he protested. "I've always looked after you, always provided for you, hent I not?"

I told other truths, too, about how I had to run the entire house on five pounds a week while the rest got spent in the pub.

"That ent true, she's making things up now, Dad. She ent right in the head."

I looked at him—who on earth was he trying to win over here?

"Making things up, am I Edward? So am I making up Dawn Potter, 54, Phillips Road, North Walsham, phone number 0693 406375."

His face dropped, going redder and redder.

"Teddy?" his dad said. "Is this true?"

"True!" I said. "Huh. That's just the half of it. Recognise these?" Then I started to slap down all the things I'd collected from his car. "What's this? A hair clip? Don't look like none of mine. Lipstick? No, not my colour. Cigarettes? Not yours? And I don't smoke."

"Is this true, Teddy? Are you a philanderer?"

He couldn't meet his dad's eye, his lower lip trembling like it would after he gave me a beating.

"You little sod you," his dad said, giving him a clip round the back of the head that pushed up a tuft of his hair. "Apologise to the poor girl this instant."

"I'm sorry, I really am," he said bowing his head. He snivelled and wiped at his nose with the back of his hairy hand.

His dad turned to me, nodding, "Okay, good. So, there we go. I can promise you, it won't ever happen again."

"Yeah, you're right. It won't." I couldn't believe he thought it was going to be as easy as a bit of crying, an apology, and then things would carry on like normal. "It won't happen again cos I won't be there the next time."

"What you sayin? No. Please?" Teddy was in full sob now. "You ent gonna go, you can't. I'm nothing without you. I can't survive without you, you know that." This earnest pleading of his was not new, I'd seen it all before.

"I'm going to leave you, Teddy. I *am* leaving you."

"No! No! You can't. Please! Please?"

"Come on, Rosemary, look at him. Think about it, he can change. It won't happen again. Hand over heart, I promise you that."

"It's true, I'll never see her again, you must believe me. I'll go and say goodbye to her right this minute. Tell her it's over."

"Really? Okay then, you go say goodbye to her—"

"I will. I will. I promise." He even started to rise out of his chair.

"Okay, off you go then. But when you get back, I won't be here no more." I couldn't believe the cheek of the man—fancy thinking I'd be weak enough to let him go off and say a final goodbye to his bit on the side and then welcome him back with open arms. He really did think he could do whatever he pleased and always get away with it.

PART III

WORKING GIRL

43

WORKING GIRL

AGED 24 (1969)

My parents finally found a buyer for their house, so yet another move was needed. This time, to a rented bungalow in Melton Constable—a small village just outside Holt. So even though the place was new, the area was still familiar. Yet, I still didn't feel comfortable and became a bit of a hermit again.

I couldn't face going out, worried about what people knew or had heard, worried about what they might be saying about me. It wasn't just going out that I didn't like, I wasn't all that keen on having visitors come round either. The new house became like my nest that I would guard. I also did my best not to make any new female friends, knowing they couldn't even trust themselves when gift of the gab, Fun-Time Teddy was around them.

Whether he'd stopped altogether or was just being more discreet, I wasn't sure, but I didn't hear no more about him messing around after the move. Nothing else changed, mind you. He was still busy spending our money, busy going out and drinking, busy swapping cars at the pub, and busy with his fists at home.

With Hazel at school and cutbacks at the hospital reducing my working week to only two days, I spent more and more of the daytime alone in the house cleaning things to within an inch of their life. I missed having Hazel with me so dearly. I often thought about keeping her off school, keeping her with me so I could look after her properly. But unlike her mother, she really took to school and enjoyed it—and of course, I had to remember my promise.

Having all that free time also meant I did far too much thinking on things. I soon realised I needed something to keep me occupied, something else that was mine, something else for me to care about, to focus on.

I'd always been careful with my money, right back from my days as a trainee even. Knowing that Teddy wasn't ever likely to have the will to save anything, I had managed to squirrel away a fair bit myself. I always had in mind it was for our future, that it would be used to buy our own place one day. But you know what I did with it? I spent it. I spent it on me—damn near all of it.

And so finally, after a childhood of dreaming and never believing, it came to pass that I bought my own horse. She was a three-year-old dapple grey who I named Silver. I kept her at a rented stable a few miles away on the edge of Aylsham, near all the workshop and factory units. And from that day forth, I spent as much time as I could down there. If I wasn't out riding, I was mucking her out, brushing her down or fixing up the stable.

When I was out riding, I could forget everything; it all seemed to trail away behind me in the wind. It was like I could even forget who I was; I wasn't anybody anymore. I didn't have a name, have a family, have anything to worry about. If it had been possible, I would've never stopped, I would've just kept going, on and on, forever and ever.

I never considered myself brave and always felt a fraud when Wendy said I was. I guess there were times when I just knew my mind though, knew what I wanted and so wouldn't think my way out of it, I'd just up and do it.

One afternoon, after a good long hack, I untacked Silver, watered and brushed her down, then walked out of the paddock and into the warmth of the day. The birds were tweeting as I looked up at the big white clouds trundling through the sky. Then and there, in that moment, I felt good. There was a comforting calm to the day, even the distant whirring and occasional muffled clangs of the machinery from the works site seemed a part of the peaceful atmosphere. I always liked the distant sound of people busy doing their things—like listening to the merry voices of a party downstairs as I lay in bed as a child.

I looked over to the factories. Long rows of big units with their massive doors open to the world and always a hive of activity. I wondered what it was they made, what machines hid inside, and how many people worked there. I carried on walking until I came to the edge of the paddock. Out front was a clutter of piled-high pallets all wrapped in plastic, the odd forklift, and rusted skip. I hopped over the fence and kept going until I found myself outside one of the units.

From the huge entrance, a path of sunlight lead into the building a few metres or so before giving way to the darkness. In fact it was so dark, I had to keep walking to find out what was in there.

It was much cooler inside, almost refreshing, as I kept going until I crossed the sharp line the sun cut into shadow. I stood blinking until my eyes began to adjust. I could make out big machines clunking and whirring away, as tiny men in dirty blue overalls fussed about them like bees in the lavender. From between two machines, a short, dark grey-haired man strolled towards me looking down at the oil-stained rag that he was wiping his hands with.

"What, you lost my love?" he said, with a pleasant smile.

"Urm, don't think so."

"What can I do for you then?"

"I... I've come for a job," I found myself saying.

Well, this stopped him in his tracks. I could see the cogs working away in his head as he tried to remember if he'd forgotten something. He cocked his head to one side. "Who told you to come in then?"

"Oh, no one."

"I see. Well, I'm awfully sorry love but we already got a coupla gels working in the office."

I told him I couldn't work in no office, that I wanted to work on the floor. He gave a little laugh and looked at me. I explained about my horse and stable, and he explained how I didn't have no experience, that they weren't looking to take anyone on at the moment. And besides, he'd never heard of having a woman work the floor before.

"And to be honest," he continued, "it ent really the place for a gel to be working—not with all these lads. Now, don't get me wrong, they're all good fellas, we wouldn't have 'em if they weren't, but you know... they're... y'know, fellas," he finished, almost apologetically.

I told him I didn't mind—I had five brothers after all.

"Anyway, love, I ent even the gaffer here, just the floor boss."

"What? You mean to tell me I've been wasting all this time talking to the monkey," I said. "Best you take me to the organ grinder then."

He gave a little laugh, wiped his hands down while he thought about it, then, "Well, if you want to hear it from the horse's mouth, let's go see if he ent busy. Come on then."

The manager was a slightly plumper man, but just as pleasant as the foreman and equally bemused. He told me the same as what I'd just heard. We sat and had a cup of tea and talked about my horse. Then I thanked them and left.

The next day, I went back to check if he hadn't changed his mind. But he hadn't. The day after that, I thought I better double-check, and the day after that, and a few more yet, until eventually, he said I spent so much time there, they might as well try and make some use out of it. They gave me a two-week trial on the line, putting television sets together in the next unit along—a place where they did employ the fairer sex. It wasn't quite what I wanted. I wanted to be a bee, not an ant, but I thought I'd give it a go, anyway.

However, when the floor manager showed me around, I thought I'd made a big mistake seeing all these women with their hands going back and forth like the clappers.

"Are you trying to talk yourself into a job or outta a job?" the floor manager said after I told him my concerns.

"No. No, I'm sure I'll get the hang of it soon enough. I'm a quick learner, you'll see." And thankfully, I was true to my word. After a fortnight, I was on the top bonus line, my hands a busy blur putting together them circuit boards. Once the sets finished the line, they sent them to Lowestoft for distribution. Just before I left they'd even started to make the colour TVs too. However, I didn't stay there all that long; I was seen as a loner by the other women, which didn't bother me. I was more than happy not to be involved with them and their gossiping and fake ways—as I saw it. I couldn't believe what they were like at times. There'd be two girls next to each other all morning, planning their weekend together, laughing away. Only later, you'd hear one of them in toilets running the other down and vice versa. I really couldn't figure out if they liked each other or not, or if they even knew it themselves.

It was a five days a week job with optional overtime at the weekends. I was able to use the car to get to and from work and the stables as long as I had it back in time for Teddy to go to the pub. But a little after a week, I managed to bump a post as I was leaving off, denting and scratching the back. I couldn't think what to do, knowing I'd get it when he found out. At my wits' end, I decided to take a bit of a risk and took it to one of Teddy's mates, Russell, who was meant to be good with cars. By the time I arrived at his car yard, I'd got myself into a right state, begging him not to say anything about it.

"For gawd's sake, stop crying gel, course I won't tell him." He'd been mates with Teddy for years, so I guess he might've known something about his temper. He managed to get the dents out, but there wasn't much he could do with the scratches.

It was horrible having that hanging over me the whole time, flinching every time Teddy spoke to me, thinking he'd finally seen it.

It was maybe a week later that he came home all riled up. I heard the roar of the car as it skidded into the gravel. Then the slam of the door. Next, he was hollering for me.

"Rose! Rose, git out here!"

I daren't not go. It was always a case of making the beating as bearable and as quick as possible. Trying not to stir him up any more than I already had.

"What is it? What on earth's the matter?" I could feel the worry on my face, there was no hiding it; it would have only taken one look to find the guilty party, stood right there in front of him.

"Here!" He grabbed me by the arm and dragged me to the back of the car. "You see that," he said, pointing to the scratches.

My heart started dancing the quickstep—it was decision time. Deny, deny, deny or come clean and dance to the music? Luckily, I dithered just long enough, as he started effin and jeffin, jabbing a finger at the scratches. See what some effer has done to my car, he was shouting. I felt ever so rotten, but I knew it was best to agree rather than try and play it down, so I threw in a few choice words about the mystery culprit too.

"I'll have to take it down to see Russell. See if he can't do something," he said, before aiming a kick at the car's bumper.

"Probably not much he could do with a scratch though is there, well... I wouldn't have thought at least?" I said, wondering how true to his word Russell would be when faced with an irate Teddy.

"And what would you know about it? You a bloody car expert all of a sudden, are yuh?"

Luckily, Russell kept schtum. But after that, I daren't use the car and would take the bus nearly everywhere I went. Getting the bus to Aylsham proved to be a right pain and added at least an extra hour and a half on to my day. So when there was news of a factory that had recently opened in Melton Constable that was looking for workers, I went along to see.

Teddy didn't bat an eyelid when said I was going for a job working with all fellas. At the start of our marriage, he'd get angry and jealous, but now he knew he had me where he wanted—knew I wouldn't dare mess around. When he told me to be somewhere or do something, you could guarantee I'd be there or I'd do it.

When I went in to speak to them at the factory, I got the same old story. "This ent the right place for girls to be working."

But having older brothers and having worked on a farm, I didn't buy into this 'jobs for fellas and jobs for girls,' malarkey. And besides, I didn't want to work with girls again. And so the crazing started, and this time it only took me three days.

They made gret big electric motors, so most of it was machine work. I remembered my mistake at the television factory, so when I saw the men working away, I said I could do that no problem.

He looked me up and down. "A pretty little thing like you?"

"I'm tougher than I look," I told him.

"All right then, I'll give you a one month trial. But any trouble and you're stret out that door, mind."

"Sounds fair to me," I told him. "I wouldn't have it any other way."

44

THE COUNSELLOR

I was put on the rivet press to start off with, which was certainly more riveting than sitting on the line—if I only had a penny for every time one of the fellas came nudging up to me with that one in my first week.

The work was fairly straightforward if somewhat samey, but I didn't mind that so much. I found once you got into a rhythm, you no longer noticed that things were repeating over and over again and that most of your day had passed you by without you really realising it. It was only the blare of the siren over the clanging and bashing of machines that would eventually snap you out of it.

When the siren sounded for break time, the whirring and pummelling of machines slowly died down, and then like woodlouse from an upturned log, the men came pouring out of all corners, scuttling across the floor to the tea station.

The tea station was the holy shrine of the factory floor. It sat just inside the entrance, so on warm days with the doors open, a path of golden sunshine led right up to it. The occasional lost screw or shard of metal would glint and sparkle along it as if it was some kind of sacred, bejewelled road. Each man would queue up waiting for his turn, then go back clasping his hands together in front of him around his steaming mug. A nudie calendar was pinned above it, which most of the men would have a quick glance at, paying their respects to that month's idol, sometimes with a muttered comment to show their appreciation.

"Don't get many of 'em to the pound, I'll tell yuh."

"Talented gel that one, make no mistake."

"Cor blimey, wish my missus had a set of norks like that."

Gathered around the tea shrine was an assortment of old grease-stained and battered chairs, ranging from an armchair to a collapsible deck chair. There seemed to be some sort of system to it—the older you were, the bigger and comfier your seat. And everyone always sat in the same place in the same chairs without fail.

On my first day, I realised there weren't any spare seats in the circle, so I went outside thinking I could find a wall to perch on. After a bit of a wander, I found an upturned faded-red plastic chair round the back. It was one of those with the metal legs that stack on top of each other, most often found in town halls. It needed a dust down and it was a bit stained and very wobbly, but it did me fine. I'd sit on my own and drink my tea just outside the massive metal doors. Although the tea assembly got some sunlight, for me it wasn't the same as being properly outside, being able to feel the breeze. I found it ever so relaxing, all the machinery gone quiet, just the gentle jostling of leaves, the twittering of birds, and the low murmurs and chortles of the workers drifting out. In fact, it was the closest I could get to feeling completely relaxed other than being on my horse. So much so, at times I had to be careful not to fall asleep.

The boys were all friendly enough, but maybe a bit unsure or even shy of having a woman about. Like I said before, I'd take working with blokes over girls any day, even though I wasn't any more included in this group. It was just a nicer atmosphere, more of a together feel and always laughs and jokes going on, rather than snips and snipes.

A couple of weeks in, I went outside for my break as usual, only to find my chair was missing. I stood there clutching my cup of tea, thinking how best to react. To be honest, I was surprised it'd taken this long for me to become a victim of their humour. I realised I had two choices, either ignore them and sit on the wall and pretend it didn't bother me none, or go over and do my old Matron routine and pretend to scold them.

As I walked back in, I expected all eyes to be on me as they tried to stifle their giggles. I looked around the circle but they were playing it well, chatting like normal—not a snigger to be heard.

I took a breath and marched over, all ready to do my bit when something familiar caught my eye. There, sitting in the congregation circle, was my little, faded-red chair, so I stopped. I looked up for a face to thank, but it was as if no one had seen me, all of them still carrying on like normal. Maybe the trick was still to come, I thought, but I had nothing to lose, so rather than standing there like a lemon, I thought, sod it, and walked over and sat down. As I did, I suddenly realised I'd made a terrible mistake.

I knew my chair ever so well, so as soon as I sat down, I instantly realised this wasn't it. I felt a blush coming on. How on earth was I going to undo this? Bold as brass buttons, I'd just come along and plonked myself right amongst them. And any minute the rightful owner of the chair was likely to arrive and be just as embarrassed as me. I was desperately trying to think of some sort of joke, make out as if I'd done it on purpose just for laughs.

I slowly looked up, but no one reacted. It seemed they were just going to ignore my rudeness until the chair owner turfed me out. It was no good, I thought, I'd just have to get back up and sheepishly make my exit.

As I picked up my mug to leave, I saw the familiar yellow stain in the shape of a fairy's wing on the front lip. Finally, I clocked what was amiss. It was my chair, after all. The only difference was that it no longer had its customary wobble.

Again, I searched for a smiling face—this time to thank them. Nothing was astir, except for their mugs of tea. I guess that's just the way it is with fellas sometimes—they can be more than capable of having a kind heart, but not always having the balls to admit it.

It may not seem much, but to me, there and then, it seemed like the world. Being accepted in that way with no ceremony or fuss, in their way, as if I was just another one of the fellas.

The following week, one or two of them plucked up enough

courage to ask me a question or two, and the week after that it was as if I'd worked there for a year already. I think what fully marked my acceptance into the group was when I had an occasion to tell them off and set them straight about how to treat a lady properly in the workplace.

One of the old boys, Roger, was telling one of his stories; this one was about the time he worked down at the cow-yard in Hevingham. Every day he seemed to have a new yarn, and every day he'd get a fair few laughs out of them. He was telling us about the time a young heifer got her head caught in a wire fence. He was saying how he and his mate were trying all sorts of ways to get her free without having to cut the fence up.

"So he's one side pushing this cow's face that was all smothered in axle grease and I'm up the other end trying to pull," he said, giving it all the hand motions too. "Trouble was, there ent much to get hold of at that end. Of course, my first thought was to grab her by the tits—since the missus never lets me grab hers no more—but anyway, all I could do was grab the tail. And then on the count o'three, my mate starts pushing and I start pulling." Again he was busy with the hand gestures.

"Wellll, I'll tell yuh, I was pulling and pulling on that tail. Putting my back right into it, pulling with all my might. Pulling like my life depended on it. Pulling like there's no tomorrow. Pulling like young Franky here does when he gets home each day after work, when suddenly... from outta nowhere... the old cow only goes and farts right in my face."

Well, near all of them fell about the place, Roger more so than any other. That was until he saw a few of them looking in my direction with rather pink cheeks.

"Oh, Rose. I'm right sorry," he said. "I weren't thinking. I dint see yuh. I... I forgot there was a lady present."

"No," I said, shaking my head. "You're not to do that."

He looked ever so upset and took a sudden deep interest in stirring his tea.

"What I mean," I continued, "is you're not to apologise. Look, I've come creeping into your world, not the other way round. You take no mind of me. You buggers carry on just like before, okay? You treat me no different to any other person in here. Have we got that straight?"

A few looks were exchanged as my little speech was considered, before most eyes turned to the two oldest fellas sat in the armchairs. One of them, Mike, took a long slurp of his tea, looked across to the other, Alan, who murmured something. Then they turned back to the circle and nodded their agreement. And so it was passed, things were to carry on as before, no bloody different. And that was that. That was me accepted into the group as one of the fellas. I got along great with most of them, many of them even becoming lifelong friends.

Now, although I was able to cut the mustard in a man's workplace, I was still a bit of a dolly bird in those days, I don't mind telling you. Yes, I wore my overalls, my hair net, and didn't mind getting grease on my face, but maybe as a leftover from my nursing days, I always made sure I was well turned out. Everything clean and neat at the start of the day, and I have to admit I usually wore a hint of makeup too. There were a couple of times when fellas tried it on, but I always dealt with it and made sure they knew it wasn't going to happen. The first time, I gave the fella a friendly slap on the wrist and asked what he was doing. I then reminded him what I said about being treated the same as everyone else.

"Or do you go around pinching all the other men's bums as well?" I said nice and loud to make sure a good few others heard. The others all laughed and the bum-pincher soon scuttled back under his log.

The second time, I was also able to set my stall out and let the fella know how it was. Though, it didn't happen on the shop floor in the public gaze this time. Whenever a job sheet was finished, you'd take the piece you'd been working on into the inspector's office. Unfortunately, he was not shy in wanting to inspect more than my work this one time.

"Working here with all these young men," I said, wriggling free from him, "and it takes a dirty ol' man like you to try and mess me around."

"If you don't like it then you shouldn't have come in here, should you?" he said with a grin, leaning right into my face.

"All right then. I won't. If you want to check my work, you can come crawling out of your little hole and check it in the workshop so everyone can see where your bloody hands are." I knew it was a gamble, but I weren't going to accept it. If it meant losing my job, then so be it, I'd just go find another one. At least that was my thinking.

The inspector hated going out to the factory floor. He didn't get on with the fellas so well. He'd rather spend his whole day in his heated office reading newspapers. One-on-one in his own territory wasn't a problem for him since he was their superior, but on the floor, he was outnumbered and out of his comfort zone. Not that they did much more than flick rubber bands at him from the gantry and give mock Nazi salutes when his back was turned.

But after that day, I never did set foot in his office with him alone again—and if anyone needed a rubber band, there was always plenty to be found around my machine after I'd had my work inspected.

Of course, it wasn't long before the fellas were asking why I got special treatment. I didn't let on and would just shrug and smile and say, "Maybe it's cos deep down there's a proper gentleman hiding in there somewhere."

One fella who was a real gent was an old boy called Ronny Jordan. He was ever so kind and thoughtful. He had a dicky leg and couldn't drive or ride a bike too well, so he was always seen limping his way to work every morning. Most mornings he'd arrive bearing gifts, such as a bag full of field mushrooms that he'd picked along his way. He'd give them out to the same close friends every day, but he'd always save some for a different person each time and make sure to stop by and have a little chat with them.

It amazed me, but some people actually refused them, said they felt funny about eating stuff from the roadside. One day, I see another nice fella by the name of Vic handing back his mushrooms saying, doesn't Ronny want to keep some for himself?

"Oh no, I don't bother. Not too keen on mushrooms, me," he explained.

He wasn't only kind-hearted, he had a good sense of humour too. In fact, he was one of the first fellas who had the nerve to play a joke on me, or at least the first to get caught. On Fridays, the fish and chip van would come down to the works, signalling a mad race between all the different factories wanting to get there first. Everyone wanting to get the choicest bits of fish, the hottest food, and the most time to scoff it down. Most of the old boys and myself didn't bother with the mad dash. For me it was all too easy anyway, as there weren't many of the fellas who didn't say, "Ladies first," and before I knew it I was at the front of the queue buying some steaming hot chips—this being the one time I didn't mind being treated differently of course.

I came back in one day with my food warming my hands and the smell of salt and vinegar teasing my nostrils when I noticed the circle of seats was still fairly empty. Then I saw that most of them were huddled around my machine whispering away, so I walked up behind them to see what was going on and saw Ronny with a rubber glove attached to the pneumatic hose. He was using it to blow up the glove like a huge gret cow's udder.

"Eer, pass us the string," he was saying to Vic.

Just as he was trying to tie it to my machine, I gave a polite cough.

Well. He spun round in surprise and let go of the glove, sending it whizzing around the factory like an angry wasp with a bad case of wind. I couldn't help myself but to laugh as he hobbled a slow escape across the floor.

He later come and apologised, and we got talking and became good friends. He was a proper country boy and there wasn't much he didn't know, or a practical problem he couldn't solve, and so very much reminded me of Little Weasel—God rest his soul. It always seemed a waste, a man with Ronny's skills pressing buttons and pulling levers all day, but it was what he wanted and what he was happy doing.

As a young lad, he worked as a smithy's apprentice and so once he found out I kept a horse he was such a great help. He knew how to shoe them, float their teeth, the lot. And he'd never want anything in return no matter how much I tried; he just loved to help people.

A lot of people thought of Teddy in the same way. He was always ready to help others out, doing them favours. Much like my mum, I guess, with her baking bread for the village. Mind, neither of them was ever likely to do it for me. Though there was this one time Teddy offered to help me out when we were re-decorating the hallway. With it being so narrow, it was too difficult a job for just me and a ten-year-old Hazel, so Teddy got involved. Between the three of us, we'd managed to get the roll of wallpaper unravelled and pasted. Next, we had to get it up onto the ceiling nice and straight. It didn't take more than two attempts before Teddy lost it and after a brief tangle with the paper ended up flinging it at me. I'd been holding up the other end so was caught in a wallpaper and paste sandwich. It stuck to my face for a second before slowly sliding all the way down my front. My first reaction was to burst out laughing, and looking up I saw Hazel was of the same mind. Not so Teddy, though. Once his temper had deserted him, it didn't often come back until something felt his fists.

"It's not funny!" he told us. But seeing him in such a grump, in such a silly situation was too much. I knew I couldn't hold it any longer so raced out of the hallway shortly followed by Hazel and we both fell about in fits of giggles.

As we crept back, we heard the metal steps being moved, the rustle of paper, a moment's quiet... then a bout of sudden swearing, "For eff's sake! You effin piece of shit!" he'd go, followed by the ceiling or wall being thumped. This was repeated three or four times before he finally gave up and went to the pub. I don't know what came over us that afternoon; we couldn't help but to laugh. It's strange that we were able to laugh at the very anger that we suffered from so much.

After a year of working at the electric motor factory, I'd become more than just accepted, I'd also taken on the unofficial role of marriage counsellor. I guess it was the first time for them to have a 'fella' at work who also knew so much about women. I did the best I could, yet I couldn't help but to feel like a bit of a fraud seeing how unhappy my own marriage was a lot of the time, but I guess it's always easier to recognise and say the right things than it is to do them. I always considered my situation different anyway, as if I had my own special problem, as if it was something that no one else would be able to understand. But anyway, this isn't about me for once.

So, the fellas usually came to me with their gripes and groans first thing in the morning. One such morning Vic came in looking like he'd seen a ghost.

"She's left me, Rosemary. My wife... she's left me and the children," he said, obviously in a state of shock. "Just gone."

I told him how sorry I was.

"I loved her. I did everything for her. The cooking, the cleaning, the money. I don't think she'll even manage by herself, bless her."

I told him just to give it time, that often these things sort themselves out, eventually. I told him to wait and soon enough she'd realise what she was throwing away and come back to him.

The next day he came back to me, pale-faced and with a far-off look in his eyes.

"She's gone off with another fella, Rosemary. That's it, she's gone. I don't even know where. How can she do that, after all these years? Her children. I'm... in pieces, Rosemary. I just... don't know what to do. You gotta help me. Nothing will be the same ever again. What is there now? There's nothing. It wasn't supposed to be this way."

"Now look here," I said, realising that despite how sorrowful and pitiful he appeared, it was time for the wet flannel to the face, "you may not like what I'm about to say, but I'm gonna say it nonetheless. Nothing is supposed to be any particular way; you make your own future. Your life is yours, and yours only. And only you can make the best of it. Despite all the crap that life throws at you, you gotta believe in yourself, and you gotta continue on no matter what, and not hide. You go and face it, you go out and hit it on the head, or grab it by the... wotsits, cos there ent no one else gonna do it for you. Of course, people can help you along the way, but eventually, it comes down to you. And I know you, Victor. I know who you are and I know *you* are more than capable of doing it."

He stood blinking at me for a few seconds. Perhaps he'd been looking for some soothing sympathy. I started to think that maybe I'd judged this one wrong and done him more damage than good. After a long moment's thought, he gave a puff of the cheeks, nodded a thanks, then walked away.

I hoped that it was enough, that I was right, that maybe just words alone could actually help him in some way.

45

THE NEW INSPECTOR

AGED 27 (1972)

If anyone was ever absent, it was usually me who was moved to cover their machine. A lot of the older fellas weren't so keen on working at a different station; they liked their routine and anything changing it could only be a bad thing in their eyes. Whereas I always welcomed the change of scenery, and therefore I was one of the few people who had a rough idea of the entire goings-on in that factory. So a couple of years down the line, as the factory started to expand, it didn't seem that out of place when I was promoted to inspector.

As the unofficial factory counsellor, I'd already climbed up a few rungs on the respect ladder with many of the men. Therefore, there weren't many eyelids batted when the news broke. Occasionally, I had a few teething problems when new fellas came in, but I generally found I could win them over after a while. There was only ever one bloke who just couldn't get along with having a woman as his superior, but it was nothing I couldn't handle. As it turned out, he didn't really get on well with the other blokes either, and to this day I can't even remember his name.

One thing I quickly learnt from my new position was that there isn't just one magical way you could deal with people. Different types had to be handled in different ways. My usual manner was just being straight with them, which was especially useful when it came to dishing out the job sheets.

"Why does he always get the plum jobs, eh?"

"So in total that's six different ones, right? So I got to set up the machine six different times in one day then?"

"This worksheet is longer than my arm! I'll be here 'til kingdom come."

"That's nothing, yesterday my job sheet was longer than Roger's peck- peck- ...pencil. Hello, Rose, mighty fine morning, eh?"

But unlike the other inspectors, I always explained why certain people got certain ones. It didn't always mean they'd go away happy, but at least they had a reason they could get to grips with. The really tricky job sheets were always called the narst'uns and would usually fall to the same few fellas. And every week I'd have the same few fellas twisting my lug about them. But I'd tell them how it was.

"Yep, you're right, it is a difficult job but that's exactly why you've got it. When I come to inspect it, I want to find it ent got a problem and my best chance of that happening is giving it to you."

"Well... yeah... but—"

"Look," I'd then say, "to be honest, the bottom line is that you're the only one I trust to do a good job on it."

"True, true. You put it like that... I guess."

"Good chap! I knew I could rely on you."

I think in the end they'd just come and moan to get the compliments.

The other thing I did different was to always take their word for it, always trusted their judgement on a job regardless whether I thought it was right or wrong. If they came back to me saying it couldn't be done, I'd happily ring up the customer and say it's impossible, you going to have to change the spec if you want it doing. I know other inspectors would be suspicious that the fella was just trying to shirk a narst'un, so often they'd force them to keep going at it. What they didn't understand though, was that it didn't matter what the truth of it was, either way, you weren't going to get a good product. If the fellas were being honest then, of course, it couldn't be done. And if it was just a case of the fellas not feeling confident about it or his heart not being in it, then you'd still end up with a shoddy product or they'd even mess it up on purpose just to prove they were right.

It was a strange double life I lived for them few years. At work, I was this confident, straight-talking, high-flying, young woman who wouldn't take no messing from anyone. Then in the few minutes it took me to walk home, the clock would strike midnight and I'd go back to being a timid little house mouse that lived in fear of her husband, surviving off the tiniest crumbs of kindness that would occasionally fall my way—as long as I didn't make too much noise when ate them of course.

If I was ever caught limping or wincing in pain at work, I'd always blame it on falling off my horse.

"That must be one wild horse you got yourself there," Vic said to me one day.

"I know, but she's my horse. I chose her. Not a lot I can do about it now, is there?"

But Vic, despite being pure and kind of heart, didn't pull any punches when he could see clearly to the simplest answer. "Sure there is, you can send her to the glue factory and get yourself a gentler one."

They worked us hard at the factory, but they looked after us too. They made sure we knew we were appreciated, and that made for a lovely close-knit feel to the place, which is something that I'd have never guessed at until I worked there. Every year come Christmas, we were each given a box and inside would be a bottle of wine and a gret ol' joint of meat. Then on the last Saturday before Christmas, they'd put on a dinner and dance evening—all free of charge, even the drinks.

I had asked Teddy if we could go along the first year, but he said no. The following two years I didn't bother asking. However, after my promotion and being fed up of all the fellas asking why I never went, I decided I really should make the effort. I went home and told Teddy I was going and I'd like it very much if he would come too, and to my surprise, he just about agreed.

I couldn't help feeling excited as we left the house all dolled-up and him looking ever so sharp in his suit. I used some of my own separate savings to buy a brand new dress that was said to be the latest fashion by the woman in the shop. It was a sleeveless, white-spotted navy blue number with a white sash that tied high around the waist. It came with choices of accessories too. Long white silk gloves and a sleek white hat with a flower sewn into the band. I bought the gloves but left the hat —preferring to tie my hair up in a ribbon instead.

Apart from the very occasional trip to the pub and dinners at his parents, we never went out as a pair. When we did though, Teddy was always the perfect gentleman, the man I fell in love with—at least usually for the beginning of the night. After a couple of drinks, you might never know we were married though, as he'd be off talking and laughing with everyone but me. I hoped this time it would be different, as for once it would be mostly my friends we were surrounded by. Of course, some of the boys knew him—or at least *of* him—it was hard not to, with him being such a character around town.

46

THE ICE DANCER

They laid on a lovely meal of roast lamb and potatoes and all the veg, followed by a bread and butter pudding with cream. For the second half of the evening, the tables were cleared away so that the dancing could begin.

Apart from sharing jokes with the young girls doing the foodservice, Teddy had been fairly quiet. He turned his nose up at my suggestion to dance, preferring to sit there, arms folded, only moving when he drank from his pints. It wasn't like him; usually he burst into a room loud and full of smiles whether he knew anyone there or not. I can't say what had got into him, whether he was worried what the fellas might know about us, or whether there was some jealousy now my workmates had become real people rather than just unknown names from my stories that he barely listened to.

We sat for a while just having drinks, but he didn't even seem to have a taste for talking, just grunting in reply to my efforts. It was torture for me watching all those people I usually enjoyed chatting to having fun and me not being able to join in. And for once in my life, I actually felt like getting up and having a bloomin good dance. Eventually, I decided enough was enough and that we might as well go home since he obviously wasn't in the right mood.

I'd noticed a few of the fellas occasionally look over at us, so I gave them a smile back, hoping it rang truer than it felt. I was worried they were finally seeing through the disguise I wore at work, seeing the real Rosemary.

It was plainly obvious to me, that going to dances and myself didn't mix, so I decided to give it one more drink, just to be polite, then we could make our excuses and leave.

"I'll get 'em in, and when I come back, I want you to perk up and have some fun, Mister. All right?" I said putting on my best Rosemary the Inspector impression. It worked with the fellas, they all liked me, they all respected me. Maybe that's what I'd been doing wrong all this time, I thought, so I even gave him a playful nudge with my elbow as I got up. He didn't reply, just grumbled and shifted in his seat.

On the way to the bar, I stopped for a quick chat with a couple of the fellas, just so they didn't think I was ignoring them, then returned to our seats with the drinks. But when I got back, Teddy wasn't there. Maybe my 'little Rosemary the Inspector' skit had put a bit of life into him, I thought. And then looking up, I realised I was right. There he was dancing away with one of the dinner serving girls who'd just finished her shift.

I tried to smile through the heart-crushing pain and anger, tried to hide it, but not for his sake. What I couldn't have was the fellas seeing me weep. I couldn't let them see me powerless and pathetic, it would be the ruin of my career at that factory, is what I was thinking.

I had to try and ignore his antics, not even lay sight on him. It was the only way. So I looked everywhere but that dance floor, my face aching from the fixed smile as my eyes roved the room.

Looking over towards the bar, I caught the eye of Ronny Jordan, Vic, Roger and a couple of the old boys. I forced my grin up another notch. Vic raised his eyebrows as if asking a question—*you okay?* I made like I was laughing at some joke and continued glazing the room with my smile.

When the song finished, Teddy came sauntering back, but I knew it was too much to expect him to ask me for the next dance. Instead, he reached for his beer and took a long glug.

"You'll have to get me another one, this one ent right," he said, passing it to me as he wiped his mouth on the back of his hand.

I had to stop myself pouring it over his head—probably wouldn't be here today if I had. Of course, I went and swapped it, bringing him back a fresh one. And we sat again in silence.

I sneaked a peek at the fellas at the other end of the bar, hoping they weren't looking our way no more. They seemed occupied, gathered in a huddle as though planning one of their work pranks. I saw Vic holding old Ronny Jordan's shoulder as he talked close to his ear, then I quickly turned away when they looked up.

"I want to go, Teddy. Can we leave, please?"

"I thought you wanted to have some fun? And I still got my drink left." He took another long glug. "I'll tell you when I'm ready."

"Scuse me, Sir," came a rusty voice. "I'm sorry to trouble yuh, but I was just wondering if I couldn't have the honour of dancing with this here lovely lady?"

I looked up to see the crooked frame of Ronny Jordan stooped in front of Teddy.

"With you?" said Teddy.

Ronny nodded politely.

"Be my guest, old boy," Teddy chuckled.

Ronny held out his hand. "Is that o'rite, Rose?"

"Of course," I said, taking it. "I'd love to."

I heard Teddy still laughing as Ronny led me hobbling over to the dance floor.

It was very sweet of him, but I have to admit, he seemed so frail I was worried he'd end up doing himself a mischief.

"I'm sorry to say I ent much of a dancer no more. Mind you, back in my day I'd been swinging yuh around like a klaxon," he said. "Anyway, those days are long gone, so you'll have to take it slow wiv me, o'rite?"

And slow it certainly was. He was the perfect gent and kept making me giggle as he talked me through his moves and harked back to his glory days.

"They used to call me Ronny the Lady Wrangler back then. They'd say if yuh didn't keep a firm hand on your lady, before y'knew it, Ronny would whisk her away to the dance floor."

"Is that right?"

"Certainly is. In fact, once word got out about my moves, they'd be queuing up outside my parent's house wanting t'know if the Wrangler was going to be at the next dance or not."

"Well, I never."

"My mother would have to come out and shoo 'em away with a wet mop, she would."

At one point, he did try to spin me under his arm, but with his hunched frame he was even smaller than me. We did manage it, but it was very much like an oil tanker turning in Blakeney harbour.

"See, you never lose it," he said with a wink afterwards.

When the song finished, I was worried Ronny would be too. He kissed my hand and said that was all he could manage. He then hobbled back to the bar, and I skipped back over to my seat and Teddy. But Teddy wasn't going to let my joy last for long.

He sat with his arms folded, leaning back in his seat, smug grin on his face, as if to say, *Ha! Is that the only person who'll dance with you? A coffin-dodging cripple.* Of course, he didn't say it. That was only my thoughts, which left me awash with guilt—was that just what I really thought?

"Don't worry," is what he did say, "I was all ready to call the ambulance." Then threw his head back and laughed.

"Scuse me, Sir," came another voice, "I'm sorry to intrude."

Teddy stopped laughing, and we looked up to see Roger the Rogue in his finest threads and a pleasant smile. "I'm sure you wouldn't have no objections if I *also* danced with the lady here?" he continued smiling as Teddy dithered. But we all knew he couldn't refuse after allowing Ronny to break the seal.

"Huh. It don't bother me none," he said, gathering himself again.

Roger took my hand and led me away. He surprised me some, being quite the dancer. He could also play the gentleman too, despite the fact he was the filthiest-mouthed rascal of the lot. As he twirled me around, I caught a fleeting glimpse of Teddy. The serving girls had all gone home, so all he could do was sulk at the side with only his beer for company. For the following three minutes, I managed to forget about him and actually enjoyed myself.

This time when I went back to him there was no smug smile or snide joke, and no sooner had I sat down and there was John from the metal-punch machine asking for the next dance. And from that point, until we left, my bum hardly touched my seat and my feet must have covered every inch of that dance floor. I must've danced with ten different blokes. It was truly magical. I felt like a princess at a ball, my heart fluttering like a thousand tiny butterflies had burst free from it. My face ached from genuine smiling this time. I could've danced right through until sunrise, even if my dress turned back to rags, my horses to mice, and I had to drive home in a pumpkin.

However, I was no fool. I knew what was to come once we left. I knew there was always the price to pay. But I didn't care, it was more than worth it. I just had to accept it in exchange for having one of the best nights of my life, is how I reasoned it.

One of my last dances was with Vic. "Thanks for this," I said to him.

"What's that?"

"This. Tonight. Thank you."

"Nothing to do with me. It just happens that you work with a bunch of blokes who know how to treat a woman properly is all."

47

~

It started as soon as we crossed the threshold. *Bam.* In the back, between the shoulders. He didn't say anything, there was no shouting, there was no swearing, no storm clouds brewing up a warning of a rough night to come, just instant thunder and lightning.

He pushed me to the ground, knocking down the wooden telephone table. Then, *Bam. Bam. Bam.*

We'd taken Hazel over to Muriel's for the night, before going to the dance, but even with her out of the house, I was still determined not to cry and scream. But when he started on me with the telephone receiver, I couldn't help myself. I was curled up on my hands and knees as he tried to get me in the stomach. I kept myself in a tight ball, so instead, I got the blows on my back. *Bam. Bam. Bam.*

Eventually, he managed to roll me onto my side. He steadied himself, leaning against the wall, panting for breath.

I looked up between my hands and hair to see if he was ready to cry and ask for forgiveness. His face was still strangely calm, hardly any emotion showing as he rubbed at his forearm.

Letting out a weary sigh, he bent down. He lifted my hair back from my face and tucked it behind my ear. He looked at me so matter-of-factly, as if he didn't recognise me, or recognise I was even human—something living, with thoughts and feelings.

He straightened up again. I heard him breathe in through his nostrils, then... *Bam. Bam. Bam.* He stamped on my shoulder, eventually pushing me flat to the ground. He picked me up onto my knees, then... *Bam. Bam. Bam.* This time stamping on my thigh.

Right in front of my face, right close to my arm, laying on the carpet was the broken leg of the telephone table. Sharp, jagged, pointed, within easy reach of my hand. But thoughts of fighting back never came into my mind.

It was the longest and severest beating I'd taken. It was the first time I feared for my life. At one point, I felt like I was drifting away. I could feel the thuds but they were more like dull echoes, as though I'd managed to shrink to the size of a thimble, curl up and hide away in the centre of my body. My body nothing more than a soft, empty shell.

48

THE DOCTOR

When I came back to the land of the living on the Sunday morning, I found myself lying in the front hall, still in my clothes. My beautiful dress ruined—ripped, bloody, and half hanging off. I threw it away.

Usually, old clothes were either fixed or torn down and saved as cleaning rags. But even though Teddy had done the hard work already, there was no question of keeping it. The gloves went too, despite the fact I'd taken them off before the beating had started. They were untouched but still soiled.

I moved slowly, as if I'd aged a hundred years overnight. My hip hurt, causing me to hobble like old Ronny. My shoulder made a strange clicking noise when I lifted my arm any higher than my chest.

The telephone was done in, and the table it sat on no better than firewood.

Blood had soaked through my dress onto the new carpet and wallpaper.

I tidied and scrubbed the evidence away as best I could. I then changed into clothes that would hide the evidence on my body and went to pick up Hazel.

Muriel made me sit and have a cup of tea after seeing me grunt and groan my way down the drive. I told her I was aching from too much dancing.

"He's got good moves ent he, my boy," she mused.

Hazel came over and hugged me. Shooting pains coursed down my spine and upper leg, and my arm hurt too much to even hold her against me.

By Monday, the stiffness and aching had got worse. I told the manager I'd had a nasty fall from my horse, so he sent me to the doctors.

The doctor examined me and told me there was nothing broken. He stuck a dressing to the wound on my side and gave me some painkillers. As he handed them to me, I noticed my palms were sweaty. I was dreading the difficult questions that were bound to come at some point. It was easy to pull the wool over other people's eyes because they never saw the bruises.

After I finished putting my clothes back on, he ushered me out and it was then I realised... the questions weren't going to come.

I was stunned. He wasn't going to say anything.

My breathing juddered and I felt my eyes beginning to well up. He was going to let me leave, scot-free. I delayed slightly, causing him to place his hand on my back as he guided me to the door. I turned to him; one final check that I was free to go— unchallenged. But it was no use, I couldn't hold back the tears anymore. I felt so alone, so abandoned.

He looked at me and sighed wearily. "You want to talk about it?"

I could only snivel into my hand.

He leaned past me and shut the door. "You didn't fall off your horse, did you?"

I shook my head as I wiped my tears away.

"Somebody did this to you, didn't they?"

I nodded.

"Your husband?"

I clasped my hands together to stop them shaking.

"This happened before?"

I nodded.

"How many times?"

I looked up. "Years."

He nodded.

"I need... I need help."

"I can't help you."

My face fell back into my hands and I buried myself in his shoulder. Why not? I just couldn't understand it. He allowed me to sob for a few moments, before gently pushing me away.

"My hair is falling out," I said. "And I'm worried, I worried for my daughter. I'm worried for myself. I don't know how much longer I can go on for."

"I'm sorry," he continued, "I can't do anything for you. Only *you* can. You need to change your situation. I can't do that for you."

I can't change my situation, I wanted to say. I was scared, scared for my life. Every time I'd tried to leave him, he bounced me about like a rag doll. And I knew he wouldn't be able to handle it if I left him. He loved me too much. This was always the hardest thing to explain to people. He was protective but not always in a jealous way, often in a... more precious way, is how I can only think to describe it. When Hazel was older, if she even wore any of my clothes, he'd go mad and try to tear them off her shouting, "They're not your clothes, their Rosie's. Take them off. How dare you."

And he never once let my mother treat me badly. In the end, I had to pretend things were okay between her and me. Even if I told him about something that happened the week before, he'd get mad and then sometimes knock *me* about. It was as though I was his prized possession that no one else could touch, but he could do what he liked with.

Walking out of that doctor's room, I'd never felt so alone and helpless. Imagining my future was too much of a scary thing. There wasn't anything there, the slope had become too steep. I'd lost my feet and was slipping further and further down and would soon run out of slope altogether. And scarier still, there wasn't anyone at the top to pull me up. The only one who really knew what was going on was my 11-year-old daughter, and I desperately didn't want her to reach out for me, as I feared I'd only end up dragging her down with me too.

I always thought I'd done right by Hazel, thought I'd protected her.

Yes, I was strict with her but I had to be. I had to do my utmost to keep her from setting Teddy off, keep her away from the edge of that slope.

The closest I ever came to standing up to Teddy was the first time he swung at her. We were watching television, and this time it was a cream-cracker. I wasn't ready, and no sooner had she crunched it than he was up and towering above her. She was more of a fighter than me and started kicking out with her legs to protect herself. I managed to throw myself in the way of his fists as he tried to bat her legs away. I landed on top of Hazel and could feel her struggling beneath me. After taking a couple of blows, I got hold of her arm and dragged her clear and shut her in the kitchen. I turned back to face him.

"This is your fault!" he was shouting as the fists rained down. "It's your fault, your fault if you get in the way!"

"You'd kill her!" I screamed back. "If you hit her like you do me, you'll bloody kill her!"

49

HER MARVELLOUS MOTHER

AGED 28 (1973)

As Hazel became a teenager, she realised that living every day with the fear of falling bombs was not normal. At the age of 12, she knew enough of the world around her to see that what we had was a one-off, that ours wasn't the normal family life that most folks lived.

And I have to be honest and say this did actually help me. I finally felt I had someone who understood my suffering at least. I didn't feel so lost and alone in the world anymore. But as always, there was the inevitable price to pay—and this one came as a complete earth-shattering bombshell, that all but obliterated me.

One day when I went to pick her up from school, her teacher came over and asked me in for a quick word. She then sent Hazel off to read a book while 'the adults have a little chat.'

She asked if everything was okay at home. My heart immediately started pounding. It was always my greatest fear that it would spill out of our nest and into the world beyond. My emotions went haywire, part of me scared, part of me feeling bad for poor Hazel, and part of me even feeling angry at her for letting on about our secret.

"So...?" the teacher said again after the silence grew too long.

My mind raced—what had she said? What had she let slip and how could I get around it? How could I explain it away? "Well, I dunno.

Why would you ask that? Is there a problem?" I said, but with a bit too much edge creeping into my voice.

"Hmm, I mean it could be nothing, but the only reason I bring it up is because it's not been the first time I've noticed."

"Noticed. Noticed what?" I didn't want to ask, I didn't want to know, but finding out was the only chance I had of covering it up.

"The bruises," she said, and then watched me carefully.

I pulled the collar of my coat up higher. I was confused. How had she seen them? I always made sure I covered up when I was out and about. My heart rate did begin to settle though, as I was well-practised at explaining these away. "Oh, I see. Well, it's cos I'm a horse rider ent it," I said with my best effort at a good-natured chuckle.

Her eyebrows narrowed. "I'm sorry...?"

"I ride... horses," I said, clutching my hands in front of my lap. This wasn't how it usually went. She hadn't responded the way most other folks did when I wheeled this one out. She knew something, I was sure of it now.

"Okay... but I don't see how that is relevant."

"Why?"

"Look. Mrs Miller, I'm just going be frank. More than once now I've seen the bruises on her."

"Her?"

"Yes, Mrs Miller. Her—your daughter."

Ka-boom.

I was shell-shocked for a good few seconds. My whole body went numb and frizzy.

"Hazel? What...?" I said, shaking my head. "No, no, no."

"So you're saying you don't know about them? You, her own mother?"

"Wh... what? No. I don't know..." And I didn't. That was the scariest thing. I didn't know.

She sighed. "I'm not a doctor, but I know enough that you don't regularly get bruises on the underside of your upper arms from falling off a horse."

I walked out of that school still in a state of shock. The best I could do was promise the teacher all was well at home and that I'd speak to Hazel and find out what was going on. I also asked if it was likely she was being bullied at school, but the teacher said that was impossible, that Hazel was the most... how did she put it—dominant personality in the class.

I couldn't speak on our way home, my head was swimming too fast. How could I have not noticed them? How could I not have noticed him doing them to her? When did he have a chance? I made sure never to leave them alone together. I mean, they played together, but I'd always be within earshot. Why had she not told me? None of it made any sense.

Once we were safely inside, I stood Hazel still and yanked off her cardy. I then rolled up the sleeves of her blouse. Raised her arms up above her head.

"My god. How did he...? When did he...?"

She didn't answer. Her eyes wide, her arm trembling in my grip.

"Hazel!" my voice was at breaking point, "Answer me! When did he do this to you?"

"He... didn't," she managed to snivel.

"Hazel! You've gotta be honest with me now. Don't be afraid," I said, trying to shake her out of it.

"He didn't do it, Mum," she said, her voice still strained but growing... almost angrier?

"What... Well... Who the hell did?"

Her eyes scrunched shut, tears rolling out of the corners.

I shook her again, "Hazel! Tell me! Who - did - this?"

She opened her eyes, dark and fierce. She looked up at me, "You. You did."

For a moment I wasn't there. I felt like the world was spinning out of control. I thought I'd gone mad. It could only be a dream—no, a nightmare. None of it made sense, none of it was real, none of it was really happening, it couldn't be. At any second, I was sure to wake up.

50

PROMISES

AGED 32 (1977)

I never once forgot the promise I made to her as a baby. In fact, I was so determined to keep it, I'd ended up losing my focus. I knew things weren't perfect for her, but selfishly, I thought I was the only one who was being hard done by.

I'd always provided for her—food, clothes, toys, without ever going over the top. I always showed her love, as did Teddy most of the time. I made her work hard without making her feel like my slave. I encouraged her to stand up for herself at school, and she was certainly more popular than I ever was and never took no nonsense from the other kids. After providing all this, I thought I only needed to protect her from the physical hurt at home and that would be enough to give her a chance at a happier childhood than what I got. But I'd been blind to what she was really going through and what it was doing to her.

I was heartbroken when she finally told me, told me of the anger she harboured. I always thought that every time I got a thumping I was saving Hazel. And thinking like this even helped me get through it, it gave me purpose and a reason for what was happening. But I'd been wrong. I'd failed her, and in so many ways.

She told me he only had to yell at her and she'd wet herself a bit. She told me that, even though she was behind a door and in a different room, she heard and felt every punch, kick and thump her mother took. She still heard every word of the shouting, the swearing, and the crying. She told me how terrified she felt in the evenings when we watched TV. How she would be playing on the carpet when suddenly I would scold her with a death stare for no reason. How she was just as afraid of me. How I hurt her. How I bruised her when I swooped down and dragged her away by the arm, then threw her into another room, discarding her, sometimes for hours, alone and crying, in the bathroom, the hallway, or worse in the darkness of the laundry cupboard.

As devastating as this was to learn, we managed to talk through a lot of things, and in the end it really helped our relationship. Helped each of us in our struggle. I realised I didn’t have to, and shouldn't try to, battle through it alone. We became a team and dealing with him became more of a game. We were in it together—working together. We'd study his face when he came home and swap glances, trying to gauge what mood he was in, like guessing the weather, trying to see if we were in for a stormy night. Finding out if we needed to batten down the hatches and see out the evening without taking too much damage.

It wasn’t long after that chat that I started to let Hazel go out in the evenings. The way I figured it was, I had no need for a personal housemaid and the less time she was in the house of falling bombs the better.

When she was 15, she started courting a boy named Paul. My family and friends couldn't understand why I let a girl her age get so serious with a fella, and I know others talked about it behind my back. I didn't care this time, as I knew the way I wanted to bring up my daughter. I didn't want her running around with no gangs. Often there was nothing worse, nothing crueller than a gang of kids. Even the nicest of kids could get swayed by the mind of the mob, doing things they shouldn’t, or wouldn't usually, just to fit in and be a part of it all. At least with Paul, I knew who she was with and he always brought her back right to the front door at whatever time I told him. She was never crawling along neighbours' hedges or waiting in dark woods or making secret pacts with people so they’d be her alibi.

He was a good lad, him and me always got on well. One day, he even came over and asked if he couldn't come live with us because he wasn't getting on so well with his step-mum. I told him, as much as I wanted to help out, I had to think of my daughter first and it would be too much to have them living together so young. However, I did let him stay round occasionally at weekends. But before I allowed this, I thought it best to take Hazel to see the Doctor and get her put on the contraceptive pill. I didn't want her to make the same mistake as me and get trapped before she'd learnt enough about life and people.

I'll admit I was a little worried at what he'd say. I half expected him to go up the wall when I told him she was but 15. He was very professional about it and didn't say anything until we were about to leave, then he stopped and sighed. Taking off his glasses and rubbing the bridge of his nose, he finally spoke his mind.

"I'll tell you something now," he began, "I wish more mothers were like you. Facing the truth and being sensible. Not even a week gone by, we had a girl of twelve in. For an abortion. Twelve." He turned away, shaking his head. "I don't think she'll ever get over it."

51

BONFIRE NIGHT

Bonfire night was always the biggest event of the year out our way. Something to get excited about as the winter weather settled in. It always seemed so much more than just one night as well. Most families would start the fireworks a few days early and were always finding leftovers to continue for a while after.

It may sound strange or may even be wrong, but I found it comforting lying in bed hearing the dull boom of fireworks going off all weekend. I'd imagine I was in London during The Blitz with danger all around me that could strike at any moment, even while I slept. I'd huddle inside my eiderdown quilt, tucking it under my feet and over my head. Completely cocooned, I would feel safe, like nothing could touch me even if my house took a direct hit.

The biggest bonfire was traditionally at Corpusty—and still is to this day, I believe. Bales of straw, old broken pallets and autumn tree cuttings would be piled high and set ablaze. The heat from the fire always amazed me. You couldn't get within twenty feet of it without feeling your face was slowly wrinkling and scrunching up like when you put a crisp packet on the living room fire.

Every year, you wondered what the firework display would be like, always thinking to yourself, well, once you seen one you've seen them all, but every year it seemed to get bigger and better and louder and longer. I guess with a year gone by between each one it was hard to really tell, so most of it was all in your head.

Nevertheless, everybody from the surrounding towns would be there. You'd walk amongst the crowd of silhouetted figures and every now and then a familiar face would pop out of the darkness, all tucked up in a scarf and hat.

There was always plenty for the kids to do, from horse and cart rides to apple bobbing. I think I sometimes looked forward to bonfire night more than Christmas, if I'm honest. Christmas was a cosier family affair, which is fine—depending on your family, of course, whereas bonfire night was one big happy time that left nobody out. There was always plenty of drinking to be done to ward off the cold, and wherever you went the whole town was full of smiling rosy-cheeked faces.

It was a bonfire night that got Wendy and me back together after a long time apart. I was worried things might be awkward like they sometimes could be, but I let Work-Rosemary do most of the talking and we soon clicked back into gear.

After the fireworks, the crowd began to drift away from the fire, which was no more than a glowering mound that spat crackling sparks high into the sky until they faded into the endless blackness above.

We nattered away for a good while, Wendy hugging herself against the cold and trying to hide the chattering of her teeth. I told her to come snuggle up to me and take warmth in my mink fur coat.

"Hang on," she said, cocking her head at an angle. "Ent you still one of those vegetarian people?"

"Yeah, going on... cor, seventeen years now," I said proudly.

"So... the coat?"

"Well, I didn't eat them."

"No, but they still had to die, dint they?"

"I guess. I never really thought about it that much. Do you think...?"

Wendy shrugged. "Dunt matter none to me. Nobody's perfect, right?"

I know that nowadays it's much more of a big thing, but back then it really wasn't, and after all, we happily trosh around in leather shoes with a leather handbag over our shoulder—and that sure doesn't grow on trees. It was also devilishly cold and I loved that coat so much. It wasn't just cos it made me feel warm and safe; it did other things too. No small part was because I'd worked damned hard to afford it, so it made me proud, showed what I could do for myself. And on the outside, it showed people I wasn't just this worthless and neglected thing that belonged to my husband.

It was long and white with a thick collar. When I bowed my head, my face would sink into the soft downy fur and it would gently tickle the underside of my chin. I'd wear my long black hair down the back, knowing full well the striking contrast it made against the pure white.

I'll admit, I was a little worried about the muddy field though and had to keep checking it wasn't getting splashed with dirt from the kids as they whizzed about with their sparklers.

"If it weren't so cold, I think I could fall asleep stood up, don't you think so?" Wendy purred as she brushed her face deeper into my neck.

"Come on then," I said, "let's go warm up in the pub and see if we can't get a drink out of Teddy."

Wendy looked around at the large swaths of people that were starting to wander back into town. "You think we'll be able to find him?"

"Oh yeah, don't you worry about that."

The low-ceilinged pub was crammed full, many folks still in their coats and gloves. It was probably the pub's busiest night of the year, I should think. People were calling to each other over the sea of heads. Drinks were being passed back from the bar through the forest of bodies, cheers going up if anyone spilled some as they went.

They had a dance hall out the back and since I hadn't heard him yet, I knew that's where he'd likely be. Wendy held my hand as we weaved and bumped our way through.

If there had been any music it had recently finished. It was still busy, but there was at least room to breathe. Most folks were gathered about the long tables rowed along each side. I had a little scan before going down the steps into the hall—but still no sight or sound of him.

Even though you had to go down the steps, the ceiling was higher in there, so it was roomier than the main pub. And therefore, when it started, there was not a soul in there that it didn't cut straight through. The background noise of happy chatter was immediately pierced.

"Nooooo! Let go of me!"

All heads turned to the far end of the room.

"Nooooo!" More panicked than angry and clearly the scream of a girl in distress.

Being smaller than most, I couldn't see, but I followed everybody else's gaze to the far end. As people nervously shuffled away from the commotion, a path began to open up. I wasn't the slightest bit surprised to see what was the cause.

He had her up against a wall, leaning over her, one arm outstretched, bracing himself. She was cowering. Head turned away, arms in front of her.

Nobody looked like they wanted to do anything. Most were pretending they hadn't even noticed and had turned back to their conversations—though still couldn't resist a quick shifty over their shoulders.

I didn't even stop to think. I didn't need to. I marched straight over.

"For God's sake, whatever are you doing to her? Leave the poor girl alone," said Work-Rosemary.

I saw the girl's frightened eyes look to me from under his outstretched arm. Teddy carried on as if he hadn't heard. "I told yuh. Dint I," he hissed. "You're just making a scene now."

"Teddy!"

And still he didn't react.

"Teddy! I'm talking to you."

Nothing. It was as if I didn't exist at all. All I could do was pull at the arm he was using to lean against the wall. And still nothing. I pulled harder, this time causing him to stumble forward and spill most of his pint.

His movement was slow and hazy as he first looked down at the floor, then to the large wet splotches down the front of his trousers, then back up to me. His eyes bloodshot. The venom burning deep within.

"...Teddy?" I managed to say before his arm shot out.

Striking like a snake, he grabbed my hair. He yanked my head back. I was looking at the dusty wooden beams for a second, but they quickly became a blur as he brought my head down onto the table with an almighty crash. He pulled me up and banged it down once more, then dragged me along its entire length, as if using me as a cloth to wipe it clean.

Everything on the table crashed and cascaded to the floor. When we reached the end, he dumped me onto the ground. Discarding me amongst the upturned ashtrays and broken glasses.

I should have known better. There's no such thing as a tamed tiger. Why I thought I'd get away with poking it, heaven knows. Maybe the drink had made me bold, maybe being in a public place had, or maybe it was not wanting to lose all those years of Wendy's misplaced faith in me. Anyway, I should've known better.

It all happened so quickly, there was nothing I could've done once I'd started it. There was only a blur as the dance hall was turned upside down, then the smashing of glass, then finding myself dazed and numb lying on the floor. At first, everything seemed to go silent and still. All I could see were people's legs slowly backing away.

I felt embarrassed, floundering about on the muddy floor in my glamorous fur coat. I tried to stagger to my feet. Wendy was staring, mouth agape. The tear-strewn girl Teddy had been bothering, stooped and with a trembling hand hooked me by my arm and helped me up. I saw her mouth moving but I wasn't hearing any words yet. I felt groggy and slow, as if I'd woken up in a dream. I stumbled slightly and reached out for the table. The drink-stained tablecloth was half hanging off and I nearly slipped back down with a jolt.

Then the sound faded back up and I heard the screaming.

It came from behind me. Like a steam train screeching out of a tunnel. It was piercing, like metal wheels scraping along metal tracks and as sharp as the jagged glass that littered the table and floor.

I turned to be met by a sea of shocked faces. Some holding hands over their mouths, others over their eyes, one or two staring at my legs.

A warm tingle shivered down my neck, down my spine, down the inside of my thigh. At first, I thought I'd wet myself, but then I saw the thick line of red running out from beneath my coat, down my calves and into my shoes.

I reached up to the back of my head, to the wet feeling growing heavier and heavier in my hair. Instead of something wet and soft, I found something hard and cold. I pulled it free to the gasps of the onlookers. The wetness became thicker and warmer as the blood flowed more freely, following the course of my long hair, streaking a dark crimson path down the back of my white coat. Wendy later described it as looking like I'd been cleaved almost in half with an axe.

I took two unsteady steps forward, trying to escape the pool collecting on the floor, but the blood trailed me, leaving red smeared footprints.

Where Teddy was or what he was doing, I don't know, as things quickly became a blur again. I only remember a few brief flashes. People stepping forward, hands on my shoulders, guiding me. A broad-shouldered man trying to clear a path through the pub. People pushing back at him until they saw the crimson, then the sea parting, suddenly everyone managing to find enough room. People staring. People jostling for a better look. People talking behind their hands as the pitiful and bloodied creature was led outside.

I remember the sudden change of temperature as my coat was stripped from me, like an animal being skinned. I tried to resist but was too weak. I felt cold and exposed and the pain started to become real as the initial shock began to wear off.

It started to hit home that I'd been badly hurt. That everyone was worried for me. That I was in need of care. That I needed to be helped.

A folded woollen jumper was pressed to the back of my head to help slow the bleeding. I was put into the back of a car, then silence as the door shut behind me. Dark forms of trees rushing past the window. Hands reaching into the car and then the bright lights and whiteness of the hospital.

Things started to come back once the doctor was in front of me, speaking to me slow and calm asking what happened.

"There was a fight, I... I got in the way. I slipped over. My own fault really," I found myself saying automatically.

Teddy was there. He looked beside himself with worry. Tears in his eyes. His lips mumbling and gibbering, like he was saying a frantic prayer.

"You've still got a fair bit of glass in your head," the doctor said as he peered over me.

I barely felt the dull touch of his hands as he parted my hair. There was little more than a brief tug as he took out the bigger shards.

"There we go, you're a brave girl," he cooed as he dropped the pieces into a metal kidney-shaped bowl. Then he paused, his hands still amongst my matted hair.

"Are you okay?" he asked, sounding a bit more concerned all of a sudden.

I was about to answer, then realised he wasn't talking to me. He was facing Teddy. Teddy's face was green and his head wavered as his neck went to jelly. Without answering he turned, stumbled, made it halfway out of the door before collapsing and taking the tall metal pedal bin with him.

"Nurse! Nurse!" the doctor bellowed.

52

GOING BACK

Teddy was mortified with what he'd done. He swore he would never touch a hair on my head again, he'd never raise a fist to me, he'd never even swear at me—is what he said. I wanted to believe him so badly, and that's why I gave him another chance. And this time he was good to his word... for two weeks at least.

People have said to me, why didn't you get out of there? Why did you put up with it for so long? You can't continue in a relationship like that and survive—surely you'd been better off without him? You had nothing to lose by leaving him.

The problem is that the worse it gets the more you shrink and hide, trying to protect yourself, protect the only good things you do have going for you. The good things become more and more valuable. The risk of losing them becomes scarier and something more real. And the longer it goes on, the more there is to lose.

In the end, it wasn't a beating that did it for me. It wasn't catching him messing around with some floozy. It wasn't someone's wise piece of advice. It wasn't anything. It was just a Tuesday like no other.

I was sat in my office. The bruises from my latest beating nearly faded—no more than pale yellow splotches. I'd just inspected a job.

The fella had left and was not best pleased that it needed a few more tweaks to pass. But I told him straight and so he'd accepted it.

I looked up at the clock and saw I had five minutes until the lunch hooter. I never usually had a spare moment at work, I made sure of that. But I was tired and thought, *sod it, I'm gonna sit here and do nothing until that klaxon calls me. I'm good at my job and I've earned this five minutes of sitting here doing nothing for once.*

I leant back in my chair and stared up at the ceiling. 32 years old, I remember thinking, 32 years old and look at me. How was this going to end? Could I keep going on like this for the rest of my life? The uncertainty... the secrets... the Jekyll and Hyde existence? At work a somebody, at home a nobody. I was damn good at my job. A job I got all by myself. No one helped me get it. And I earned my own money. I bought my own things. I paid for everything. But then there was everything else. So how did it all balance out in the end? What was I? A success? A failure? Something in between? Or was I just a shameful old fool. I'd escaped my mother's clutches only to fall into Teddy's. *If you fool me twice*... isn't that what they say.

32 years old. I still had at least half a lifetime ahead of me. This got me thinking all the way back to my earliest memory of being 3 years old in that small hospital in Cromer and having to learn to walk for the second time in my life, even after being told I might never be able to again. Maybe it was because I was so young and naive that it didn't bother me, that I didn't stop to think or question things before climbing the mountain a second time. But if 3-year-old me could do it, then why the heck couldn't 32-year-old me. I would be the stupidest person alive if I didn't grit my teeth and take those first steps and learn to walk all over again and scale another mountain. Ain't nobody else was gonna do it for me, it was my life, my future, my decision.

"Edward Douglas Miller," I said out loud, "you don't own me, and I don't owe you. We are finished. I am leaving you."

~

I told her straight out. I told her I was leaving Teddy because he'd been mistreating me, and then I asked if I could stay with them for a while.

"You wouldn't listen to me, would yuh?" were her first words. "Your own mum. Told you he was no good, dint I?" She could barely hide it. For so long she'd put up with the verbals from Teddy and the embarrassment of him talking down to her and now finally she felt like she'd won.

"Well, I know now. I made a mistake."

"Well, I knew it from the beginning." She dried her hands on a dishcloth and lent back against the sink. "And now your chickens have come home to roost, hent they," she said folding her arms.

My chickens...

Even in my darkest hour, she had no empathy, couldn't see me as a victim. Always the enemy, always at fault. But I couldn't even get angry with her anymore. I'd already conquered that mountain. I saw her for what she was now, and I pitied her and her twisted ways of thinking. But if it made her happy, made her tick, then so be it. More pity her.

Something that did worry me though, was that the warped way her mind worked was something I had too. I had to stop myself from biting back and telling her that she hadn't won, that actually, me crawling back with my tail between my legs was *her* defeat. They'd each had me for equal halves of my life, both seemingly hell-bent on wearing me down and destroying me. But after all was said and done, I'd come back to her—the lesser of two evils. She didn't hold the fear over me no more, not after living through Teddy's reign. I wasn't afraid of the dark, and that's all she was. Whereas he was the monsters that hid in the darkness.

I held her gaze. "So, is it gonna be okay for me to stay here or not?"

"Well, I s'pose we got room. I s'pose you got no other choice. But—"

"I can always stay with Wendy if it's a problem."

"No, no, no," she said, stepping forward from the sink. "You'll stay here, what'd people think? Not staying with your own mother in your time of need." She lowered herself into a chair at the kitchen table as if it were some great effort. "Mind, we still gotta okay it with your father," she sighed. "We'll just have to hope he's in a good mood is all."

I rolled my eyes and left the kitchen to fetch my bags.

Dad knew something was up as soon as he walked in. He didn't say anything, he just waited.

"Rosemary's got something to ask you. She's only gone and—"

I butted in. "Dad, is it okay if I come live here again, please?"

"Of course, don't need to ask." Then, like always, he went to pick up the paper from the table.

We waited as he opened it and shook it straight. Mum and me must have been thinking the same thing, cos at the same time we looked to each other before turning back to him.

Then finally he spoke, "You left him then?"

"Yeah."

"Thank God for that," he replied. "He's no man."

"What? What d'you mean?"

Dad had never once offered his thoughts on Teddy before.

"Laying hands on a woman," he said, shaking his head. "Coward."

"You... knew?" I couldn't believe it. I was speechless. My face began burning up, but whether more from embarrassment or anger, I couldn't say.

"Don't you think someone said something, him knocking you about in the pub like that?"

"Then... why..." I swallowed. "Why did you never say anything before?"

He cocked his head to the side as he gave it further thought. "Cos you never did."

What do you say to this? What do you think to this? In some ways there was a weird feeling of relief that I hadn't been alone all that time, but what did that matter now? There was the shame too, that people had known my secret all that time. And worst yet, there was the hurt that nobody had lifted a finger to help. It really seemed that back in those days it was some kind of taboo to interfere with a couple's affairs. I couldn't help thinking, what if he had really done me in? What would they all be left feeling then, after none of them did anything?

It was Dad who spoke next. “I figured if you wanted us to know, you'd tell us. And if you wanted help, you’d ask us. Simple as that, ent it.”

If only. But I had to believe he believed that.

After that day, I assumed that everyone knew. That my private business was all over town. Which only made me wonder, did my brothers know? Five brothers and not one of them had done a thing about it. I knew in my heart of hearts that my dad and my brothers loved me, but why? Were they scared of Teddy too? The closest anyone came to standing up to Teddy was, of all people, my mother, and she still came off second best though.

53

MY BIRTHDAY

AGED 33 (1978)

Hazel and me had to share a bed in the small room at my parents' house. There wasn't much space for the both of us, so we could only bring a few of our things. This meant there were times when Hazel would have to go back to the bungalow to pick stuff up as we needed it.

The first time, I was worried Teddy might do something, might take it out on her. Might even keep her hostage to try and make me come back. But Hazel said it would be fine. She had that same confidence as him. When she said something, you knew she really believed it, so therefore, you couldn't help but to go along with it without question. However, an hour after she left, I started to feel different and I was in two minds whether to phone the bungalow or go down there myself. I left it another ten minutes but couldn't bear it any longer and phoned. It rang for some time, letting me fear the worst. Half of me desperately wanted to hang up as soon as possible, but my worry for Hazel saw me through.

"Yes," he answered irritably. "It's Teddy. What d'you want?"

I was relieved to hear the grumpiness in his voice, rather than anger or tears.

"Teddy... it's—"

"Rosemary! You're coming back?" he said, instantly perking up. I could almost hear the sparkle in his eyes. "Please, Rosemary, you can't leave me like this."

"If I came back, you'll end up killing me. Now, is Hazel there?"

"I won't, I promise. I can change, you know I can."

"Hazel please. I want to speak to her."

"Come over tonight and let's talk about this."

"Just let me speak to Hazel."

"She's cooking me dinner at the moment. Come over and eat it with us, just like a family should."

I politely and firmly insisted until she came to the phone. She told me she was going to cook dinner and pack his lunch for the next day, then leave. I should've hung up as soon as I said bye to her, but Teddy grabbed the phone back.

"I'm gonna pick you up when you finish work tomorrow."

"No." I could feel the receiver becoming clammy in my hand. "No, Teddy, that's not okay."

"Alright, I'll come into your work and see you then. You prefer that?"

"No."

"Right, so I'll see you at five then."

All day it was preying on my mind, and my mind was praying he'd forgotten. When the clock struck five, I rushed out into the car park, hoping I could get rid of him before the rest had washed their hands and come out.

But there he was, sat in his car. His thick hairy arm resting out of the window.

"Come on then, let's go for a drive."

I shook my head.

"Please, Rosemary. Just to talk."

"I can't."

"Don't be silly, just get in."

"I'm not getting in." Be strong Rose, be strong like Work-

Rosemary, I was telling myself, that's who you are—that's who you really are.

"I ent gonna ask again." He closed his eyes for a moment, took a breath and then looked back at me. "Please, Rose. I don't want to get angry. I don't want to make a scene." I saw him look past me for a moment.

I turned to see a few figures coming out of the workshop, chatting as they made their way towards the car park.

He looked back to me. "Well, what's it to be?"

And so I got in the car.

Once we were on the road, his mood changed. He was upset and saying nice things, telling me he couldn't manage without me.

"Get a housekeeper then," I told him.

"I don't mean to look after me, I could get anyone to do that. It's you, I can't live without you."

We drove around the country lanes for close to an hour. I mostly listened to him making promises and telling me how much he loved me, but I knew I couldn't allow myself to entertain his words. Occasionally, he rested his hand on my thigh. I could feel the warmth of his strong fingers; it still felt normal and natural.

Soon the petrol started running low. I told him I had to be back to make dinner for the family and made him drop me off around the corner from my parent's house.

"Just like old times, eh?" he said.

As I was getting out he pushed down on my shoulder. This time his touch caught me off guard and I flinched. I looked back at him and he looked hurt.

"Sorry. I just... I just wanted to ask if you could do this for me?" he said, reaching for a bag of laundry. At first, I thought it was one of his jokes. He looked so pathetic, like a kid asking to have his laces tied—so I took it.

Of course, he was phoning me the next day saying we had to meet again so he could pick it up. I told him it hadn't dried yet and I'd let him know. Instead, I sent it with Hazel the next time she went to fetch some clothes and cook for him.

I made a rule to myself not to take anything else from him. Having rules helped, made things more concrete, easier for us to understand, I thought. I was doing well. I was making decisions. I was being strong. He'd tried it on and failed. He'd learn.

The following day, I was in town after work, having just picked up some groceries. I was walking back to the bus stop when my arm was gripped tightly from behind.

"Next time," he said, pressing his mouth right up against my ear, "if you say you're gonna meet me, you better bloody well meet me."

I tried to hurry away from him, but his grip was too tight and he matched my pace. The both of us were locked, hurrying along the pavement as if we were just in a rush not to miss the start of a movie.

"You want me to come see you at work, is that it?" he said in a harsh whisper between gritted teeth. "Is that what you're wanting?"

His arm moved quickly in front of him, striking my midriff and then my hip. We passed by an old couple coming from the other direction; he stopped his swearing and I looked away.

I saw my bus come to a stop ahead of us. A few people already waiting. I slowed, bending as though the pain had doubled me, then I suddenly pulled free and dashed over the road, hoping he wouldn't chase me down in public. He stayed. Watching until I got on the bus.

Leaving him hadn't solved all that much. He kept finding me and he kept knocking me about. He started to blackmail me into meeting him, and I daren't not be there in case he came good on his threats to come into my work. Deep down I suspected he wouldn't, not with all those blokes there, not after the way they'd stood up for me at the Christmas Dance—but I still wasn't willing to risk it.

When my birthday came around, as usual, I wasn't in no mood to make a big song and dance about it. In fact, I didn't even tell anyone who hadn't already remembered. I booked a day off and made plans to meet Wendy for tea and cakes. Mum left early in the morning without so much as a note, but I was glad to have the house to myself and took my time getting ready. I turned up the wireless and ran a long bath. Afterwards, I laid out the few clothes I had there so I could best select my outfit for the day. What with the wireless blaring and my god-awful singing, I didn't hear the car.

I saw the movement of a figure through the net curtains and thought it was just the postman. But then came a fast and firm knock. As it was the daytime, a weekday, and no one knew I wasn't at work, I didn't think for a second about checking who it might before I opened the door.

"What the hell are you doing?" he said, looking me up and down. The anger in his eyes already lit.

"How d'you know I wasn't at work?"

"Who are you seeing?" He pushed his way inside and stuck his head around the corner.

"Teddy, pleas. What's going on?" I said, following up behind him. "Why ent you at work?"

"I ent gonna ask a third time. Who are you seeing?" He stepped right up close to me.

"Wendy. I'm going out for lunch with Wendy."

"What, dressed like that? Don't give me that crap. Who is he?" he said with specks of spittle firing into my face. "Well?"

"No one. Wendy. I'm going—"

"You're lying." His lips began to curl and he drew breath in through his nose.

"Teddy, no. Don't you dare. Not today."

Then... in his eyes, there was a faint flicker of light blinking through the red mist.

"Not today, Teddy. Not on my birthday."

His brow narrowed. He looked down and realised he was gripping my upper arm. I felt it loosen. He stopped. For the first time, *I'd* stopped it—stopped his anger.

He studied my eyes, trying to work out if I was telling the truth. Then looked my dress up and down. The tension in his shoulders broke and he let his hand fall.

"I wasn't. I wouldn't- I wouldn't do that. Not on your birthday, you know that?"

Huh! At least there's *one thing* he wouldn't do on my birthday, I thought.

"Well, I should take you out for a pub meal then," he said, as he re-straightened the collar of my dress.

"I've arranged to meet Wendy."

"In the evening. I'll pick you up."

"No, Teddy. I don't want to do anything. I just want to go and have tea and cakes with my friend and that's it."

"But it's your birthday. You saying I can't do anything for you on your own birthday?"

"You didn't even know it was my birthday 'til I told you."

"Yeah, but I know it now, don't I."

I told him I had to leave, but he kept blocking my path, kept trying to persuade me. I didn't let his words in and kept repeating that I was going to meet Wendy. Eventually, we got to the backdoor and I managed to push past him. But before I was halfway up the garden I was yanked back by the ribbon in my hair and the fists were flying.

54

A PROBLEM SHARED...

AGED 34 (1979)

Hazel had started spending more nights per week at the bungalow than with me at my parent's house. She said she preferred to be with me, but it was too much living in a tiny room with your mum, especially since she was courting.

Even though I wasn't living with him, it still seemed like we saw each other just as much. There was always an excuse, a threat or demand, and I'd be there at his beck and call. My moment of clarity had been nothing more than a muddy puddle in disguise, and every time I looked into it there was my sorry tear-stained reflection staring back. I really didn't know what to do. There was no way out. I used to dread finishing work, never knowing whether he'd be waiting for me. I started leaving through the back, but it wasn't long before he started waiting down the road instead.

One such afternoon, he came and took me away in his car, but this time he was all quiet. There was none of his hijinks followed by promises he'd changed, or no angry accusations and thumps on the thigh. I thought maybe he'd accepted it, that even though he knew he could control me, I wasn't ever going back to him.

Eventually I spoke, thinking I could speed things along, get him started and get it finished for the day. "Teddy, we can't keep doing this. This isn't helping either of us, is it?"

"Please, Rosemary, just come back, please. I promise everything will go back to like it used to be."

"That's exactly why I can't."

"I meant... before. When it was good. The good times."

"The good times? Were there good times? Teddy, I hardly remember anymore."

"I'm only asking for one last chance."

"You've had all of your one-last-chances and you've never took a single one of them."

There was no reply. Even the man who had an answer for everything couldn't deny the truth of this.

"What are you doing with your money?" he asked instead.

"Saving it."

"Why?"

"Cos that's what you do with money."

"And then what?"

"I dunno..."

"You gonna meet someone else, aren't you?" His voice was beginning to waver. "You'll meet some other fella, won't you?"

"No. Not for a long time yet. I need some time without a man."

"You will. You'll meet someone else and then you'll realise." He wiped at the bottom of his eyes with the back of his hand. "You'll realise just how bad I've been to you." He'd started to sob. "You'll never want to see me again. You'll forget all about me."

I don't know how he did it, or whether it was all just me and my soft heart, but it was the same as when you see a helpless, tearful child. I couldn't help it. I felt so sorry for him. I wanted to make things better for him. It was so hard having to always remind myself what he'd done to us.

I couldn't think how to reply. I knew I couldn't give him the foothold he was seeking, but at the same time I didn't have it in me to twist the knife and tell him he was right. So I said nothing.

All was quiet apart from the hum of the engine and the air rushing in from the window.

I noticed he was staring at me.

"You can't even talk to me now?"

"There's nothing to be said. Please, just take me home."

Still, he was looking at me.

There was a scrape of stones and a bump.

I braced my hand on the dashboard and saw the grass verge all too close to my window. I quickly looked to Teddy. He glanced forward for a second as he corrected the steering wheel.

"Teddy. Please. Look where you're going."

He blinked slowly, staring at me, blank-faced.

"Teddy, I'm serious. Please. You'll crash."

"So."

"So—you'll kill us."

"Good."

"Don't say that."

"Why? I mean it."

"Don't be stupid."

"If I can't have you, then what's the point in going on? If you're gonna go off with some other fella, what's the point."

I couldn't keep my eyes off the road, as if I could somehow make up for him not paying attention.

"Teddy. There's a corner."

He looked forward to take it.

"I'm gonna do it," he said flat and calm. "I'm gonna kill us. I'm gonna drive us into a wall and stop us both from suffering."

I was petrified. He'd made threats before but always in anger, never in such a cold, calm manner.

"Stop the car!"

"No."

He gradually pressed his foot down on the accelerator. The road began disappearing beneath the car, faster and faster. The hedges grew blurrier and blurrier. Air from the window rushing in—cold against my skin.

"Teddy..."

Ahead, the road bent to the right before ending at a t-junction where an old squat oak tree sat bang in front of us.

I studied his face. He was staring blankly ahead. The car still gathering speed. I looked to the door handle, but we were going too fast already.

Any doubts he was serious evaporated when I next looked up.

There was no way we could stop in time. There was nowhere to go. We were going to crash.

You always hear that time slows down when faced with death, and it was true for me. So many thoughts were able to flash through my mind, each one clear as day. I thought about Hazel, imagined some doctor or policeman telling her the news that both her parents were dead. I thought about my brother, Billy, in London, he'd have to come back for my funeral. Then from somewhere, I thought about Aunt Sylvie, even though I hadn't thought about her in years. I'd always clung to the idea that one day I'd make the effort to go and see her—would she ever know I'd died? I thought about my horse, Silver—who would look after her, where would she go, would Hazel take her on? I thought about Wendy. I thought about Matron. I thought about how guilty Tracey would feel hearing the news. I thought about Teddy as though he was someone different, not the person sat next to me trying to kill me. I thought about the past Teddy, a young, good-looking, smart-mouthed patient at the hospital. A dream guy, like a movie star. A guy I could never have dreamt of marrying. I remembered how lucky I was, the envy of all the other girls. Teddy and Rosie. There goes Rosie, being taken out to the pictures by her older boyfriend with a car. Drives out to the lake. I thought about the times when he stood up to my mum and gave her what for. When I had to show him how to unblock sinks and gutters, and how impressed he'd been with me. Then the times he'd hit me, kicked me, swore at me, cheated on me, lied to me. Ruined me.

These thoughts all occurred in a matter of seconds, but they made me feel weary, made me feel tired of life and its constant ups and downs and false hopes. I'm ashamed to admit it, but for a brief second, I almost felt ready to hit that tree. But maybe I was just accepting it because I had no choice, and that's what I always did.

"Take me back." A voice edged with panic cut through my

thoughts. I returned to my body, returned to the car, not ready to die just yet.

His knuckles were white from gripping the wheel. His arms locked straight. His mouth began to twitch. He started to shy his head away, readying for the impact.

“No,” I answered.

He scrunched up his face and he let out a coarse and pitiful wail. The tree loomed large, filling the windscreen. He stamped down on the brake. But it was too late.

Screaming, he yanked at the steering wheel. One way, then the next —sending me slamming into the door. The tyres screeched and the car began to slide. We hit the low grass verge with an almighty bang and cannoned through the hedge, glass shattering, then a moment of darkness before bursting through into the light of the wheat field beyond.

We didn't speak as we drove home in his scratched and battered car. When he dropped me off I could barely open the car door, it was so bent out of shape. My hands were shaking so much it didn’t make things any easier. I wasn't yet in tears, but I was finding it difficult to catch my breath, my chest juddering and jittering with every try. I wanted to get out as quick as I could but I didn't have control of my body; it wasn't able to keep up with what my head was telling it to do.

Teddy was silent. He didn't react. He didn't look at me, just stared out of the glassless windscreen.

When my foot stepped onto the road, it felt harder and more solid than I'd ever remembered. It reminded me of the only time I'd been on a boat and how reassuring it was to finally step back onto the wooden jetty.

I was just about out of the car when he spoke. He was still staring out of where the windscreen should’ve been.

“Maybe,” he said, “I'll do it now. By myself.”

I didn't answer. I didn’t even look at him, because in that moment I didn't care, and for a brief, shameful second I wanted him to, I wanted him to end our problems.

55

GOING BACK

I warned Hazel. I told her she had to stay with me all the time, that something had changed, that things could get dangerous for her. But she said she was fine, that she could handle him. She said that she knew he was very far from perfect, but he was her dad and that still meant something. Said that he needed her, that she was worried he couldn't handle losing both of us, it would be too much. It left me worried sick the whole time, but there wasn't much I could do once she had her mind set to something.

As for me, I stopped answering the phone and my parents would hang up if it was him. I'd stay late at work just so I finished at different times. I started wearing hats and old clothes he wouldn't recognise when I went around town, and as much as possible made sure I wasn't ever alone. This worked well for a time, but I realised it wasn't a long-term fix.

When Perry and his wife Karen came down from Mansfield to stay in Norfolk for a couple of weeks, they insisted on taking me out, saying I couldn't let him make me a prisoner in my own home. When they took me to the pub, we'd have to check for his motor first. Even if we didn't see it, there was still the fear that he'd recently swapped it.

But luckily, he was mostly a creature of habit and stuck to the same places.

There was one time we went right out of our way to go to a pub he wouldn't be at, but lo and bloody behold there sat the red Triumph he drove at the time. I started having what must've been a panic attack. My breathing went haywire, I started babbling and my whole body was trembling. And so we had to go home. Yet another night out spoiled by old Rosemary the ruiner. Instead, we spent the evening at home drinking tea and eating biscuits.

"Come and stay with us for a while," Karen said. "You can't live like this."

But I refused her. I had my girl, my job, and my horse to think about.

"Y'know he come speak to me yisty," Perry said as he slowly stirred his tea.

Just for a second, I wondered whether that's how he'd known what pub we were going to. Somehow, he had an uncanny knack of not just finding me, but being in places before I even got there. However, I quickly shook this stupid thought out of my head. Not my own brother, surely.

"He knows he's been bad to you," he continued. "He was right honest, saying how he sees why you won't forgive him. He says he could change, that he's realised now how bad he's been. He said that—"

"What are you trying to say?" Karen cut him off, suddenly sitting forward.

"Well, nothing..." Perry said, "I just... just promised I'd say to her what he said to me. He does seem ever so sorry y'know."

Teddy's emotions were always so raw that when he was upset you could see it was real, you could see his suffering, see he was laying himself bare. And even though it was considered unmanly in those times, Teddy never cared, and other fellas seemed envious... or even impressed that he could show his true feelings like that with no shame. Either that, or you'd look on him like a lost child in need of help, which is something too hard to ignore. It just ent natural to be cold to someone who is suffering like that before your very eyes. And then of course there was his charm. It was honestly like he could hypnotise people, make them think completely different, control their thoughts even. But what others didn't see was how it happened with all his emotions, with the anger, the rage, and the lust. And he couldn't control them, they controlled him—he was their slave.

In too many ways, Hazel reminded me of him. She'd definitely picked up his stubbornness and strong will. Unfortunately, I could also recognise his rage in her too, which was another reason I wasn't keen on them living together. Sometimes I had to stop myself thinking about it because it caused me to have confusing thoughts. Was that really the only reason I wanted them apart? Or was I really worried that she might start to side with him and turn against me? I'd try and convince myself it was only her safety I cared about, and that was more than a good enough reason to try and get her out of there. But he was her father and they shared the same blood—which was something I had to answer for. Of all people, I knew I had no right in telling her what she could and couldn't do. I wanted to protect her—not control her.

I guess Perry said something to Dad about my panic attack. He came home from work the next day, washed his hands and said he was going to drive me to the bungalow. He loaded up the car with empty boxes and sacks and told me we were going to pick up every last bit of my stuff. Then there'd be no reason or excuses for him to try and get me over there anymore. There'd be nothing left to remind him of me. It would show him I was gone for good.

Dad had his surprising moments. Just because he was quiet and browbeaten, it didn't mean he was stupid or didn't care. But to be honest, I wasn't sure about his idea at first. The last thing I wanted to do was to go to that house, but it did seem to make sense to draw a line under it, show him it was over—forever.

We drove in silence. I recited nursery rhymes in my head to keep my panic controlled. But as soon as we turned down the road leading to our old bungalow, a surge welled up inside. My hands became clammy and my heart started racing.

"It's okay Rosie, he ent gonna hurt yuh."

"I can't do this," I said, clutching at the lap of my dress.

"Yes, you can."

We arrived. His red car was in the drive.

I looked to Dad. He nodded slowly and got out.

I stood behind him as he knocked on the door. But then he took a step back so we were side by side. I felt like I was at school and was waiting outside the headmaster's office.

Teddy answered. He didn't even acknowledge my dad at first. "Rosemary. You look really pretty today."

This caught me off guard. It wasn't what I was expecting.

"You used to say that all the time," I said.

"And I always meant it, and I mean it now." When he spoke like that, it made me feel like we were the only people there, sometimes the only people in existence.

Teddy stepped forward, finally offering his hand to my dad. "Trevor, good to see you again."

Dad looked down at his hand—then shook it.

"We ent gonna be long. Just come to pick up the last of her stuff." He reached into his pocket and took out his roll-ups.

"That's fine. I won't bother you none," said Teddy as he stepped aside to let me in.

Dad waited in the drive, smoking and loading the car.

When we finished, Teddy asked us in for a cup of tea.

"I'm all right," said Dad, "but you go ahead, Rosie."

I wasn't sure. I wanted to ask Dad why he said that. I guess it was to show him we were being civil.

I made a pot of tea and went through to the lounge. Hazel was lying on the sofa reading a magazine, her bare feet resting on the arm, which obviously didn't bother Teddy anymore.

It was the first time the three of us had been together in the same room for nearly two months. It was a bright, fresh morning. The sun was shining strong beams through the net curtains. The smell of Dad's roll-up and the sound of chattering birds drifted through from the open front door.

"It's nice this," he said, "the three of us together. Like a proper family."

I looked to Hazel, but she was idly flicking through her magazine.

"If I could do things again it would be different, it'd be like this all the time." He rubbed at his face. "I realise what I had now. I know what I lost."

And in that moment, I knew I'd had to leave. I had to do what we planned. I had to get my stuff and leave. "Well, I think it's about time I got going again," I said, putting down my untouched cup of tea.

"Please, Rose. I know now, I know what life is like without you and I can't bear it. I promise if I touch you one more time, then you can go and I'll only have myself to blame." His brow was furrowed, his face broken. A little boy asking for help.

Hazel hadn't spoken and only moved to re-cross her legs. She had been living with him without any trouble—so was it just me? Was I being selfish by not letting her have a normal family life? Was I, in fact, going back on the promise I made to her all those years ago?

"Please," the little boy said again, "you can't do this to me."

"I don't know, Teddy..."

"Why? Why not?"

"How is it gonna be any different this time? Tell me that?"

"Cos it is. Cos I know what I'll lose if I do it again."

The three of us together in the lounge—it seemed normal and right. I wanted it. I wanted it so bad. A normal, happy, proper family. But could he change, was it possible after all this time, all these years?

I'd managed to change. I'd been living a repeating loop over and over again, and then one day I managed to break free from it. If I could do it, maybe he could. Maybe he really had reached that point too. I knew that he was capable of being the husband and father we wanted. I knew he had it in him, and now he also knew I had it in me to leave him. Things seemed clearer than they had before.

I can see how it frustrates people, how weak I seemed to them, giving him chance after chance, never learning and always forgiving. Some people can't understand why the first time a husband lays a hand on you it isn't the last. Why ent that the cue to get out of there and never look back. But unless you're there, unless you experience it, feel it, how can you begin to pass judgement.

Everybody wants to be happy and has this picture in their mind of how they want their life to be, and that's a powerful thing. We get one go at life. One go at finding happiness. And sometimes you'll do anything to make it so, from whatever you've got available. You'll take every chance you can.

I loved him and had been with him for sixteen years, and despite the bad times outweighing the good, that amount of time forges a bond. I'd lived with him longer than my family; he was the one person I'd spent most of my life with. You feel so connected, as if the two of you are becoming part of the same person because you've shared so much.

Or maybe it's just me, maybe it's just because I'm soft, I don't know. But he was the father of my daughter and the only man I had ever been in love with.

56

SURRENDER

Sniffing away the start of his tears, he knelt down on the floor in front of me. "Don't make me beg," he said. "You can't deny it. It's what you want as well."

"I... I know, but..." I found myself saying.

"There's no buts. It's what *we* want. It's what we all need."

I scrunched my eyes tight, trying to fight it, trying to keep my head straight. But it was my heart—my heart was a whir, urging me on, almost buzzing with eagerness for the promise of a happy future.

"So what do you say, Rosie?"

"I guess..."

"It's the right thing. Come on, let's go get your stuff outta the car, yeah?"

"I... I..." There was movement behind him. Hazel on the sofa. She'd lowered her magazine.

I was staring into Teddy's teary eyes, but I could see her behind him. She sat up. She was looking at me. Waiting. This poor young girl from a broken family. She deserved better. I owed her. I'd made a promise to her.

"Come back to us, Rosie," he continued.

Behind him Hazel mouthed something, but all I could make out was the word *mum*.

"I guess..."

"It's what we *all* want. It's what we all need."

I looked above his head as if in thought. I looked to Hazel. There was no doubting she was her father's daughter. Her eyes had narrowed, her bottom lip was pushing up in a pout. She fixed me with a fierce stare as her head moved from side to side, slowly and deliberately. *"Mum - don't - you - dare,"* she mouthed. Her shoulders rising slowly up and down with her breathing.

"No," I said, swallowing. I could feel my leg juddering and my heartbeat quicken. "No, Teddy. It's... it's over. You've had your chances. Now it's my turn, my chance to try for a happy life."

His face disintegrated in an instant. "No... No... No, Rose. Don't do this to me."

Behind him Hazel was now nodding furiously. *You do it, Mum! You bloody well do it!*

I stood up. "I came here to collect my stuff. And that is all." I wanted to run, but I calmly walked to the lounge door. I turned and nodded to Hazel, who gave me a wink and the thumbs up and then dipped back into her magazine.

Teddy had his head in his hands. I saw a tear fall from between his fingers onto the carpet. I stood half in, half out of the doorway. Part of me wanted to just leave without saying a word, but I told myself to be civil and proper. "Goodbye, Teddy."

His head rose from his hands and I could see the demon had entered his eyes. "NO!" he screamed. Then was up on his feet and rushing at me.

Boom. Like a freight train, he hit me. Pushing me through the lounge door and into the kitchen. I started to fall backwards but managed to grab the sink. He kicked my legs from under me and down I went. Then he was on top, straddling me. He grabbed a fistful of my jumper and pulled my upper body clear off the floor.

I heard Hazel screaming up behind him, "Let her go!"

Then, to my horror, she started pulling at his shoulders. He swung his arm back, casting her aside, sending her crashing into the table and chairs.

"Look!" he screamed. "Look what you're doing to us, you stupid bitch!" And then, for the first time in the sixteen years I'd known him, he hit me in the face.

The pain was instant. Red splotches filled my vision. I thought that was going to be it, that he'd crossed that final barrier and that there was nothing else to lose.

He hit me again, but somehow I managed to move my head and instead he struck my neck causing my head to bang onto the tiled floor. He picked me up by the scruff of my jumper with two hands and shook me, banging the back of my head down repeatedly until I heard the crack of a tile.

I was outside myself, screaming and screaming, my bladder went and I was sure I was going to die. I was screaming so hard my throat hurt. I honestly thought that I was done for. I just hoped, unlike her stupid mother, Hazel would have the sense to get out of there and never come back.

He stopped shaking me. I opened my eyes to see him pulling back his fist. But before it came, there was a distant roar. Teddy turned his head as the roar grew louder, echoing through the tiled kitchen until clear words could be heard.

"COME HERE, YOU FUCKIN' ANIMAL!"

Through my blurred and blotched vision, I saw my 60-year-old dad hurdle a fallen chair. His soil-stained fingers close around Teddy's throat. And lord knows how, because Teddy was no small man, but next he was dragging Teddy out of the kitchen, his arms flailing, his heels kicking in an attempt to stay upright.

I managed to get to my feet. I was still beside myself, thinking the two of them would be slugging it out in the drive. I'd always feared my dad getting hurt by doing something stupid like standing up to Teddy. It was part of the reason I'd kept everything from my parents for so long. In my eyes, Teddy was invincible—and I guess Teddy thought the same way too. No one had ever successfully stood up to him.

I got to the hallway at the same time as Hazel; her face mirrored my own dread. We raced to the front door.

Dad was stood bristling on the step. Teddy was on the gravel flat on his back, looking up wide-eyed in shock. He got up onto his elbows, grabbed a handful of stones and launched them at my dad. Dad turned his face, but Teddy's aim was poor and they rattled and cracked off the kitchen window.

"I ent scared of you, old man."

With a growl, Dad feigned a lunge. Teddy flinched and fell back again. On the second attempt, he got to his feet.

Dad reached into his pocket and took out his tobacco pouch.

Teddy started laughing as he picked bits of gravel from his bleeding elbows. Shaking his head, he turned to his car. "Huh. This ent the end. I'll get yuh. I will," he said before getting in and spinning large brown scars into the drive as he went.

As Dad licked the cigarette paper, I could see his hands were shaking. But it didn't matter none, because standing there, on the doorstep, that morning, my dad looked huge to me, a real colossus.

The next morning, I went straight in to speak to the manager. He was sat at his desk opening the morning post with a deer-horn letter opener.

"What, you some sort of film star now then?" he said, looking up at me briefly.

"Sorry...?"

"Not like you to wear sunglasses."

"Oh, I see. Well..." I took a deep breath. "There's something I need to tell you."

"Go ahead, just like the elephant, I'm all ears," he chuckled to himself.

"I'm handing in my notice."

He paused halfway through opening an envelope and looked up. "Is that your joke?"

I shook my head.

Then he smiled at me. "I see," he said as he made me wait while he finished opening the letter. "Well, I guess maybe it's overdue and certainly not undeserved. I'll tell you what, leave it with me and we'll get something sorted out by the end of the week."

"Sorry...?" I'm not really sure what reaction I'd been expecting, but this one completely flummoxed me. Maybe he didn't hear me right, was all I could think. "I'm gonna have to leave the factory. Leave my job."

"It's fine, Rosemary, don't worry. We have already been talking about it. You'll get your pay rise."

"My what? No, I don't want more money. I really am going to have to quit the job."

He paused again, but this time he put down the letter opener. "Why on earth would you want to do something as silly as that for?"

"It's... complicated. It's... too difficult to explain."

"Well, you better have a good go, cos I ent about to let one of my best workers just up and leave like that," he said, giving a snort.

I sighed. Then removed my sunglasses.

"Oh dear. Whatever happened?"

And so I told him. Told him almost everything. Told him I had no choice but to leave. I could see in his face he didn't quite know whether to believe it, but the eye wasn't telling no lies. He told me to wait outside for a second, made me promise not to go anywhere.

"Okay," he said when he came back in, "what we can do for you is this—you can have one month's leave and then when you come back we'll give you a ten percent rise. How does that sound?"

I was tempted, it sounded like it could work, but deep down I knew if I was going to do this, I had to do it properly.

"Okay," he continued, then took a breath, "three months and fifteen percent. How does that strike you?"

"I... I can't. I'm sorry. He's won, he's beaten me. I'm broken here. I've got to start again. Once I leave, I can't come back."

I'd worked there eight and a half years. Without that job, I don't think I would've survived. It'd given me so much—a sense of worth, value, respect, friends. But there was only one way out, only one way to leave Teddy for good—and that was to leave Norfolk for good.

57

A NEW START

Curled up in the back of the car, I could feel every bump and lump until we left the country lanes. I kept the blanket tucked tightly over me the entire journey—safe in my cocoon. Once or twice he asked me if I was okay, but other than that, we hardly spoke. Nobody outside of the family knew, not even Wendy.

When we arrived in Norwich, he found a parking space down a side road out of the way. He took my case from the boot and we followed the slow drift of people making their way towards the bus station. It was a rare event that I went into the city, and I knew it was probably going to be the last time for a fair old while too.

The bus station was full of noise and people milling about. In a way, it reminded me of the old cattle yard with all those great hulks lumbering about, jostling into their stops like cows at the trough. The deep rattle and hum of idling diesel engines like their slow croaking moos, and the occasional cough of fumes like dust kicked up on dry a summer's day.

"What'll you say when people ask where I've gone?" I said to Dad.

He took a long draw on his roll-up. "That you've moved away."

I felt bad for not telling anyone, but I knew how easily word spread, even if people didn't mean it to.

"And you'll steer clear of Teddy, won't you?"

"I'm too old for scrapping."

"And you'll look after Hazel. Don't let Mum... you know."

"She'll be fine."

I'd begged, pleaded and cried for Hazel to come with me, but things were going well with Paul so she felt she couldn't leave.

After Teddy had driven off that Saturday morning, we immediately started cramming Hazel's stuff into the car too. With me gone, she now had the room at my parent's to herself. I'd asked her what she was going to do, was she going to see Teddy anymore. She said she hadn't decided yet.

We stood leaning against the wall waiting for my bus to come. I told Dad he could go, but he insisted on staying and I'm glad he did, as it was him who spotted Mr and Mrs Glennings, a couple we knew from Melton. But the first I knew about it was when he grabbed my hand.

"Let's go."

We scurried around the corner and he peered out to see where they were. I was so scared of him finding me, I couldn't even have anyone knowing which bus I was getting on.

I started to worry. "What'll I do if my bus comes while they're still there?"

"Get the next one."

Luckily that didn't happen, by the time my bus arrived they'd gone, and then very soon after that, so was I.

58

MANSFIELD

Even though I was all those miles away, I was still a nervous wreck. Whenever someone came knocking at the door, I'd drop whatever I was doing and would be off, shooting upstairs before you could blink.

"You're in Mansfield now, Rosemary, he can't get yuh here," my brother would tell me. But I just wasn't willing to take that chance.

With Perry and Karen both being at work during the day, I found it really difficult being there by myself. I kept all the curtains shut and the doors locked, but then there'd be a noise, maybe just a neighbour in their garden, a drink can skipping down the road in the wind, a plant idly tapping at the glass. I'd try and tell myself it was nothing, but when you're listening for him, you can't help but to hear him creeping about the outside of the house trying to get in.

One particularly windy day it drove me so crazy that I went around the entire house and whipped open all the curtains and tied up the nettings. From then on, this was how I preferred it—being able to see everything. I'd then pace around the house like the sorry-looking leopard Hazel and me saw at Cromer zoo one time. I'd do laps of the house, upstairs, downstairs, regularly checking out of every window.

I was fine when I was out. I felt comfortably lost while I was going about looking for a job. Everything was so different and new. The way people dressed was different, the way they spoke, even the words they said.

It was nice that no one knew me, that no one was nudging their husband as I passed, saying, *that's the one, that's her. The one whose husband beats her, the one whose husband cheats on her, the one whose mother is an old tart, the one whose daughter is a delinquent.*

I took the first job I was offered and found myself inspecting jumpers at Meridians. I worked on a line with this young girl called Estelle. It wasn't as interesting as my old job, but it was something and brought money in to pay Perry for my board. It also got me out of the house and into somewhere I felt safe. Work had always been a safe haven for me, sacred ground where he could not come, where he could not get to me.

I don't think I'd been working there a week when Estelle turned to me one morning and said, "You know what, I gotta say, this is the most bloody boring job in the world."

I laughed and agreed.

"No, I'm serious," she continued. "If I see one more bloody jumper, I swear I'm walking out here at lunch and getting me a different job."

I picked up the next jumper off the line and held it up in front of her, smirking away.

"Aye, that's done it. I'm leaving."

And you wanna know something—we bloody well did.

We went out at lunch and got ourselves a job working at Metal Box—just like that. In a matter of minutes, Estelle had made a decision, taken action and made a change. I guess I had too. But in truth, I'd just tagged along, not actually believing we'd go through with it.

Metal Box was a massive old factory. It was five levels with something like five hundred people working per floor. The main redbrick building was a huge block with large crisscrossed white windows. The factory site was built into an old quarry, and because of the protection this gave, it was used to make ammunition and shells during the war. Being built into the quarry also meant that the top floor was actually level with the roads and was well-hidden from a distance. The only thing that could be seen was the famous clock tower with its green lead dome. Most workers and locals used to set their own timepieces by it, and apparently there was uproar one Christmas when the big Roman-numeral clock wasn't wound on during the break.

Once the war was over, the factory started making metal tins for toys, biscuits, tea, the lot. I got a job working on a press and it was no more glamorous than inspecting jumpers, but it was a nicer place to work. There was always a vibrant hubbub of chatter with so many people working there. You felt like you were part of something big and alive. If you didn't work there, it could be guaranteed you knew someone who did. The place was like a town inside a building. On the bottom floor were all sorts of shops and services, from a hairdresser's to a dentist's.

I've got to say, the people up that way were all marvellous, everyone would talk to you and be ever so friendly.

"Aye, that's cos the further up north you go, lass, the friendlier the folk," Estelle had told me with quite some authority.

I was a little bit in awe the first week or so, having never experienced anything like it. Estelle took me under her wing and was great. She was so confident and always knew her mind. And even though she was in her early twenties, I'd follow her around like she was mother duck, letting her make all the decisions, just going along for the ride—and a ride it certainly was. She had such a short attention span and always did whatever made her happy at the time.

When she found out I was 32 and didn't have a fella, she nearly ended up killing me, I tell you.

"There's nowt for it, you coming out wi' me and the girls tonight," she told me.

They were all youngsters, so I did my best to keep up with them as we went from pub to pub, pub to nightclub, nightclub to nightclub. Estelle was like a friendly sergeant major. It was always, "Finish them drinks, ladies," and "Come on, to the dance floor, lasses."

We'd put our handbags in a pile on the ground and dance in a big circle around them. The first time they took me out, I'd started to feel tired and saw it was nearly one o'clock in the morning. Knowing we had work the next day, I asked what time we were going to leave.

"Not before it closes," she'd shouted back in my ear.

"When's that then?"

"Three o'clock."

Three o'clock! I couldn't believe it. This went on for another two months. In the end, I couldn't cope and had to calm it down. Even though it was nearly the death of me, I enjoyed it ever so much. I'd seen a completely different side of life I never knew existed.

It was after another three months that I got a call from Hazel. I could immediately tell she was upset.

"What's he done? Tell me he hasn't—"

"No, it's bloody Paul. We broke up."

"Oh thank goodness," I breathed out, releasing a massive knot from my chest.

"Mum!"

"Sorry, I meant... I'm just glad you're safe." Teddy had almost become a faded memory now, and the only time he was able to enter my head was when I phoned Norfolk.

A week later, Dad was driving Hazel to the bus station in Norwich, albeit without needing to hide her in the boot with a blanket over her head. Perry didn't have the room to keep the two of us, so Hazel and I got ourselves a council house. In the months we'd been apart, I'd tried to speak to Hazel on the phone as much as I could, but it was still amazing how much she'd grown and changed in that short time. She came to me in Mansfield, as a near as damn it, a full-grown woman.

Now, truth be told, I probably didn't handle her right to start off with. I was so pleased to have her with me that I let her have a very loose rein. I was always aware of making sure she felt her life and her decisions were hers alone. And more importantly, at that time, I wanted her to enjoy being in Mansfield, enjoy being with her mother more than anything else.

However, at first, she was in a right grump over her and Paul parting ways. I'd go and wake her in the mornings before I went to work, only to come home and find she still hadn't got up. Even though she spent most of the time in bed reading magazines, she always seemed to be tired and I rarely got to see the nice side of her. She'd snap at me for the littlest reason and I'd usually let it go. It was very much like living with a grumpy old dog at times, tip-toeing around my own house. But at least this grumpy old dog only ever barked.

"You're her mam aren't yuh?" Estelle said to me one day. "So you grab her by the lughole, pull her outta that bed and tell her to get herself a job. She needs to get out and meet people. Get amongst it. She'll probably not take that kind to it, but it'll be for her own good."

There I was, a 34-year-old who had been a mother figure for the last twenty-odd years, taking advice on how to bring up my 18-year-old, from a younger woman with no children. However, when I thought about it, I could see how it made sense. I'd never really had a teenage childhood myself, I'd skipped all that, whereas Estelle's teenage years weren't all that far behind her.

I didn't dare go as far as grabbing Hazel by the ear, but I did go home and give her the ol' wet flannel and then whipped off the bedcovers.

"Right, young lady, I've had enough. You gotta get yourself a job or you're going back to Norfolk. The choice is yours."

The next day she came in with me and got herself a job at Metal Box. She certainly didn't need much time to settle, getting on like a house on fire. She quickly made lots of friends and was earning good money for a girl her age. I was so proud. She was such a good worker. I like to think that was something of me reflected in her. Mind you, if I thought I'd gone a bit wild when I first came down, well blow me! It wasn't anything compared to Hazel.

Except for her board and her magazines, I'd say every penny went on going out at any given opportunity. While she may have got the hard-working genes from me, she certainly got the temper and drinking genes from her father, so was often getting herself into fights during a night out.

"Well, what was it this time?" I'd ask her in the morning, seeing she had lost several buttons and had a bald patch from where a clump of hair had once been.

"The way I talk again, ent it," she grumbled, as she blew the steam off her coffee.

It was something that had never bothered me. I'd always found it funny and laughed back at their accent whenever I copped it for my Norfolk one.

"Sounds like an old farmer dunt she," they'd laugh.

Of course, I let Hazel know how I felt about her behaviour, but she was her own person and old enough to start living by her own decisions. However, later that year, just before Christmas, I thought it was all about to come to ahead.

They certainly did see in Christmas up that way. There was a buzz all around the place starting halfway through November. The week before the Christmas break, the amount of work done at the factory would start to tail off. But the managers never seemed to get onto us that much—it was as if they expected it. Then after work it was straight into the pubs.

Hazel and her gang had been going out every evening in the week leading up to Christmas itself—until one night I got a knock on the door just gone eleven.

I was a bit fearful at first, being home by myself and with the knock being so firm and almost impatient. I peeped out from the lounge window, as I could generally see most of the person at the door if there wasn't a pea-souper (what they called the heavy fog up there) laying siege to the town. Just as I was leaning in to get a look, he knocked again, which caused me and the curtain to flinch.

"Rosemary Page? Is that you? You in?"

It was only the bloomin governor of our department. He was a big barrel-chested man who always looked like he was leaning backwards even when he was walking.

I opened the door to his tired and sunken features.

"I know it's late, love, but I got your daughter in the car. And it's fair t'say she's a little worse for wear."

"What, she hasn't been fighting again, has she?"

"Fighting? I bloody hope not. Drinking, more like it."

"Oh, I'm so sorry."

"Well don't be, just open the door wide and I'll go get her."

We dragged her murmuring and giggling up to her room, then came back down.

"I'm so, so sorry about this," I said to him. "I really am. Did you want a cup of tea before you go?"

"Got no time for a brew, I'm afraid."

"But... what's gonna happen to her?" I asked.

"I'd say she'll have a mighty bad skull ache in-morning, and best you take an old bucket in there, case she throws up—again."

"I mean... her job... it's a wonder you're not gonna sack her."

"Sack her?" he said, rolling his eyes. "Blimey, if I sacked her, I'd have to sack fifty more. She isn't the worst of them by a long shot. I feel like bloody Father Christmas, 'cept I'm delivering drunk girls to families all across the land instead of presents."

Well, the following morning, I'd be dammed if I could get her up. Not even the wet-flannel trick worked. Eventually, I had to leave her—so at least one of us would still have a job to pay the rent come the end of the month. All day I was in a tizz, wondering what should I do. I couldn't really tell the governor she was ill since he'd been the one who brought her home. I decided I just go offer an apology and hope that might help.

"She's here now," he told me. "She crawled out from under her rock just after lunch. Cheeky young devil, that one. Strolled in as bold as a peacock and said, 'afternoon all,' sat at her machine and started working as if nothing had happened."

"Oh dear. I see. Please... you have to give her another chance though. She just got carried away cos of Christmas."

"It's the same as I told you last night, she's not going anywhere."

"Well, are you sure?"

"D'you want me to give her the sack?"

"No, of course not."

"Look here, she's lightning on that there machine, she'd caught up with the others in no time. If she weren't doing her job, or more than her fair share of work the others wouldn't stand for it anyway, and she'd be out."

I was so happy she hadn't got the hook, but I did finally put my foot down and stop her going out during the weeknights.

59

GOING BACK

AGED 37 (1982)

Can you believe, it wasn't for another three years before I first went back to Norfolk.

My youngest brother, Daniel, sometimes drunk with the fellas I used to work with, and once he let slip I was coming for a visit they started badgering him, asking whether he was going to bring me out. So in the end we arranged a get-together at the pub.

It was lovely to see them all, and from the outset it felt like I'd never been away. There wasn't any of this politeness and testing the water and such—we were joking and taking the mick from the get-go. None of them much had changed. Roger was still as foul-mouthed as he'd always been and Ronny Jordan still sweet and hobbling about, though quite a bit older—and a bit more hobbly.

I was offered so many drinks I could've got pissed as a newt three times over. After the first lot, I went to the toilet and as I was making my way back I saw them all huddled together and hiding something.

"Come on then, boys, what is it? Don't be hiding nothin from Inspector Rosemary now."

"We just got you a little present is all," said Vic.

"Something to remember us by when you bugger off back to... Timbuktu or wherever it is you're holed up," said Roger.

"I think it's only right that Ronny should be the one to present it to you though," Vic said as he let him hobble out.

"Oh, really fellas, you shouldn't have. There's no need," I said, thinking they were gonna present me with an ornamental lamp or a nice decorative plate. But no...

From behind his back, Ronny brought out a bright yellow rubber glove filled with air and bolted down onto a metal plaque and engraved *To Rosemary, from the Fellas.* Even if it wasn't quite what I was expecting, it certainly made me laugh some. We carried on drinking, but I switched to the lemonade after a few because I didn't want to make a fool of myself after all those years.

"That's not like you, is it Victor?" I said, noticing he'd also switched to the soft stuff.

"I gotta be careful as well, I ent been out in near three years. I just ent used to it no more. What with the wife gone and the two kids, I don't hardly get a minute to myself."

"Blimey, you oughta come up to Man- Ma- my way," I managed to blurt out just in the nick of time. "They'd drag you out every night of the week if you told them that."

"Actually, Rose, I've been thinking... well, I was wondering if you'd like to come to the dance out in Melton on Saturday night? With... me, of course."

"Oh..."

I know it wasn't the politest way to answer, but he'd blindsided me with that one for sure.

"I ur... you see, most of the fellas will be going along too. I just thought I'd look a bit of an old fool dancing by myself."

"I tell you what, if Daniel will come with us too, I'll go."

Since leaving Norfolk, I'd hardly given fellas much of a thought and I was more than happy about that. I did like Victor—a lot. He'd always been one of my favourites from work. I'd always admired the way he'd dealt with things after his wife left him in the lurch. He was a thoughtful, honest, and caring man. Very selfless and could also surprise you by making you laugh when you least expected it.

Knowing I would be going back to Mansfield after the dance meant there wasn't much chance of things getting awkward or complicated, so I dug deep for my inner Estelle and said why the heck not. And besides, I already knew Vic wasn't a bad dancer.

~

It was fantastic, and Victor the perfect gent. He didn't once refuse to dance with me; he didn't dance with the waitresses; he didn't buy me a drink then ignore me for the rest of the evening or even beat me up at the end of it. Then again, neither did Teddy when I first started going with him.

I'd noticed Daniel keeping a protective eye on me over the course of the night. I nearly went over to him at one point to tell him not to fuss so much, that Victor was a good guy, and he should concentrate on enjoying his own evening.

As the night began to draw to a close, Daniel came over and said it was time to be heading home.

"Fair enough," said Victor. "But I was just wondering though, if you wouldn't mind that I take Rosemary to your house? If Rosemary don't mind, that is?" he finished, turning to me.

Daniel's eyes flicked from Victor to me and back again. I don't think there was a lot to read in my face, as I wasn't sure myself. "She'll be fine coming with us, I think," Daniel replied.

"Of course," Victor said, dipping his head momentarily. "Thank you, Rosemary, it's been a lovely evening and hope it ent too long before you come see us again."

"Come on then, Rose," said Daniel, already heading for the door.

"Wait," I called out, having not yet moved. I'd stayed facing Vic. In a weird way, it seemed it was my body and not my head that had made my decision.

Daniel turned back.

"Actually, I think I will let Victor take me home."

"Well... better to come with us, I think. Don't you?" Daniel said motioning with a nod.

"Go on, go with your brother, Rosemary."

"No. It's all right."

He took a moment to look Victor up and down again. "If you're sure, Rose," he finally said.

Victor was a big strong man, much in the same way Teddy was, but more similar to my dad in terms of personality. He was quiet, but you knew the strength was there without him ever having to show it. He drove in a very proper and calm manner, even though he'd had a few drinks. I almost suggested he should speed up a bit just so Daniel wouldn't be worrying where we were.

When we got there, Danny's car was parked outside his bungalow and the kitchen light was on. Victor stopped behind his car and pulled on the handbrake but left the engine running.

"Well, thank you very much, Victor. I had a lovely time."

"You're more than welcome."

And then there was a pause. I wasn't sure what was expected or what I wanted. "Say thanks to all the others too."

"I will," he nodded.

I couldn't help feeling like he was waiting for something, maybe to say something.

"Well, I guess that's it really," I said.

"I reckon."

"Okay," I replied.

"Goodnight then, Rosemary."

"And goodnight to you, Victor."

"The door handle is down by your knee," he said, pointing to it.

"Oh yeah. I'm used to it being higher up is all."

I pulled the tab and the door cracked, allowing the cool night air to blow against my bare ankle. I pushed it open enough to step one foot onto the ground; then I looked at him again.

"Okay," I sighed. "I'll give you a kiss, on the lips, but no more, mind," I said pointing my finger at him.

He held up his palms. "I wasn't expect'n anything. But if that's what—"

And so I kissed him. On the lips.

We held it for a few seconds, then I got out. Victor waited until I was inside before he drove home. It was a strange one, all right. It was nice. It felt comfortable, but also a bit wrong in a way. I mean, I'd only ever kissed one man in my entire life before that moment.

~

Being back in Mansfield was also a confusing one, I was home but I wasn't. I couldn't work out whether I was coming or going, as they say. But once I got into the house, slung my bag down and got the kettle on—that certainly felt good.

I loved Norfolk; it was the place I was born, where all my friends and family lived, where I'd lived my whole life. But I was relieved and felt relaxed being back in Mansfield. I guess because it was my safe place. It was untouched. Nothing of him existed there.

It still took a day or two to get into the swing of things. It made me realise how calm and sleepy Norfolk was. Everything moved at its own pace and nobody was in a rush to get anywhere. Whereas in Mansfield there was always something going on, there were always people everywhere you went, and they always seemed to walk and talk a lot more and a lot faster.

Being back at working again was just what I needed. Things were much better when I had something to distract me. I still enjoyed my time off, especially on Friday afternoons as we were allowed to finish at 1:30 pm if we weren't behind on any orders. Usually, I'd go meet up with Hazel, and like all the other girls we'd go and get a Chinese.

The Friday after I'd got back, I was sat with Hazel, but she didn't seem all that interested in what was happening in Norfolk. She was busy prattling on about what I'd missed.

"You ent even listening to a word I'm saying, Mum."

I apologised, saying I must still have my countryside head on.

I saw her looking at me closely. "Nothin happened, did it? While you were there?"

Surely she couldn't have heard about me kissing Victor already, I was thinking. "Well, what on earth do you mean by that?"

"Y'know exactly what I mean. Did you see him?"

"Victor?"

"Victor? Who the hell's Victor?" she said before shovelling a forkful of noodles into her mouth. Most of the girls would try and use the chopsticks, without much success, so it was always a good source for a giggle. However, Hazel wouldn't even bother trying and always made sure she got a fork.

"Victor. Y'know, the fella I used to work with. I told you about him before."

She couldn't remember and wasn't much interested and started talking about how Janet picked up the wrong bag from the dancing circle and was so drunk she didn't realise until she got home and couldn't get her key in the door.

"Mum. You still ent listening to me, are yuh?"

"Sorry," I said, shaking my head.

"Not bloody Victor again?"

"No. Of course not," but she must've seen my cheeks redden.

"Huh. So you like him do yuh?"

"Don't be so daft." She was a canny one, that girl, because I hadn't even really realised it myself. But yeah, I had been thinking about him —a lot.

60

A PROBLEM SHARED...

I took another trip back a month later, but not to see Vic. Instead, I'd made plans to visit Wendy.

Wendy had been telling me about a new car she'd got herself and these wild plans about driving all over Norfolk for various adventures. When she arrived at my parents, I think we must have laughed for a good five minutes before we managed to say anything to each other. I couldn't quite believe it—she turned up in a sky blue, plastic pig (as they used to call the three-wheeled Robin Reliant cars), which, wait for it, was covered in huge pictures of Mickey bloomin Mouse.

"I ent gettin in that!"

"Why on earth not?" she said with a sulking pout.

"Well, someone might see me for a start."

"D'you want to walk to Hayden then?"

Shaking my head, I got in. If I'm to be honest, I was actually more worried about what her driving was going to be like than the fact we looked like a couple of twerps. And... she didn't disappoint on that front either, as the first thing she did was crunch the gears.

"Sorry! I'm always forgetting which one is backwards," she said as she nestled the rear end of the car into the opposite hedge.

She weren't so bad once we got going. It was a bit wobbly over the bumps, but that was probably due to it being one wheel short of a proper car. Wendy made me giggle as she kept making *woo* noises every time we went over a hump. I wasn't entirely sure she realised she was even doing it.

The sky was pure and cloudless, and there weren't any other cars on the roads. We undid the windows, letting the fresh spring air blow through our hair, and in that moment I knew I really did miss the Norfolk country life. I allowed myself to think what it'd be like to come back—I wasn't planning it—just thinking about it, trying it out in my head, you know.

Unfortunately, Wendy wasn't much of a navigator and quite often we found ourselves stopped at a crossroads so she could squint up at the signposts. We weren't in no hurry, so I left her to it, thinking she needed the practice. After a while though, we'd taken so many turns, down so many high-hedged lanes they all started to look the same and even I wasn't sure where we were.

"Well, I did promise you an adventure, dint I?"

"You got enough petrol, I hope," I said, with imaginings of us pushing a giant blue Mickey Mouse into the petrol station with a crowd of people all gawking at us.

"Which one tells me that? Is it that one?"

"Aha. I know where we are now," I said, recognising an old concrete military pillbox. "You want to take a right here and follow it down, and then eventually we'll come through into Corpusty."

"How embarrassing, you've been away all these years and still know the roads better than me, don't yuh?"

"Oh don't be silly, I only know this way cos it's where my friend Russell has his car garage." I pointed it out as we went past and I told her about the scratches I'd got in the motor that time.

"Well, I ent gonna be letting you drive this beauty now you told me that, am I?"

I told her I wouldn't want to anyway, in case it toppled over going around a corner.

We decided to go and have tea and cakes somewhere for lunch, then plan the rest of our adventure.

"What we need is a bit of music, Wendy," I said, trying to tune in the radio. I bent down, straining to make out the needle. I kept twisting the knob until music started blaring out. I'm not sure what the song was now, but I do remember hearing Wendy's voice above it, as she gave a sudden, *woo!* With my head still down, fine tuning, I hadn't seen the little bridge and felt my stomach move up inside my body as we trundled up and over it.

"You all right?" she shouted.

"You could've bloomin warned me," I shouted back. I then turned to the rear window to look at the offending bridge. But I couldn't see it. Instead, what I saw was the front of a dark grey car steaming up behind us at a fair old lick.

I remember thinking, what's his game—these lanes are far too narrow to be overtaking. But it kept coming closer and closer, growing and growing, until that's all I could see through the back windscreen. Then. *Whoomph.* It hit us with an almighty bang.

We were jolted forward, jarring against our seatbelts. Wendy let out a terrified scream and her arms went into a wobble. The car veered from side to side as she grappled with the wheel.

"It's okay. It's okay," she said as she straightened it up again. "You okay, Rose?"

But, the poor girl didn't know yet.

"What was that? Did I go over something?" She glanced over at me. "Rose...? Are you—"

Whoomph.

"My god! What the—" She looked behind, then started screaming and didn't stop.

I'd never seen Wendy lose it so badly. It frightened me— what was happening to her. I could feel all the hairs, cold and prickling, standing up all along my arms and down my neck.

"My god! Who is it? What are they doing? What do they want?"

"Me," I said.

As soon as I said it, I felt like crying. I felt so sorry for Wendy; she hadn't done anything. It felt like I was infected, that I had this horrible disease I'd never be rid of. I wasn't a safe person to be around. I was someone best to steer clear of for your own good, a tainted friend. I was the family dog who'd got rabies.

Again. *Whoomph*.

"What's he doing? He'll kill us." Wendy screamed as she battled the steering wheel. The tears were flowing, her lips trembling, her knuckles white. "What do I do? What do I do, Rose?"

I knew exactly how she felt, but I couldn't help us. We couldn't stop, we couldn't escape him. All we could do was carry on and hope to get through it. But all you want to do is be able to click your fingers and in an instant be at home tucked safely under your bedcovers.

"Help me. I can't see. I can't see." She wiped her hand at her eyes. "Oh, Rosemary."

I realised I had to do something. I had to be the calm one, be the Rosemary she thought I was. I took a moment; I took a deep breath. My demon, my problem.

"It's okay, Wendy," I said as calm as I could manage over the noise of the radio and her sobbing. "It's okay, he don't want you. He won't hurt you, it's me he wants." I took another deep breath. "Stop the car," I said firmly. "Stop the car."

Wendy didn't answer; she didn't even look at me. Her face streaming with mascara.

"Look, at this rate he's gonna kill us both. If you stop the car, he ent gonna hurt you. So, stop the car—please."

She clenched shut her trembling lips. She breathed hoarsely through her nose and narrowed her eyes. She adjusted her grip on the steering wheel, then her knee rose slightly before she slammed her foot down on the pedal.

I felt myself pushed back into the seat as the hedges streamed past our windows faster and faster.

"I am not going to let him get you," she said with grim determination.

I'd never seen her angry and it didn't half make me jump. She leaned right up close to the windscreen, her arms shaking with effort.

I looked back and saw his car shrink away just for a moment. Then he came at us again. I couldn't see him because of the reflecting sun, but I knew.

Whoomph. With our extra speed, the impact wasn't as bad.

"Is that all you got, Mister Teddy," Wendy screamed out of her window.

Whoomph. Again.

Then we had to slow for a bend. The bend was long and sweeping, the country lane narrow. I was so glad there wasn't anything coming from the other way. As the road straightened out again, Wendy stood back on the accelerator.

"Come on, Mickey! Faster. Faster," she shouted, pushing her body forward as if it would give us some extra go.

I peered back, waiting for the grey faceless beast to appear. The corner faded behind us and still nothing came from around it. "I think... it's okay. It's okay, he's gone."

"You sure?"

"Yeah. He's gone." I finally turned down the blare of the radio and caught up with my breathing.

Wendy slowed the car. All was quiet. We waited. Wendy's foot hovering and me leaning back, checking out the rear window.

"He's gone."

Just like a phantom, disappearing as suddenly as he'd appeared. In one way, I was glad I wasn't alone, otherwise I might have thought I imagined it all. Although the dents and cracks in the back of Wendy's new car left no doubt.

Wendy spun around to see for herself. "He's not bloody there, is he?"

"I'm so sorry."

"I told yuh. I told you he weren't gonna get you. I dint let him get you, did I?" Her red blotchy face was positively beaming.

"No, you didn't. You did good, you did a real good job." And I could feel my own face halved by a broad, uncontrollable smile. Then came the laughing and woohooing—bumps or no bumps—as we waved our arms out of the windows and cranked that radio right back up again.

61

THE UNWELCOME VISITOR

After the car incident, I didn't much feel like seeing Victor—not that I'd made plans to, anyway. I just wanted to crawl back up north and hide under my Mansfield-shaped rock. However, the afternoon before I was due to leave, I did bump into Roger. Dad had stopped to get some petrol, and with it being such a pleasant day I got out of the car to stretch my legs.

"Well, blow me. If it ent rosy Rosemary? What you doing back here already? And why the f- f- ...heck, dint you tell us?" he finished, spying my dad.

I explained I'd just popped back to visit an old friend.

"And you dint have time for the fellas. We had such a good laugh, dint we?" He looked at my father and then in a quieter voice. "Especially Vic," he said with one of his roguish winks.

"Actually... do you think... you could maybe not tell Victor I was down?"

"Oh. Right. I see. Well, if that's what you want."

"I'd appreciate it."

It wasn't until I was on the bus and had time to think the conversation over again that I realised how that might've sounded to him, and it wasn't what I meant at all. I prayed that he'd keep his word and not tell Vic. Roger was nice as pie once you got to know him, but he wasn't half a blabbermouth.

Once I was back in Mansfield, I told myself to forget about it anyway. The run-in with Teddy had reminded me I'd never be safe in Norfolk and that men, in general, were nothing but trouble. I'd been doing just fine without one all this time—in fact, it was my longest run of happiness I'd ever had.

The only problem being, I wasn't so good at forgetting about stuff. I always managed to find time to mull things over and over in my mind until they drove me half bananas. And so, within the month, I'd booked another bus ticket back for the weekend. I made no excuses this time and no plans to meet up with Wendy. I knew full well I was going to see Victor.

I didn't have any romantic plans to sweep him off his feet, I just wanted to see how he was and let him know I hadn't forgotten about him and how kind he'd been to me at the dance.

I took the Friday off, and that morning I made myself up all nice, putting on a dress and some make-up as if I was going out for dinner. I then took the early bus to Norwich, then a taxi from Norwich to Melton—which cost more than the bloomin bus from Mansfield. I got the taxi to drop me off at the factory and arrived twenty minutes before finishing time. I sat out on the wall, trying to keep my hat from blowing away. It was only then that I realised I hadn't really thought things through—Victor might already have plans, or more than likely need to go home to pick up his kids and cook them dinner.

When the klaxon sounded I stood up and straightened my dress. Moments later, the men started lumbering out and heading towards the car park. I saw one fella straining to look at me, maybe wondering what on earth the silly woman was doing loitering outside the factory units, so I dipped my head, hiding further under my hat.

When I saw him, I got all nervous for some reason and didn't do anything. I didn't want to go running over or shout because I thought that'd be very unladylike. I guess I'd been hoping he'd just... notice me. I watched him as he started to go around the corner towards the car park and knew I had to do something quick.

"Urm, Vic? Hello? Victor," I called out and luckily he stopped.

He turned and squinted. "That is you. It's Rosemary. You all right?"

"Yeah, I'm good thanks. You all right."

"Yeah, I'm good thanks."

"Good, good," I said.

"Well... it's good to see yuh. Take care now." And with that, he rounded the corner before I could make a sentence that wasn't mostly made up of the words 'good' or 'thanks'.

I stood there, confused. Had I got it all wrong? Or had he met someone else already? Or had it just been some workplace wager to see who could get a kiss out of old Rosemary first? These are the things that go through your head, even though none of them made sense. The last time I'd seen him, he was the perfect gentleman and was keen to see me again. It was like being 15 years old all over again. I just couldn't figure it out—even though I had plenty of time on the long walk to my parents' house.

I felt a right wally, all dressed-up traipsing along the country roads. In fact, I felt so silly that I started hiding behind hedges every time a car came—my new tan shoes getting filthy.

By the time I made it home, I'd got myself right worked up and was angry at Victor for not even having the decency to stop and talk to me. Surely we were still friends? Surely he must've known I'd come to see him? Why else would I be there all dolled-up to the nines.

I got thinking about all the important men in my life, and how topsy-turvy they all seemed. They always have you believing it's the women who are the crazy ones, but I'd beg to differe. From the beginning, there was my brother Billy who was my best friend growing up, but then turned into my worst enemy for a few years, then changed back to being my friend before buggering off to London. There was little Daniel who I had mothered for so long, and now it was the complete opposite. There was my dad, who was this fearsome angry ogre when I was little, ignored my plight when things first started getting really bad, but then turned out to be my knight in shining armour and was the only man I knew who seemed to have a real heart after all. But then ultimately wasn't even my real dad. And then of course there was him—Teddy.

I felt so foolish. It didn't matter how many times things happened,

I never learned from my mistakes. I was destined to keep making them over and over. I could all too easily imagine what Hazel would say when I got back. Thinking about this, I realised there were times that I'd do well to learn from her. She always knew what she wanted, was never in doubt and always strong-minded. What would she do? She wouldn't stand for it is what. She'd go round to Victor's and let him have both barrels.

I went to get changed, but then thought, would Hazel bother? So I threw my hat down and went into the shed and got on Mum's bike. It'd been a fair while since I'd been on a bicycle—in Mansfield, you could get a bus to most places, or if not walk. It wasn't easy with a dress on, but I hitched it up and set off. Despite my bad temper, I quite enjoyed the ride, the wind against my face, whizzing along at a great speed knowing it was all my own doing. It reminded me of the early days at the hospital. My feet going around and around, my knees up and down, faster and stronger. I was going such a speed I only had to shift my weight to lean round the corners. I zipped over cattle grids with no more than a sudden buzzing *burururur*. I shouted a warning to two youths picking blackberries as I zoomed by. "Mind yourselves! Mad Mother coming through!"

I pounded uphill and coasted down. I even overtook a tractor at one point. Its large back wheels were taking up most of the lane, but in no mood to stop, I took to the grassy verge. It was lumpier than I thought and caused me a good wobble and moment of panic, but I remembered from my youth how it was best to relax your arms and bend your knees, moving with the bike, let the bike tell you what to do. And sure enough I made it, cutting in front of it onto the lane and giving the farmer a big single arm wave. I didn't look back, but could well imagine the look on his face as this woman, dressed in all her finery, came zipping past out of nowhere.

As I got nearer to Victor's, I had to remind myself that I was supposed to be angry. I thought back to how he'd ignored me and the long walk to my mother's, and it soon did the trick.

I arrived at his bungalow and shoved the bike up against the fence, marched up to his door and gave it a fair good rap. He wasn't going to be able to ignore me this time.

I waited.

Then I began to wonder, what was going to come out of my mouth when he answered?

I knocked again—bit harder and a bit longer.

When the door was finally opened, it opened slow and wide and there was Victor holding a spatula, wearing a floral apron and a pair of tatty old pink bunny slippers. I nearly lost it for a moment, but managed to stifle my giggle.

"Whatever is it, Rosemary? What's happened? Are you okay?"

"No, I'm bloody not. What d'you think you're playing at? Ignoring me like that when I come all the way down from Mansfield, especially to see you."

"Now, now, Rosemary," he said, "I certainly did not ignore you."

"Well... you might as well have done!"

"I'm fairly certain I said hello to you. And goodbye."

"And is that all I deserve? All I'm worth?"

"I could ask you the same question but—" he stopped and raised his palm, "but I'm not going to, not when you're all het up like this." He lowered his hand. "Now, my daughter's inside scared half out of her wits from all that banging, so could you kindly calm down, then tell me what's got into you?"

"You. You... bloody... man."

"Please, Rosemary. I can't have you swearing in front of my daughter like this. If you wouldn't mind, I'd like to ask you to leave, okay?"

"Oh, don't you worry, I'm leaving. I know where I belong and that's back in Mansfield. And if that's what you want—fine."

"Actually, no, it's not. It's very far from what I want. But I also don't want you ranting and raving and scaring my family."

"Well, you're in luck, cos I'm going." And with that, I turned and stomped back to my bike. He stood quietly, watching me in his apron and slippers. Then I left.

Well! There was no need to tell myself to be angry on the way home. It wasn't until I was up to full speed and the rhythmic clunk of my pedals and the constant buzz of rubber on the road that I managed to calm down some.

I then heard what he'd been saying—heard what I'd been saying. I also realised I'd only gone and told him I was living in Mansfield. I couldn't believe I'd let it slip after all these years of keeping it schtum. I just hoped that I'd been ranting so much he hadn't realised, or hoped he was sensible enough not to tell anyone.

Then I heard the way I'd been speaking to him—like some kind of madwoman, some raging, uncontrollable female version of... well.

Yet, still, he'd been so calm and gentle, not once raising his heart rate, let alone his voice. I heard his words again. His first response was concern, his first thoughts for his family and... had he said it...? Did I hear him say he didn't want me to go back to Mansfield?

I stopped pedalling. Deep in thought, I slowed right down until I had to put my foot out for balance. I lowered the bike. What had I just done? I lowered myself onto the grassy verge. What must he think of me? He'd probably never want to speak to me again. I felt it coming. I hugged my knees up to my chest and the first of my tears tumbled onto them.

Everything seemed so clear. My mother had been right all along—I was broken goods. I wasn't ever going to be good enough for any man. Yes, I suffered my fair share of crap, but worse, I'd let it affect me, let it beat me. I was just as much the problem as anyone else. I wasn't even fit to raise a daughter the right way. I was better off alone. I didn't need anyone. I only needed my work, it was the only thing that brought positives to my life, the only time I felt like a normal person.

The noise of the tractor trundling down the lane didn't register, but the uncertain voice of the farmer did break me out of my thoughts.

"Miss? You all right there, Miss?" he called down.

I didn't look up. I just nodded my head and beckoned him away with my arm.

"You... you sure? Did you come a cropper?"

I shook my head.

"Do you need some help?"

I needed help all right, but nothing he could help me with. I shook my head and beckoned him away again.

"If you're sure?" He didn't say anything for a few seconds, then I heard the tractor clunk into gear and rattle away.

Shortly after, I got myself up before anyone else came along. I'd made more than enough of a scene already and embarrassed myself enough for one lifetime.

Dad was just getting home when I got back.

"You all right?" he asked, craning his head forward as I hid mine.

"I'm fine," I sniffed.

"Okay then."

And that was it.

I made a pot of tea and sat at the table with him. We sat there for some time, not saying anything. It was nice, him just being there.

The quiet was eventually broken by the shrill ring of the phone. Dad looked at me, then got up.

I could hear him answer it in the hallway.

"Who's calling?" he asked. Then, "Ent sure. Wait."

He came back to the kitchen, "Victor?"

I shook my head. He waited a moment, then went back. "Not back yet. Okay... ...yep."

He slid the number in front of me. "Wanted to check you're okay. He... do anything?"

"No, he didn't do nothing."

Dad sat down and returned to his paper, and the following day I returned to Mansfield.

I thought it was best to just let things be. He'd get the idea and get on with his life and soon forget about me. I told Hazel about it, about my decision. She scoffed at me like I was a sulky teenager putting on her parts and said suit yourself.

"Well, do you think I'm doing the right thing though?" I asked.

"Only you can answer that one."

"Then, yes, I'm doing the right thing. I've had enough of being hurt and hurting people. It's better for everyone this way."

"If that's what you think."

"Well, I do."

"Then what's the problem?"

"Well, nothing."

She was sat crossed-legged on the sofa, filing her nails.

"What?" I asked.

"I dint say nothin."

"Well, why you looking at me like that?"

She gave a weary sigh and dropped her hands to her lap. "That's his number right?"

"What is?"

"That bit of paper sticking out the phonebook."

"I don't know, is it?" I said with a shrug.

"If you weren't still thinking about him, you wouldn't still be talking about him. And if you really dint want to call him, you would've thrown away his number."

"Well, I'll throw it away then."

"And besides, you wouldn't be asking yourself these questions if you didn't already know the answer. So, if you don't get his number and call him, I bloody well will."

"But... I can't. Not now. Not after what has happened."

"Oh for god's sake." She threw down her nail file, jumped up and walked over to the phone.

"No. Hazel, what are you doing?"

"I warned yuh. Now is that a four or a seven? I never could read granddad's writing."

"Seven. I mean... no, Hazel, please don't."

"It's ringing."

"Hazel, please!"

"Still ringing. You gonna speak to him? Otherwise I will."

This was threat enough, so I took the phone but didn't bring it to my ear. I could hear the muted *brrrp, brrrp*. I looked to the kitchen clock; maybe he'd be out with the kids. *Please don't be in, please don't be in,* I was praying. But then the faint *brrrp, brrrp* stopped with a click. There was a moment of silence and I thought maybe it had rung out.

"Hello?" Came the distant voice.

My breathing quickened. I didn't know what I could say to him.

"Hello? Anyone there?"

I took a step toward the telephone table and turned the receiver, ready to place it back in the cradle.

"Is that Victor?" Hazel shouted across the room. "It's Rosemary, she wants to speak to yuh, but she's too chicken and don't know what to say."

I couldn't believe it. I was mortified.

"She wants to—"

"Hello! Victor. It's me. Rosemary," I blurted out just to stop her.

"What is this? Is everything okay?"

I was so embarrassed to begin with. Even though he couldn't see me, my face was shining like a sunburnt tomato. He said he didn't think I was stupid or mad. He said he liked me a lot and wanted to know if I felt the same. I told him I thought I did, but I wasn't in no position to rush into anything because of what I'd been through before. After saying this I left a silence to see what he'd say, see how much he knew or had been told. He said he'd heard that Teddy hadn't treated me right, that he wasn't a real man, that the things he did was something that he couldn't even think about, let alone do. He said all he wanted from a woman was honesty—he was a straightforward man, who said what he meant, and meant what he said, and only wanted to be treated the same way. He said he wasn't into playing games, except for the odd game of darts. I laughed, but Victor didn't let on whether he was meaning to be funny or not. It helped though; it helped me relax, to actually be able to talk to him like a normal person. He then said we should be doing this face to face—not over a wire. And I said maybe it was best to get this chat out of the way first so next time I came to visit we could start afresh.

62

NORFOLK

AGED 38 (1983)

Soon, I was going back every month to see him. I'd go down on the Friday or Saturday and then like Cinderella at midnight I'd disappear back to Mansfield on the Sunday. I'm surprised he stuck with it, as I didn't half treat him mean. When I came to Norfolk, I'd stay at my parents' or Perry's, and I still refused to give him my address or phone number in Mansfield. When I was gone, I was gone.

I cared about him ever so much but I wasn't sure if I ever wanted to be involved with a man properly again. After finally having what could be called a normal life, I wasn't in any rush to risk losing it.

When Easter came along, I had a week off work and stayed at my parents' house, seeing Victor at every chance. This week was different though, rather than always going out and doing something, we did the ordinary things and it was nice. It was good to see that side of life with him, see that we were a good match. And then at the end of the week, with the ballroom clock creeping towards midnight, Victor drove me up to the bus station.

"Come on then," I said after he'd kissed me goodbye. "You can see me onto the bus like a proper gentleman for once." I don't know why I always made him drop me off down the road, he knew I went to Mansfield. I think maybe it was just so there was some doubt involved still. I guess it gave me some sort of feeling of control over my half-secret.

He didn't say anything but I think he recognised the significance. We kissed again, he looked up at the front of the bus and gave me a half smile and sighed, "So, you're off home again then."

"No," I said. "This is my home. Norfolk's my home."

Whilst I'd been spending my time doing the Cinderella act, Hazel had met a new fella and got engaged. I was glad that she hadn't got the same trust issues as her mum, but it was different with her, she always seemed to be the one wearing the trousers in her relationships.

With Hazel's engagement in mind and the fact she wouldn't be able to keep the house on by herself, I talked to her. I told her how I was feeling, how I wanted to go back home.

"You gotta do what makes you happy, Mum."

And so that was that. Victor came up one Saturday to Mansfield and picked me and my stuff up. I'd told him there was no need to drive all that way, that I could do it by bus, or if not get my dad to do it, but he insisted. I guessed he just wanted to be chivalrous and the like, so I didn't realise we'd got our wires all in a muddle until we turned off the Corpusty Road.

"Oh..." I said, when I realised.

He looked over to me briefly.

"Urm... Victor?"

"You forgot something? I guess it's only five hours if you want to go back for it." He smiled—but I didn't.

"Where are we headed?"

"Well, home of course."

I looked at him. "*Whose*... home?"

He let the car slow to a halt. He stared out of the windscreen.

"I'm sorry. It's just too soon."

"Too soon?" he said, turning to face me.

"We don't know each other well enough yet, is all."

"What are you talking about, I've known you fourteen years. What about Easter? What about—"

"No. I mean, me and your children. You can't just move me in like that. It'll be some shock for them. They gotta get to know me, get to like me. They gotta want me to move in. You see?"

He thought about it and nodded.

I got him to drop me off at my parents' house, but that wasn't where I was staying either. I'd made arrangements to live with Wendy for a bit. Unfortunately, Victor wasn't the only one who'd been making assumptions. Mum, predictably, went up the wall when she heard my plan to move in with Wendy.

"What'll the neighbours think? What'll they say!" Blah, blah, blah... she went on.

"You know what, Mum, if I was you I would be more worried about what the neighbours say about you and all your bloody antics over the years." I don't know where this came from. But it came out so automatically, so confidently, that it blew her clean out of the water.

She was too stunned to come back at me. She flustered for a second or two as I began picking up my bags, trying to get some wind in her sails. She then turned to my father for support, but he had his head down, smirking away as he concentrated on topping up his narrow-spouted oilcan.

"I don't want to keep Wendy waiting," I said, "but if you want, I'll come over Sunday and help you with the dinner." I wrote down Wendy's number. "Just give me a call and ask." I handed my gawping mum the scrap of paper. "See ya, Dad."

"Mind how you go, Rosie."

My old workplace were delighted when Victor told them I'd returned, and they offered me my old job back—the job I loved, the job that paid me handsomely, the job that saved me. But I told them I didn't want it. The reason I gave them was that I didn't want to work with Victor, if one day I was going to have to live with the old bugger too. Though there was some truth in this, the real reason was that things had changed. I didn't need it anymore. The job had always been so demanding and stressful, and when I was with Teddy, I needed that. I needed to have something to help me forget about my home life; I needed something that relied on me, something that gave my very existence some sort of value.

Instead, I got a job sewing up coats in a little shop on the edge of town. The couple that ran it were lovely and kind. It was a nice peaceful place, no great rush to get things done in time, or no need to satisfy a near impossible spec sheet.

Victor had become good friends with Daniel and his wife, and so the four of us would go out together. Even though Victor and I were officially courting, I never stayed overnight at his. But I had started to get to know his children and eventually we went on weekends away together as a family. It did seem strange returning from being joined at the hip, only to go our separate ways at the end each time. It was after the third such time when he pulled up at Wendy's house and said what he always said.

"So, I guess I gotta lug your bloomin cases indoors again."

"You know what, Victor, no. Not this time."

"Oh, so you're gonna do it yourself for once?"

We sat in the car and talked it over with the kids. They seemed to be okay with it, though I couldn't help sensing Debbie was a bit wary. I think she'd got used to being the female figure in the house and was unsure about sharing that role. Thomas was fine; I think he'd missed having a mother around.

Debbie did her fair share around the house, but apart from that she was actually quite lazy and also a bit tubby. She didn't go out much and seemed content staying in and knitting or doing a jigsaw—even on a lovely warm day. Victor said he'd tried to get her interested in other things, but she just wasn't having it. Now, the last thing I wanted to do was come across as controlling, or seem like I was telling her what she could and couldn't do, but I decided to have a go.

At first, I thought about it as if she was one of the fellas—which tack would be best used to deal with her? I found firm and friendly to be the one that worked. Not asking her, but telling her, and knowing full well in my head that what I was saying was right and that I would not be taking no for an answer. And then chuck a little funny in at the end if I could, so she didn't feel she was being scolded like a dog.

And so, I set her some new rules, such as not eating an entire packet of biscuits between her meals, and whenever I went out I made her come with me. I didn't have to force her, but I could see what Victor meant. She'd give a slow shrug and say, "All right then," then trudge about after you.

When we were out buying things for the house, I'd always ask her opinion on which one she liked. Of course, I usually got the same response, "I don't mind," or "I don't care." However, I kept persevering. And then one day I took her to buy some clothes for herself, to smarten her up a bit. I was imagining it was going to be a long day but after a time she got into it and was choosing things she liked and telling me ones she didn't.

I eventually helped her go through a bit of a transformation, gain some confidence and be herself. Without all the biscuits between meals and being a bit more active, she lost her podge too, and with a new wardrobe she turned out to be quite the looker.

I was happy with the way things were and saw no need to risk upsetting the applecart, but Victor was keen for us to get married. He wanted that family unity. For so long they'd been a fractured family. He said he wanted to be whole again. Of course, this was something I ultimately wanted too, but I guess the scars were deeper for me, so I had to tell him I wasn't ready yet.

It was hard for me to completely trust Victor during the early days of our courtship. Even when he went to the toilet when we were out, I'd be asking him where he'd been and why he'd taken so long. Heaven knows why, he'd never been the type to do anything to suggest otherwise.

I carried other scars with me too. There were occasions when he'd put his hand on me, and if I happened to be away in one of my daydreams, I'd jump right out of my skin. Once I even wet myself a bit —but I never told him that one.

I heard that Teddy had got a new girl living with him, and finally, finally, I thought it was all over, that our history could be filed away and forgotten. But Teddy still hadn't accepted me leaving and continued to make attempts to get me back. He still seemed to have that uncanny knack of being able to find me, as well.

One day, I was sat on Sheringham beach with Hazel, my dad, and Daniel. Hazel was pregnant, so her and her new fella, Colin, had decided Norfolk was the better place to be bringing up kids. It was her who saw him lurking by the seawall, watching us, waiting to get me on my own, no doubt. I apologised to the others and tried to carry on like he wasn't there. But I could feel him. Just knowing he was behind me made me feel so vulnerable and nervous. I obviously did a bad job at hiding it though.

"Come on," said Daniel, "let's move down the beach a bit."

We did just that, but lo-and-behold ten minutes later there he was lurking in the background.

"Right!" Hazel leapt up, dusted the sand off her hands and marched over.

She came back five minutes later. "Well, I'm supposed to tell you that he wants to talk to you for just a few minutes. But if you do, I'll save him the bother and bloody thump you myself."

It took a second or two for us to decide if we could laugh at that one. But we all did.

63

WINDOW SHOPPING

The next weekend, Victor and me decided to go to Betty's of Holt for some kitchenware. As we drove down the high street we were surprised to find a parking spot almost right outside Betty's. It was tight, but Victor managed to back in between a green Morris Traveller and a yellow Honda Ceptor.

I got out and walked up to the window of a lamp shop as I waited for Victor. An ornate brass table lamp had caught my interest, but it was difficult to see with the brightness of the yellow Honda reflecting so strongly in the glass.

"Here, Vic, I was just thinking that if—" Then I stopped.

"If...? ...Rosemary?" Victor said coming up beside me. "What's up, the cat got your tongue?"

"We have to go!" I said, hurrying back to the car.

"What are you talking about, we'll only be twenty minutes."

It wasn't a cat that had got my tongue, but rather a dog that had caught my eye. "No. We have to go. Now."

"Don't be silly, come on."

I checked up and down the street. "Please?"

"Not 'til you tell me what's got your goat. What is it? You forgot something? You left the stove on?"

"No. *That...*" I said, making eyes towards the Honda we'd parked in front of, "is Teddy's car." I checked the street again.

"You think so," he said in his normal unflappable manner.

"I know so."

"I thought he drove a blue Ford?"

"So did I. But look, that's the cigars he smokes—"

"Don't mean a thing."

"—and *they* are his mother's dogs." Curled up on a familiar but faded tartan blanket were his family's two skinny little whippets. "Now, please can we go?"

"Nope," he said, walking towards the shop entrance.

"You don't know what he's like," I said, not daring to leave the side of Victor's car.

"He ent gonna touch you. I wouldn't let him. And he knows that."

"Victor, please? *For me*?"

"Rosemary," he turned to face me, placing both hands on top of my shoulders. "You know I'd do anything for you, and that is exactly why we are gonna carry on as normal and do our shopping. You can't let him affect you like this no more." He lifted my chin up with the crook of his finger. "Look at me, the only way is to face your fear, and show him you're not afraid anymore."

My heart was racing, every nerve jangling and willing me to get out of there, even if it meant getting a bus or walking home by myself.

"Nothing is going to happen, I promise. Now please, *for me*, will you kindly accompany me into this here shop?" He held out his arm.

I gripped it with both hands and pulled myself close against him.

"Okay then," he said, casual as you like. "Let's go shopping."

"Wait. At least move your car. Park somewhere else, it's all I ask."

"Not on your nelly. Finding that spot right outside the shop's the best bit of luck I've had all month."

"I know what he's like. He'll do something. Mark my words."

Victor just shrugged as he held the door open for me.

I needed to know if he was in there but couldn't bring myself to look up from my shuffling feet. My knees felt weak, so I held on to Vic like a walking frame as I tried to control my breathing.

As soon as we entered, my eyes scanned and stopped on every

person, double-checking before moving onto the next. As far as I could make out we were safe, but that didn't mean he might not come in at any minute.

Victor started looking at a bone china tea set. “Which ones? I like the patterning on these small ones, but those ones have got the bigger handles, easier to get your fingers in. What d'you think?”

“Yeah. Fine,” I said, checking back to the door.

“Which ones though?”

“What? Both.”

Victor sighed and put down the delicate teacup. “Look you're not up to this, are you?”

I nodded quickly.

“Okay, we can come back and choose next weekend then.”

A massive weight shifted off my shoulders. I wrapped my hands back around Victor's arm and tried to guide him out of the shop. But he didn't move.

“Since we're here though, I wouldn't mind having a quick look at the jumpers. They're upstairs, c'mon.”

“No. Please?”

“Look, I don't want to waste that good parking spot, and I need a new one. I managed to get an oil stain on my favourite beige one. Can't be eating Sunday dinner with an oil stain on my jumper, now can I?”

I looked to the stairs leading to the second floor. Breathe, Rosemary, breathe, I said to myself.

Victor smiled at me pleasantly. “Should I get another beige one, or try a different colour this time?”

And before I realised it, I was being led to the stairs.

I had my eyes closed most of the way up, which meant Vic had to help me like an old lady who could barely walk. At the top I didn't want to open them, I didn't want that dilemma again of checking for him. It's strange though, how quickly your eyes are drawn to the familiar, like some magnetic force, or some extra special sense that you don't even know you have. But sure enough, there he was. The very first person I clapped eyes on. He was with his new girl, Jackie. She was playfully telling him off, swatting his shoulder as he held a bra up to his chest and wiggled it about. It took less than a second for him, out of nowhere, to turn and look straight back at me.

As soon as our eyes met, his cheeky half-smile crumbled to ash, then from the ash rose a fiery look of pure anger. He locked onto me, staring daggers, stabbing straight into me, pinning me to the spot. I couldn't move. I had no control of my legs or my body.

"What about grey?" Victor said, not even so much as acknowledging the threat. "Rosemary?"

I couldn't reply.

Victor then stepped in front of me, between us, breaking the line of sight. The relief of being snapped out of Teddy's snare was all too brief, because I then had no idea where he was, how close he was. I moved quickly to peer around Victor, but Victor blocked again, moving in the same direction.

"Maybe green would be better," he mused. Then in a more deliberate tone, "Rose. I'm speaking to you. I want you to help me. I want you to help me choose a jumper. Can you do that? For me?"

I looked up at his kind, soft eyes. "Okay... I guess... I mean, yes."

"Good. That's all we have to do. Look at the jumpers and help me choose which colour best suits me, okay?"

I nodded.

It took all my will not to look at Teddy directly, but I did always keep him, or at least Jackie, in the very corner of my eye, just to be sure, just to know where he was.

The few minutes in that shop seemed like hours until Teddy finally dragged Jackie downstairs.

"What about this one—hundred percent wool?" Victor said holding up a paisley sweater.

In the end, Victor bought the jumper and two pairs of socks, and then finally we could leave. As we left the shop, the first thing I did was peer down the road and breathe a sigh of relief to see his car was gone. But the relief was short-lived...

"Oh no. I told you. I told you. Look!"

At the rear of our car, the pavement glittered with a thousand pieces of smashed windscreen glass.

"I told you! I told you he'd do it," I said, holding my head in my hand.

"It's okay. It's no problem," Vic said as he fished for the keys in his pocket.

"What do mean, *okay*? How can this—"

He held up his hand to hush me. "It's okay. He'll just have to pay for a new one is all." His calmness was incredible. But it didn't change what Teddy had done. And that he was *still* able to affect us, always staying entangled in my life. Maybe I could persuade Victor and the kids to move to Mansfield, I started to think. It seemed the only way to escape him.

"Rose?" Victor called from the back of his car, "come here a minute."

I couldn't imagine what else he'd done, but as I went around, I was left speechless.

"What... on... earth?" I eventually said.

"Beats me," sniffed Victor.

"But how...? It doesn't make any sense."

"I told you, didn't I," he said as he opened the door for me. "Are you getting in or what?"

"But... but... all the glass."

Victor shrugged. "Well, it's obviously nothing to do with us. Come on, I'm hungry."

Later that evening, I got a phone call from Teddy's mother. We exchanged the usual pleasantries, but then she seemed very keen to know how I was, if I was okay.

"Honestly, I'm fine. Why are you so worried?" I asked.

"Well, it's just I'm guessing you may have seen Teddy today, is that... right?"

"Yeah, that's right. We did."

"Ah, that explains it then."

"What do you mean?" I asked.

"He came home in such a foul mood none of us dared ask him, but we guessed he must've had a run-in with someone."

"I only saw him, nothing happened. We didn't even speak."

"Oh? Well, he came back with his knuckles all pouring with blood and no back windscreen in the Honda."

64

HE WAS NO MAN

I continued chatting with Muriel for quite some time in the end, as I had some of my own questions I wanted answering. And the answer to one of them proved to be quite a bombshell. She as good as told me that it was my own mother who'd been tipping Teddy off to my whereabouts over the years—my days off, my destinations, and my timings and such. It came as a shock, but the more I thought about it, the less of a surprise it was. At least it meant Teddy the Phantom didn't actually have mystical powers.

Truth be told, it didn't bother me as much as it should've. I didn't care enough to waste any energy in wondering why she would do that, never mind how. The more these things came out, the more I saw her for what she really was, and that her love wasn't the prize I'd been looking for. I mean, what value is there in the respect of someone who doesn't even seem to have any for herself and her own doings. I pitied her even, cos at the end of the day, she was the one who had to live with herself, and at the end of her time, she was the one who'd had to make peace with it all. And I'm not quite sure she did, bless her.

I realised enough to know that something must've happened to make her the way she was. I knew enough of the world to know there ent many people who are just out and out nasty buggers for no reason.

Often, it seems to be the case that they've been the victim of something, or have been twisted out of shape through a bad experience or even their own guilt and regret.

It was the Alzheimer's that got my mother in the end. But before this took hold of her, she suffered a lot from rheumatoid arthritis—which kept her housebound. Things never thawed between us, but I'd regularly go check in on her, do a bit of cleaning, cook some meals, wash her feet, play some of her favourite records for her and whatnot.

She'd sit in her armchair facing the window, the television on in the corner, even though she never seemed to watch it. The volume knob was always turned all the way down, with her preferring the company of the music from the wireless as she sat looking through the net curtains at the world passing her by.

I felt more like her carer than her daughter. At her best, she was irritably civil but never grateful. She wasn't short of visitors and always came alive whenever they popped over for a quick cuppa. She loved nothing more than to hark back to stories from the years gone by, especially her days in London as the ever-popular pub singer—her memory for the details quite remarkable. Once they left though, she would instantly fall into a glum sulk. After a while, I noticed the stories would be getting repeated to the same visitors, though the details mostly remained spot on. However, soon even these started to get muddled, and that is when I decided it might be my last chance of getting some meaningful answers out of her before it was too late. I didn't harbour much hope but thought why the heck not give it a go.

I was all but finished with my jobs, had given her feet a wash and even let her have a rare afternoon sherry in hopes of loosening her tongue. And then I asked her. Asked her straight out who my real father was.

"No. I don't know. I don't know what you're talking about," she said, just as I'd expected. She folded her arms like a grumpy toddler and stuck her tightened chin to the air.

"So you don't even know?"

"No," she said, closing her eyes defiantly.

"No idea? Not even a guess?"

"No."

I turned away and picked up their faded wedding photo from a dresser in front of the window.

"Good," I said, nodding. "I'm glad of that." I saw her head turn sharply towards me in the reflection of the framed glass. I gently put down the photo and straightened the lace net curtain. "It's better that way, cos I'm more than happy with the father I ended up with," I continued, gazing out of the window, idly running the bottom of the curtain in and out of my fingers. "Trevor is the only father I've ever needed."

"Huh. Your father?"

"To me he was, and always will be."

"Your father," she said, in an almost snarl. "If only you knew the truth."

I didn't speak. I just waited.

"Huh. He was no real man."

With my back to her, I continued to wait.

"A man doesn't do that—what he did. Not a real man. Except for *him—your* father." She let out a long sigh and went quiet.

And still, I waited.

I heard her begin to shuffle. Sniff. Mutter. Then she started up again. "It was his fault. All of it. It wasn't mine. I wanted to help, you know me, I always help when I can, you can't say that I don't. No one can say that 'bout me, not now they can't."

Even though it seemed like nonsensical ramblings, I let her go on.

"It was *him*, your father the coward. I couldn't even drive at the time, let alone drive a lorry. It was all him. I even told him to look out. But it was too late. It was too dark. We couldn't see him, 'til it was too late of course."

"Who...?"

"We didn't know at first, thought it was just a deer. Then..." The saggy skin of her chin trembled, her eyes screwed shut for a moment as she shook her head as if trying to rid herself of a pesky fly. "We thought he was already done for, anyway."

"Who...?"

"Nothing we could do about it after the fact, was there. But anyway, it was his idea, it was him who took the pushbike. I never even touched that."

The lace material lay still in my unmoving hands.

"I wouldn't... I wouldn't do that. He took it. Don't even know what he did with it. And afterwards, after that young girl found him, well, I did my best. I tried to help *her* out, I did. No one can say no different. Well... I mean... of course I *wanted* to help poor June out."

The curtain fell from my hand. I slowly turned to face her.

Arms still folded, she stared up into the opposite corner.

I just watched her—until her eyes flicked towards me a couple of times.

"What?" she snapped.

I didn't offer her anything. No words. No expression.

"It was difficult. There was nothing I could do. It was... I was..." Her eyes fell shut briefly once more. "I wanted to help her out, but I couldn't because..." Then they fixed on me with that hawkish glint. "Because of you! It was more *your* fault than mine," she continued. "She lost hers—poor June, then *you* of all people come along instead. A bad seed from a bad apple. You were probably even there when it happened—inside me. So how could I face her? The last person she'd want to be seeing is you, after what *your* father did. And what he *made* me do. It would... it would've been... perverse, that's what. Having *you* there, reminding her every time she looked at yuh, every time she looked into your eyes, and your... dark hair—the obvious black sheep of the family, we couldn't hide that behind a hedgerow, could we? So what do you think she's gonna feel every time poor Juney sees you? Can you even imagine what that's like? How difficult that is? Huh?" Her mouth began to twitch and her head bow. "To be reminded of it, every single day," she muttered as she cast her eyes to the side.

"The Horse?" I said in an almost whisper.

"No," she snapped, before refolding her arms.

"Uncle Denny. You mean it was—"

"You don't know anything," she cut in. "You don't even know your own father for a start. So don't start thinking you're wise. It's all nonsense, anyway. No one would listen to you, so don't you start spouting off that big trap of yours."

I didn't have much else to say to her; my head was swimming the wrong way in a whirlpool of colliding thoughts. There was so much to deal with, without even thinking about poor old Uncle Denny and Aunt June and the unborn baby they lost all those years ago.

Finally, after half a lifetime, I had my reason, but that didn't make things any easier. Admittedly, there was some kind of relief in at least knowing that after all this time it wasn't *who* I was but *what* I was that had poisoned my pond. But this only caused me more pain, knowing it was something that was never in my control. Maybe I wasn't to blame, but that meant precious little when I'd spent my entire life doing exactly that. I'd already walked that path, already climbed that mountain; I'd already bore that burden to the end. And having spent my whole life struggling and learning how to deal with it, how to manage it, how to carry it, I'd finally got to the top, only to learn it wasn't even my burden in the first place.

I did everything for her. I gave everything to her as a child, and yet the only thing she shared with me was her torture. A torture so strong she could never see past it, couldn't ever just give me a chance, just give it a try, to try and see me as just her daughter —Rosie.

Before I finished the call with Muriel, I asked her a final question too. I asked her if she couldn't have a word with him, mother to son, and get him to stop. Make him realise it was over for good.

She told me that Teddy had only been following me cos he wanted to tell me to come and pick up the last of my belongings. Apparently, his new girl wasn't happy having those reminders lying around the house. I couldn't believe after all these years he still had stuff of mine. I told Muriel to throw it away. She said she'd tried once, but never again, that he was like a dog guarding a bone. She said he'd only let me take it away.

When I told Victor about the conversation, he asked me when I was planning on going over.

"I'm not," I told him straight out.

"As you like," he said with a shrug and then turned and opened a kitchen drawer and began to rummage inside.

"Well, what do you mean by that then?"

"By what?"

"You think I should go, don't you?"

"I don't think anything," he said. "It's your decision, not mine."

"But, if you were me...?"

"But I'm not you. Only you are you."

"Okay, but that's your advice though? Isn't it? To go."

He sighed. He shut the kitchen drawer. "You want my advice do yuh? Well, okay, here it is. Now you may not like what I'm about to say, but I'm gonna say it anyway. Your life is yours, and yours only. And only you can make the best of it. Despite all that it throws at you, you gotta believe in yourself, and you gotta continue on no matter what, and you don't hide from nothing. In fact, you gotta go and face it, and sometimes you gotta go and hit it on the head, or grab it by the wotsits, cos there ent no one else gonna do it for you. Now, of course, there'll be people to help you along the way, but eventually, it comes down to you and you alone. And I know you, I know who you are, and all the things you've achieved already by yourself. And don't be mistaken, this isn't me *believing* in what you can do, this is me *knowing* what you can do." He opened the drawer again and took out an apron. "Or at least this was the advice I once got from someone much wiser than me, someone who I've always respected dearly from the day we met."

"But..." I swallowed, "that wasn't me."

"Yes it was."

"No. That was Work-Rosemary. I hate to destroy any of the nice illusions you got of me, but you deserve the truth. And the truth is, that was all but an act."

He tilted his head to the side and raised his eyebrows. "You really believe that?"

"I'm sorry, Victor," I sniffed. "But that's the real truth of it."

"Well then, so I guess that means that the real Rosemary was the timid girl who let her mum boss her around and let her husband beat her up?"

I felt myself recoil as his words hit me. *Let them*! Like it was my fault. Is that what he really thought? Everything was beginning to unravel and fall apart in my hands—the pieces dropping and breaking across the floor. I was too shocked to speak.

"That wasn't the Rosemary we all knew," he continued. "The real Rosemary we knew didn't let anyone get the better of her. The real Rosemary always had an answer, always found a way. *One of a kind*, they'd say. *Do anything for you*, others would happily tell yuh. *A real good'un, and no one would argue the toss of that*. The real Rosemary always knew her mind."

"Stop. I don't understand. I don't know what you mean. I don't even know what you think anymore," I finished, my voice wavering.

"Were you not listening to me? It don't matter what I think. I can't make these kinds of decisions for you, only Rosemary can, the real Rosemary. Go bloody ask her what to do, not me." He put the apron over his neck. "Sorry, I didn't mean to raise my voice. Now, if you can't make your own decisions, how about helping me with mine instead? What d'you reckon I should do for dinner?" He opened the sink cupboards. "A few of the spuds are starting to sprout," he said, holding one up for inspection, "so should I do roasties or knock us up a cottage pie?"

The next day, I asked Victor to drive me over there, but he said no. So instead, I asked Hazel. Once Daniel got wind of it, he joined us too, and so the three of us set off.

When we arrived, Hazel and Daniel started to get out of the car.

"No," I said to them. "I have to do this alone."

Hazel sighed and folded her arms on top of the roof, giving herself a clear sight of his front door.

With it being an arranged thing, I was able to get a bit of control over my emotions and the physical reaction he caused in me. I walked up the path. One foot after another. *Keep your head up and always look forward.*

Of course, my heart was still trying to jump into my mouth and my stomach turn somersaults, but I knew I had to do this one last thing. I had to be strong. I had to show him I was strong. Show him the real me.

"Rosie!" he smiled, breathing out a long breath with almost giddy relief. He invited me in, but I told him to just gather my things up in a box.

"Oh come on. Don't be like that," he said, his irritation showing already.

I stared at him blankly and waited a good long second. I wasn't going to get entangled in his words and persuasions. I had to stick to my guns. "Teddy. It's simple. You either go get my stuff in a box or I leave."

"Rosie, come on—" he began to whine.

I turned away.

"Okay, okay. Wait." He shouted for Jackie to collect up the stuff.

"Here." I passed him the mottled tan comb with the missing tooth. "This is the only thing of yours I hadn't thrown out already."

"What is it? A comb?"

"You don't remember, do you?"

"Well, I remember what a comb is."

"But you don't recognise it?"

He shrugged. "Is it mine?"

"It was, once. A long while ago—but in a different lifetime."

He took it from me, inspected it for a second, before casting it aside on the hallway telephone table. "So, tell me, why won't you come talk to me no more?"

"Because there ent an *us* anymore, Teddy. We're done."

"I won't hurt you again. I promise you that."

"I know. And I believe you now."

"You do?"

"Yeah, because I won't ever let you."

"No, but this time I mean it."

Jackie came up behind him with the box. He ignored her until she finally nudged it into him. Teddy barely glanced at it. Then, what he said next, I couldn't quite believe. "You know, you needn't take anything out of this house."

"What on earth are you talking about?"

"This is still your house. You can move back in, this can be our home again."

Finally, he had me at a loss for words. Poor Jackie, she was still stood there behind him clutching my box of things. I felt so sorry for her and just prayed she weren't going through what I did. From what little I could see of her face, there didn't seem to be much reaction to all this, but I did notice she couldn't bring herself to make eye contact with me—not that I blame the poor soul.

"No, Teddy. You wouldn't want me back anyway."

"I do! I'm telling you right now that's what I want."

"Teddy, the person who walked out of your door the last time ent the same person stood here now."

His cheeks were twitching. I could see he was struggling. His head began to sway as he tried to hold it together.

"Ple- Please, Rosie?"

"No, Teddy. It's too late now."

"What do you mean? What do you mean by that?"

All I had really meant was, there was nothing that could change my mind, but suddenly I found myself saying something else entirely...

"It's too late, Teddy, because me and Victor are getting married."

His face went. His bottom jaw started trembling and he let out a pitiful groan. I felt so sorry for him, for I no longer saw the fearsome, handsome, charming man who could talk his way out of any situation and into anyone's heart. Instead, I saw a confused little boy who liked to throw his recorder out of the train window and couldn't use a washing machine.

Jackie placed a hand on his shoulder, but he shrugged it off, making her spill the box onto the floor. Instantly, Teddy dropped to his knees and began scrabbling around picking up spilt cosmetics and trinkets.

"Teddy..."

He looked up at me through tear-filled eyes. He held out an all but empty bottle of perfume. "It's yours!"

"Not anymore, Teddy. You need to throw it all away. Burn it on a big bonfire. I don't want it. And you don't need it."

All he could do was shake his head, "Rosemareee. Nooo."

"I'm leaving now. Goodbye, Teddy."

I felt like a passenger in my body as I walked away from him. I felt like my legs would give way beneath me at any moment, but they stayed their course. I could hear my heart pounding in my eardrums, my chest heaving with every loud breath.

I got in the back of the car.

"What... what about your stuff?" asked Daniel, turning around to me.

"I didn't come here for that," I said in a broken voice.

"What happened? What'd he do to yuh?"

I wiped the beginning of a tear from my eye and composed myself. "Nothing."

"Mum?" Hazel persisted. "Just tell me. You okay?"

I took a moment before replying, "I'm fine."

"Well, what's going on then?"

"Me and Victor are getting married, is what's going on," I said, finally letting go of my emotions completely, not sure whether I was laughing or crying.

"Really? Come here, you soppy old cow," said Hazel as she leaned into the back and wrapped her arms around me.

And so in the end, despite the numerous times he'd asked me, poor old Victor was the fifth person to find out we were finally gonna tie the knot and make our family whole.

EPILOGUE

I got the call at 2 pm. I was at work.

"He wants to see you," is all she said.

"Well, I don't really want to see him."

"But..." she snivelled.

"I'm ever so sorry, but that's just the way it is," I told her.

"I don't know what else to say to you then."

"There ent anything left to be said, I'm afraid."

I felt terrible after I put the phone down. I felt so, so, sorry. There ent no use saying I didn't. I'd known him since I was all but a kid.

A short while later the phone went again. This time it was the hospital staff.

"He's asking to see you, Mrs Manning."

And this time I couldn't find the words to reply.

"This is just to let you know that if you don't come now, there may not be another chance. Of course, it's entirely your own choice."

Teddy had been in the hospital for a few months. The fast-living and forty cigars a day had finally caught up with Fun-Time Teddy, and he'd got the cancer. Jackie couldn't cope; she was an alcoholic and had trouble enough caring for herself. Teddy had refused point-blank to eat the hospital food, so in the end, it was me who had to cook him his meals and then look after Hazel's little Shane, while she took them into the hospital for him. Several times he'd asked for me to visit, but I'd said my goodbye to him already. There was nothing good that would've come from it, not for either of us.

The day of the phone call was different though, and Victor understood. He was gold, in fact. He came and picked me up from work, then looked after Shane while Hazel and I drove to the hospital. He said he'd come pick me up anytime if I needed to leave.

When I arrived, there was quite the circus going on. There were so many people around his bed and hanging out of the doorway, it was as if it was the pope himself in that room. Everybody turned to look at me when we arrived. As usual, it seemed he hadn't been shy in letting them know what he wanted.

It was the first time to lay eyes on him in a few years and there was no denying it was sad to see what was left of this big powerful man, a man who'd always been so full of life. The picture I'd been carrying of him in my mind didn't marry up to the person lying in bed before me. His sallow face was so thin it had taken on a different shape. His eyes had become sunken, but they still hadn't lost that sparkle and they lit up as soon as I walked in.

"There she is! There she is," he said, reaching out with his withered arms. "My best girl. Always my best girl."

I didn't really know what to say to him in all honesty. I told him how Hazel had brought me up to the hospital and that Victor was looking after Shane. It was just something to say. I didn't like it one bit —all those people watching. I could feel their intrigue, finally getting a ringside seat to what they'd only heard about from the rumour tree most of their lives.

"Right, come on. Out you get, you lot." This was his mother. "Give 'em time alone, come on now."

I almost protested, but then I saw it in her eyes. If not for him, at least for her. And then before I knew it, we were alone. Just Rosie and Teddy.

For that time only, I had to forget I was married to Victor and forget Teddy too was with someone. I just had to be with him for a while. But he didn't get it all his own way; I wasn't about to give him an easy ride out.

"I never stopped loving you, y'know," he croaked.

"Then why, Teddy? Why all the fists and the other women? Why d'you do it? We could have had something good. Things could've been different." And I really meant it. I wasn't just saying it to beat him up. I really wanted to know if there was an answer. "I was earning bloody good money, I looked after you. We could've had our own place together, a happy life together. It was all there for us. We could have had it all, Teddy." I held his hand. "Just tell me why?"

"I... don't know why," he choked through his tears. "Cos I loved you—cos I love you. More than anything I ever had in my whole life."

"Then why couldn't you just treat me right, treat me fair?"

"Cos, I didn't want to lose yuh."

"But you hurt me."

"I wanted to protect yuh, you were mine. I had to."

"Love isn't about owning, it's about sharing."

"I couldn't. I couldn't share you. Not with no one."

"No," I sighed, "I don't mean... never mind." I stroked his thin, limp hair back from his forehead. "You just don't get it, do you?"

"Maybe I don't."

I then waited while he got through a series of weak, rasping coughs.

"But what I do know is," he continued, "is that we were meant to be together, my Rosie. Forever. Our whole lives. Cos I know you better than anyone. I know you—"

"No, Teddy. No, you don't. You don't know me, that's the whole point. You don't know the real Rosemary because you never got to meet her, cos you wouldn't allow her to exist. You always had to be in control. You suffocated her, just as she was starting to grow."

His face crumpled and he began shaking his head. "No, that ent true. You're wrong."

"Oh right, yes, I see. Of course, you're right again, Teddy. What was I thinking," I said stoney faced.

He scrunched his eyes shut, head turning away from me.

"There was so much more to me when I wasn't with you," I

continued. "You never even got the best of me. Other people did, my workmates, my friends, Hazel and now little Shaney."

"So... so what is it you want to hear?" he croaked. "That I'm the bad one? That I'm sorry?"

"No, Teddy, it doesn't matter anymore. I only care about the now and the future, cos I finally have what I always wanted."

"And soon... soon you'll finally be rid of me. Be able to forget all about me," he said, staring across the room.

"Huh, fat chance of that," I said mustering a smile. "Not with Hazel and Shaney about. Chips off the ol' block and no mistake—the pair of them."

His gaze never left the far wall, though his cheeks occasionally twitched as I spoke.

"Only yesterday I was helping little Shaney get dressed, but he was none too keen. So as soon as my back was turned, he bit me on the bum. The little bleeder. Yep, he's growing into a right character, that little lad. I'm sure he'll be able to achieve whatever it is kids dream of being nowadays. I'm sure the future will be bright for him. And Hazel too, I'm so proud of her and what she's become—considering what she went through. They're gonna be a happy family, for sure."

Even the tears stuttering down his cheeks seemed weak and fragile. Several times his jaw quivered as if he was about to speak, but no words came.

I placed his hand back on his lap. I leant forward and kissed him on the forehead. "Goodbye, Teddy."

After I left, they said he spoke no more and passed away the following day.

Thank you to my family & friends, and all those who helped in the journey of this novel becoming a reality.

About the author...

W.S. Ishida was born and bred in the Norfolk countryside and feels a strong affinity towards this beautiful and quiet part of England. When not sat at a desk writing, the author enjoys nothing more than long dog walks along the beach and sitting outside under the stars on a warm summer's night with a glass of red wine (or two).

~

Message from the author

If you enjoyed this novel, please help others find it by leaving an honest rating and review on your preferred platform, such as Amazon or Goodreads.

Reviews and star ratings are essential in enhancing discoverability and legitimacy, so I will be immensely grateful if you can take the time to do this for me.

They also provide me with invaluable feedback from the the people who really matter - you the reader. Even if they are only short comments about your general feelings on the book, it all helps.

If you would like to receive updates on the author's future projects and giveaways (such as short stories related to the novel and featuring Rosie as a child), please sign up for the newsletter. Please be assured that your email will never be shared and you can unsubscribe at any time.

Author website - **wsisihida.com**